"Life is too short to stuff a mushroom."
or:
THE SUPERWOMAN PHILOSOPHY

A Superwoman isn't a woman who can do anything, but a woman who avoids doing too much.

Conran's Law: Housework inexorably expands into as many hours as you have to fill—plus half an hour—so it never gets done.

Housework is something that nobody notices, until you don't do it.

If you're going to be lazy, you have to be efficient and fast.

It's amazing how much better a room can look even if you don't actually clean it, but simply tidy it.

No one should waste her life on the treadmill of housework.

Remember that the whole point of housework is to keep the place functioning efficiently as a cheerful background for living—so live!

SUPERWOMAN

SHIRLEY CONRAN

Illustrations by Jan Mitchener

*This low-priced Bantam Book
has been completely reset in
a type face designed for easy reading, and
was printed from new plates.*

SUPERWOMAN

A Bantam Book

PRINTING HISTORY

Crown Publishers edition published August 1978
2nd printing............August 1978
3rd printing............October 1978
4th printing....November 1978
5th printing............January 1979
Literary Guild edition, January 1979
Preferred Choice Bookplan edition, April 1979

*Serialized in the New York Post, November 1978,
Los Angeles Times Syndicate, February 1979 and
in Newsday, April 1979.*

Bantam edition/October 1979

ISBN 0-553-12556-7

*Bantam Books are published by Bantam Books, Inc. Its trademark, consisting of the words "Bantam Books" and the portrayal of a bantam, is Registered in U.S. Patent and Trademark
Office and in other countries. Marca Registrada. Bantam
Books, Inc., 666 Fifth Avenue, New York, New York 10019.*

PRINTED IN THE UNITED STATES OF AMERICA

For My Mother
IDA PEARCE
with love and thanks

Acknowledgments

For helping me to prepare the United States edition of *Superwoman*, I am greatly indebted to a Superman, Michael Demarest, for his help, support, hard work, and meticulous attention to detail.

For her guidance and enthusiasm, tact and patience while editing this edition, I would like to thank Linda Price of Bantam Books. Linda Impelli of Bantam was equally long-suffering and tolerant.

I would also like to thank John Prizeman, George Seddon, Marcia Gauger, Helen Hinkle, Raissa Silverman, Rebecca Boroson, Audrey Ball, Doris Kinney, Mileva Ross, Lorana Sullivan, Rosie Lewis, Terry Duke, JoAnn Walters and Lisa Lockhart, as well as Jenny Noll who typed on and on and on and . . . on . . .

CONTENTS

SUPERWOMAN

INTRODUCTION
by Mary Quant

I Hate housework.

I Love cooking, bathing children, brushing dogs, polishing things, and even occasionally scrubbing floors. But not housework.

I Need an immediate return on work done—congratulations or even violent criticism. But no one mentions a squeaky-clean bath and I would have thought a dirty bathroom means a clean me.

Most of my life has been spent running away from household management without much success. A busy working life may be a good excuse for not doing it, but it remains undone nonetheless. The inevitability of it appalls me, but here we have somebody who can laugh at it, do it, or dodge it.

I have known Shirley Conran since we were first grown up. The quantity and originality of the domestic catastrophes that have beset her can only be matched by the brilliance with which she has dealt with them and the funniness of her accounts of them.

She is clearly uniquely qualified to write such a book as this.

If only this book had existed when *House and Garden* came to photograph my first flat! I was inordinately proud of it, but the editor glanced around and asked, "Are you moving in or moving out?" Shirley is always either moving in or moving out, but it never shows.

She advises on a great many problems I never knew existed, but I live in a bit of a mist. I am the only person I know who can happily not answer the telephone; I never open letters unless they are from lovers, and I didn't read a book about childbirth until after the event.

However, having laughed my way through *Superwoman* I am going straight out to buy a filing cabinet. I can't find my passport or my cheque book, I am no longer allowed a key to my own house, and there is a terrible smell in the basement.

Thanks to Shirley Conran's *Superwoman* all this is going to change.

OUR MOTTO: Life is too short to stuff a mushroom

THE REASON WHY

What is a home? A home is a myth. A home is a not-so-Golden Gate Bridge, one damn long, never-ending cleaning job, that nobody notices unless you don't do it.

No matter what they claim, no one can tell you how to make doing the dishes a sensuous experience, but until the women's movement comes up with a mechanical housekeeper, *somebody's* got to do the dirty work.

Superwoman is a book about housework and how to avoid it. It is the basic minimum of household information that you can get away with. However, it is also a COMPREHENSIVE* reference work, and SHOULD CERTAINLY PAY FOR ITSELF BEFORE YOU'VE FINISHED READING IT.

Superwoman is a book for people who have to house-

---

* Which is why some information is duplicated, if needed, in two different sections.

keep but who prefer to do something else. It will help you do all the housework you can't avoid, as quickly and painlessly as possible. It started out on the British bestseller list for 44 weeks and has been an international bestseller.

The title *Superwoman* is ironic because no one woman can accomplish all the work that the traditional housewife is supposed to do. (I don't believe she ever existed.) A Superwoman isn't a woman who can do anything, but a woman who avoids doing too much. She knows her own limitations and sticks happily within them; she realizes that life is untidy and so are the children in it.

A Superwoman chickens out. She knows that perfection is hell to live with, and her standards are her own, rather than the idiotically unrealistic ones set by TV commercials, magazines, mothers-in-law, and lying friends. (Interwoman competition can be as cruel, as grueling, and as unnecessary as any of the competition in the traditional male rat race.)

Because there is a growing anxiety and depression among ordinary women which results from the impossibility of living up to newspaper and magazine propaganda about women who effortlessly organize a career (not "job" you note), husband and children while still finding time to keep a 24-hour-perfect hairstyle, "Superwoman" was originally an ironic title, because no one could achieve everything that the traditional woman is supposed to. These days, housework is not confined to one sex or one class. We *all* have to do it.

The Superwoman's reason for avoiding housework is in order to have more time for herself. Because, as well as being the supporting cast of the entire family show, YOU ARE THE ONE AND ONLY STAR OF YOUR OWN LIFE.

So a Superwoman is sensibly selfish. She looks after herself and she doesn't overwork. She knows that only by caring for herself will she be in good shape to look after all the people who depend on her. It took me years to acquire the discipline, control, and iron will that was necessary in order to stop doing things for other people and start doing things for myself. At first I told myself that I didn't have the time. But then I figured even if you work a regulation 40-hour-week and sleep 8 hours a night, you *still* have 72 hours a week left over (which is almost *twice* as long as a working week) in which to do something stimulating and rewarding, or at least just SOMETHING.

Naturally, a Superwoman does as little housework as possible, and this can be quite difficult. You have to be well organized to keep housework in its place, which, as far as I'm concerned, is firmly underfoot. Good organization doesn't just happen naturally, any more than good sex. You have to learn how to do it and put in a lot of practice, like the piano. I make no secret of the fact that I would rather lie on a sofa than sweep beneath it; but you have to be efficient if you're going to be lazy.

Some may suggest that women don't have to be well organized in order to be efficient, but I know of no job, whether it's running a factory or bathing a baby, that isn't easier, quicker, and more enjoyable if you think about it logically in advance—and that's all that efficient organization is.

Many women don't like organizing themselves because it involves a bit of forethought and self-discipline. But organization needn't mean a rigid plan brought to the fine pitch of a presidential visit. There must be a plan, but keep it a loose plan, one you can scrap or alter whenever it doesn't fit in with reality. Life is like a British summer —you have to grab it quickly, before it disappears. This means being flexible enough to drop everything and get out into the sun while it's still shining—which it never does on schedule.

Some women think that some of the things I suggest are too simple to write down. I disagree. You never know what you don't know.

A Superwoman aims at simplicity. Simplicity in organizing and living her life, in doing without things that (accumulatively) threaten to take over her life. Simplicity in using sensible things that ease labor and worry.

Some men ask me how I dare write a book about what women already know. This sort of man believes that he was born with a total and unquestionable knowledge of the combustion engine, how to broil a steak, and how to make love, whereas his womenfolk were born with a built-in knowledge of housework. But who did teach those women? Obviously, their mothers . . . well, who taught *them* . . . and when? . . .

Far, far more of today's men are *really interested* in housework. I have spent the last two years talking to men around the world about it. At first I thought that they were buying *SUPERWOMAN* so that their wives could scrub floors better, (swine) but they pointed out that today many men *have* to do housework if they are bachelors or divorced (sometimes with children) or widowed. Many modern men are certainly willing to help do the system-support work in order to help their wives, and all boys should be taught to do so. (Don't stop at potty-training: teach them how to totally clean up after themselves.)

Anyway, dig into this book as you need it. Some sections are labeled SKIP THIS UNTIL YOU NEED IT. When you do read one of these sections, read it slowly. Do not allow your eyes to skim over it; be prepared to read the section twice—it might save you a lot of money by clarifying the intricacies of moving or by explaining how your electric meter works. It certainly won't be riveting literature, but I hope it's easier to understand than anything else you may have tried to read on the subject.

A recent household management study by the International Labor Organization, which was investigating equal opportunities and treatment for women workers, showed (apart from exploitation) that full-time housewives spend an outrageous average of fifty-five hours a week on household chores while women who work outside the home spend roughly thirty hours on home chores.

Of course, this may mean that the employed women work faster, and/or it may mean that they do less work. As far as I am concerned either possibility is to be commended.

I've been surprised to hear many women say that they keep *SUPERWOMAN* by their bedside. One mother of five, who is a vet, told me that when she has finished she just starts again. I am delighted that *SUPERWOMAN* seems to have helped so many women and also that psychiatrists are prescribing it for patients who can't cope. Perhaps these women are expected to cope with too much: perhaps they are the ones who expect too much of themselves, therefore it does no harm to check on your work load and your system.

Some information will be found in more than one part of the book, which shouldn't be surprising since it was condensed from a quarter of a million words of *notes*. I hope I've sifted out all but the essentials—and here they are, gathered together in one book, instead of in piles of odd, torn-out newspaper clippings and bits of magazine articles that you can never find when you want them.

It's doubtful whether all the advice in this book will apply, or appeal, to any one woman, for it was not written for a specific woman, and, in any case, a woman's circumstances constantly change. Some women go out to work (full or part time), some don't; a few start some kind of business on the side. Some have husbands, some have lovers, some have both. Many have children, some don't. Some women may feel that they have the worst of all possible worlds with no husband, no lover, several children, and a full-time job. For this reason I have tried to cover problem areas and their solutions from mild to extreme. By the way, I have mentioned prices and costs as little as possible because, no matter what the politicians say, Old Mother Conran predicts that world prices will continue to go up and up and up.

I don't pretend that housework is fun because on the whole it isn't, although there are some aspects of it that are pleasant. Getting up early, preparing breakfast, setting the table, darning, spring-cleaning, and arranging flowers would never be a strain for me. But I find routine cleaning tedious at the best of times and clinically depressing at the worst. Because it is so dreary, it is quite easy to forget to do it, or even forget *how* to do it. Twenty years of blood, sweat, toil, and tears haven't helped me to eliminate housework, but they have taught me a few tricks to lighten the load.

Parts of this book are taken from my own home notebooks; parts of it are the summed-up experience of 20 years as a designer and editor on leading British national newspapers.

To get the best out of this book it's important to know your own limitations, allow for your weaknesses, and ignore the impossible, milk and honey standards of the unnaturally superperfect television housewife.

A routine helps you to know what you haven't done. You must also learn what will galvanize you into action to get that work done, what carrot will coax you into doing it.

My methods are probably not yours. There may even be those who find them appalling. Fine. What works for me might not work for you, but one of the tricks of sorting out what's best and fastest for yourself is to criticize someone else. Then, SHAZAM! You may have suddenly analyzed and perhaps improved your own system. *So please deface this book*. It is a working book. Add to it, cross things out, make notes, and scribble your own ideas in the blank pages at the back (they were the easiest ones to write).

Finally, no one should waste her life on the treadmill of housework. So decide how much you're prepared to do and when. Four hours a day? One day a week? No time at all? (A high aim, I feel, but good luck to you.) Decide how much mechanical help you want, how much it will cost, and how you're going to get the money to pay for it. Don't use this help to raise your housekeeping standards. Use it to create more free time to get out and enjoy yourself. (One Superwoman told me, "I make it a rule that when my kids are out I'm out as well.") Remember that the whole point of housework is to keep the place functioning efficiently as a cheerful background for living —so live! Decide on something positive, or simply pleasurable, to do for *yourself* with the time you save. Otherwise life . . . just . . . slithers . . . a-w-a-y. . . .

ORGANIZATION

DO YOU SINCERELY WANT
TO BE ORGANIZED?

A tycoon millionairess once told me that she found a business easier to run than a home. I'm sure she's right. I've never yet been able to make housekeeping show a profit; but my system is to run it in the same way as I run an office, with a planned budget, and with purchasing and filing departments (all me). This is not nearly as clever or complicated as it sounds. Any sane woman in a perfect world wouldn't bother, but if like me you've lost 2 vacuum cleaners and $280 worth of laundry in one year, you'll know it's worthwhile to keep track.

EQUIPMENT: All you need to get organized is a writing surface, a chair, a kitchen drawer, a large cardboard box, or a bit of shelf space on which to store two wire office trays or a couple of shopping bags (IN and OUT). You will

11

also need an office accordion file with about 16 pockets in which to start a filing system, envelopes, carbon paper (so you get file copies of the letters you write), 2 big note-books, and 1 small notebook for your purse. You will also need a slim little appointment book to carry in your bag in which to record such vital things as orthodonist, eye doctor, and pediatrician appointments, dates of PTA meetings, telephone numbers, expenses, and anything you want pegged to a date, such as birthdays.

SHOPPING LISTS: Tape a shopping checklist of food and household items you often buy in the back of your address book. Keep a shopping notebook in your kitchen. Expect —or rather, exact—no cooperation from your family. The only family rule is: Everyone must write in the shopping notebook what is *about* to run out. This works, because the family doesn't see it as a chore, but as a sensible necessity. They know if they don't do it, they'll run out of peanut butter or whatever they're about to use up.

MAIL: I throw incoming mail in a wicker basket on top of the refrigerator and outgoing mail in a string bag hanging by the kitchen door. I open the mail immediately after breakfast and deal with small items by postcard. When the string bag looks full enough to warrant a trip, I take it to the mailbox.

It's easier to write a line than a letter. Try to write thank-yous on pretty postcards as soon as you can, while you're still feeling grateful. I know a lawyer who keeps her post-cards *already stamped* in an elegant basket by her bed. Also use postcards for Christmas thank-yous; my last year's list was polished off in half an hour. Then, too, don't forget the plain but convenient prestamped postcards you can buy at the local post office.

Weightier things such as bank statements get thrown into the IN tray for Monday morning, when I do all my office work, belated thank-yous, and general organization. Anything that doesn't get done on Monday doesn't get done. There is always another Monday.

BILLS: Always save business letters, bills, and receipts (otherwise what proof have you that you paid cash to the man who repaired the sink when his firm sends you an invoice for it six months later?). This is especially necessary in this unnerving age of automation: computers *do* go wrong, and people with (or without) computers can be inefficient.

I may be paranoid, but I've noticed that computers never make errors in my favor. (When you've been invoiced $100 for a genuine suede camel saddle, which you haven't even dreamed of, let alone bought, remember that it can take 6 weeks for a computer to answer a simple question such as, what proof have you that this was ordered?) Keep carbon copies in your bill file of correspondence concerning bills-in-question. Don't ever send them the receipt that proves you've paid; if you do, you may lose your proof. Send a Xerox copy.

WORK LISTS: My work notebook is just a list of nonfood work to do and reads "Buy name tapes," "Order lampshade," "Get new sink stopper," etc. I never promise to do anything unless I have scribbled it down in a handbag notebook or workbook. This often stops me promising things.

Go through these notes every Monday morning, ticking off a job when you've done something about it, and crossing it out when it's completed. Write work lists on righthand pages only, and make any notes about the job on the left-hand pages. So when the cleaner promises to have your purple skirt ready, check the note; but not until the skirt has been picked up do you cross it off completely.

Supposing the right-hand page says "Query telephone bill," on the left-hand page jot down the date and name of the person you discussed it with. If the argument goes on for weeks you can always flip back to that left-hand page and make dated notes of the continuing saga (it helps to have a wrist watch with a day and date calendar). I go through 6 notebooks a year and I keep them: They take up very little room in a grocery carton under the couch, and it's amazing how useful they are.

Make sure all articles are checked in and out of your home (things sent to the cleaner, appliances picked up for repair). Get the proper person (family member, tradesman) to sign your work notebook for anything he removes; date it. The busier you are the more you should make it a rule always to keep track of who has what and where. When signing for any parcel always add "not inspected" or "not tested," whichever applies. Jeer if you must, but this sort of efficiency takes little time and can save a lot of trauma.

The only New Year's resolution I keep is to look at my yearly list—things to do on January 1. Sometimes you may feel too frail to cope with things on January 1, in which case do them as soon as convenient.

This list may look dreadful, but I find that mine (reproduced here to offer you inspiration) took only 2 hours to sort out last year. On January 1? No, on February 14.

NEW YEAR CHECKLIST

- Insurance: personal, house, health (if not paid by employer).
- Membership renewals.
- Check passport is up-to-date.
- Arrange service of air conditioner and electrical appliances, such as dishwasher and washing machine.
- Service car if necessary.
- Transfer important items from old appointment book into new appointment book. These might not be only family birthdays but also such vital reminders as "October 1: Check roof, gutters, chimney." "Clear leaves from now through fall." While you're at it, you might make a little list of these items and Scotch-tape it into the back of your diary, where it's easy to transfer from year to year. (The leaves always fall.)

Fill in your personal New Year Checklist here.

....

....

....

....

....

....

....

....

....

....

....

....

....

....

INCOME TAX: The New Year is a good time to start organizing your income tax paperwork, simply because nobody else will do it; and accountants just love you if you can get your work in before the April 15 crunch! If you use an accountant (perhaps, like me, you work at a part-time business), at the end of your financial year the minimum you should send him is the following.

ACCOUNTANCY CHECKLIST

- Checkbooks, stubs properly filled in and list of entries from current checkbooks. (Even if you haven't finished your current checkbooks by April 15, send them off and start new books.)
- Bank passbook and payment receipts.
- Any other bank correspondence.
- Order books (if this applies).
- Receipts in date order (if you have a lot of receipts, subdivide them into 12 clear plastic folders, each labeled with the appropriate month. The more of the accountant's work you do yourself, the less it costs you for expert time).
- Appointment book.
- Cash-flow position at end of year.
- Other items as follows:

....

....

....

....

....

....

....

....

....

....

....

....

....

....

NEW ADDRESS BOOK: Some people write out a new address book (saving the old one) every January, sadly weeding out the dead and discarded. Not a bad idea to do this occasionally because then, when you lose your handbag, you can go back to your old address book. If you use a Rolodex Card Desk Index system, it makes your ruthless weeding that much easier.

NEW APPOINTMENT BOOK: In my new appointment book I jot down all seasonal items, transferring them from year to year. (For example, "April (or whenever) rake up lawn, sow 18 lb. coarse shade-grass seed. Ignore existing grass, which looks messy for a few days, then springs back to life. Hose well immediately after.") I also jot odd notes in the back of the book, knowing that I won't read them until the year's end: a Christmas present list, a list of the current medicines the family is dosing itself with, the collar sizes of my favorite men, and the various sizes of my family.

Writer Katharine Whitehorn wants me to recommend her one-and-only organized habit. Write your name and address and "Please, please return" in the front of every single notebook, diary, or address book you ever use. These have frequently been returned to her by restaurants, taxi drivers, friends, and strangers.

THE DRAWER WITH THE ANSWER TO EVERYTHING

Filing is a word that makes most women suspicious, but what *else* do you do with the china every morning? It's not only a good idea but in home emergencies absolutely essential. Don't be frightened by the idea of filing. The verb only means putting things in a sensible place where you can find them quickly and easily. Four years of my filing fits into 1 suitcase.

Know your limitations, and don't plan a filing system that is better than you are because you won't stick to it, and you will find this depressing.

What follows sounds amazingly neat and tidy, but it

isn't. Most of my vital work seems to be on the front of old envelopes (backs already used for shopping lists). If I stopped to type or write them out they would never get done; it's easier to shove any old scrap of paper into its correct place in the system than to have it lying around.

SIMPLEST FILING SYSTEM: This might just be an alphabetically indexed document wallet or a personal file briefcase. My humble system started with three folders labelel "IN" "OUT," and "PENDING," and 1 kitchen drawer that deserved its peeling label, "The drawer with the answer to everything." It contained an accordion file with 16 compartments, which is the minimum for any fun-loving, file-hating harassed woman.

What to put in your files: Everyone's individual filing system is a different sort of organized chaos. Once you've started it, the only thing you will have to remember is that this repository, whatever its size or situation, is from now on *the one and only safe place in the house.* Any scrap of valuable paper (except money) should be in it, even if it's just saved in a huge envelope labeled "For sorting out sometime."

How to file: Below is one example of a filing system; yours will vary according to your circumstances. Incidentally, I never think about filing anything in alphabetical or date order, or it would never get filed, but if you always shove the latest document in the front (i.e., nearest you) of the compartment, the file will automatically be kept in date order.

File 1: *Guarantees and Warranties.*

File 2: *Instruction Leaflets.*

File 3: *Health.* Any relevant correspondence and a little notebook listing children's illnesses with dates; also health certificates, inoculation records, doctors' and dentists' visits, medical bills and payments, health insurance records. This is also the place for pets' inoculation records, in case your dog gets arrested for wandering: your fine may be doubled if you can't prove that Lassie has had a rabies shot.

File 4: *Licenses.* Those requiring yearly renewal, such as dog license, etc.

File 5: *Linen, Cutlery, Crystal, and China Lists.* If you care about these things. I do. I like to know how much disappears each year.

File 6: *Personal.* This includes recipes, diets and all their magical incantations, like the note that you wrote to yourself saying "1 slice of bread a day = 365 slices a year = huge hips."

File 7: *Useful Things Torn out of Magazines.* Advice on how to clean your jewelry, how to revive your cyclamen; a list of all-night rave places in Paris, and how to get 10 days in Hong Kong for $351, all-included. This file is never used, but I find it a comfort.

File 8: *Important Documents.* What's important is a highly personal decision. My file contains passports, stocks and bonds (we have one), marriage and birth certificates, insurance policies, tax records, and similar potential drama along with the first (and only) love letter my first husband wrote to me . . . Ah, well, on with the filing.

File 9: *Money File.* Stick bills in one pocket, leaving the other side for bank statements, used and unused checkbooks, and savings account books.

File 10: *Expenses.* This is an optional for most housewives, but if you run your own business you must keep all expense records, however trivial, for income tax purposes. Your accountant can't win the battle without the maximum ammunition.

File 11: *Paid Bills.* Just put them in (always at the front of the file), and sort them out only when your accountant needs them or when your "friendly" utility or telephone company is accusing you of not paying that electricity or phone bill, when you painfully remember writing a check. (This mix-up is frequently the result of our neglecting to put that multi-digit account number on the check, partly because there isn't room for it and partly because we were so cross at the time.)

File 12: *Household Addresses.* This file contains a sheet of paper with a list of names, addresses, and telephone numbers of importance to you and to anyone else who is temporarily in charge. For example: doctor, dentist, veterinarian, garage, fire department, police, hospital, taxis, plumber, landlord, local city or town hall (for complaining about nonremoval of garbage, etc.), oil company, electrical repair shops (incidentally, there is some merit in buying all electrical appliances from one firm, if possible, as you can then establish a friendly, first-name relationship with *one* complaint department instead of with several), window cleaner, TV repairperson, local shops, laundry, dry cleaner, railway station, bus station, airlines, nearest all-night drugstore (if you're lucky enough to have one), local movie houses and theaters (ditto), odd-job man, and so on, according to your own idiosyncratic needs. (You may have some of these listed under How to Get Hold of the VIP's in Your Life, see p. 356, but the above also serves as a guide to your establishment for anyone who isn't familiar with it.) If you're as forgetful as I am, you'll probably refer to this all the time.

File 13: *Photographs of Portable Valuables.* It is a sensible idea to take snapshots of good silver, paintings, jewelry, and antiques. With crime on the increase and insurance premiums soaring at the rate of the latest Apollo, furnishing the police with these photos can often lead to their recovery—as Zsa Zsa Gabor advised me pointing to her bed, disappointingly strewn with *photographs* of her jewelry.

List of Family Numbers. Could you describe your valuables from memory at that agitated moment when you'd just been burglarized? Could you include the brand names and serial numbers of TVs, stereos, and watches? If not, you might, given the strength, time, and patience on a rainy afternoon, draw up a list of your family numbers. These might include social security, dog license, passports, drivers' licenses, insurance policies, mortgage number, cassettes, stereos, TVs, cameras, watches, bicycles, slide and movie projectors, cars. Almost anything mechanical and stealable has a serial number somewhere on it. Note these numbers with a short description of the object.

You might also include any car or motorbike license plate numbers. For some reason, the police think you're a candidate for a straitjacket if you can't remember your license plate number, but some brains are pondering mightier things, such as whether to file love letters under "X" for kisses and did you remember to put the key to the outboard motor in your jewelry box where the baby can't grab it to teethe on.

List of Items You Keep in Your Purse. Another good idea is to list such items together with their identification numbers. Credit cards, bank card, checkbook, union card, library card, car insurance certificate, auto club card, commutation ticket, driver's license, medical insurance identification card, social security card, blood bank membership card (which lists your own blood type and can be a life-saver if you or your family need blood after an accident).

At this point you may remember that the "noble savage" happily walked around without any cards at all and you might feel a yearning to drop out of the system. But remember that if the noble savage unexpectedly ran out of blood, he dropped dead. In case of theft this list also makes it possible for you to quickly inform the police, credit card companies, and bank to cancel or replace these items.

FAMILY NUMBERS

MY PERSONAL NUMBERS

....

....

....

....

....

....

....

....

....

....

....

....

....

File 14: Keep an envelope or plastic bag full of assorted adhesive labels for files, jam jars, etc. If you can bear it, wander around your home with string and labels and remove unused keys from furniture and suitcases, labeling the keys as you go and putting them into a plastic bag. This saves time when you are trying to keep, find, and/or identify keys that are rarely used. In this file I also keep a list of people who have a front door key, however temporarily—burglaries are most upsetting and unsettling.

Use the additional compartments for your own specialized files, e.g., a gardening schedule.

It's also a good idea to put the compartment file into a fireproof box, then into the drawer, for obvious reasons.

That is the minimum efficiency method. Read on if you feel you can take something slightly more grandiose. If, for example, you have complicated home help or do stalwart voluntary work or are running a cottage industry (I know a girl who started a thriving lunch business by selling pizzas out of her kitchen window to the office workers in the factory opposite).

More advanced filing: The advanced filer uses a proper filing cabinet. You might—as I did—use an old orange box or a wire crate, until I bought a secondhand filing cabinet and resprayed it scarlet. Now, if anyone asked me what I would save in a fire I would say that cabinet. In any case, yours should be a fireproof strongbox.

I was encouraged to buy that filing cabinet (of all ridiculous things to have in the house) by the beautiful historian Lady Antonia Fraser. She said that it took her two years to get around to buying one and another year to summon up the energy to fill it, but that it really does work and she can find something like the dog license in a minute. But only *she* can find it, because Lady Antonia believes in surrounding herself with a certain amount of uncertainty, if not mystery. So, she has a secret system which only she understands: bills, for instance, are not filed under B but under U for unpleasant.

My filing cabinet is a four-drawer clanger. The top drawer is for tedious business: files labeled "Insurance," "Accountant," "Receipts," "Bills;" the second drawer is for my writing work; the third drawer has files labeled

"In/Out," "Pending," and "Voluntary Work;" the fourth drawer holds family things such as photographs, letters and school reports.

You think that's going too far? Matriarch Rose Kennedy kept a card index on *each* child.

CLEANING

WAYS TO SAVE TIME AND MONEY

"Conran's law" states that housework inexorably expands into as many hours as you have to fill it—plus half an hour. The only sure way to make extra time is to get up earlier, but you're not going to, are you? So the other thing to try is cutting out anything that isn't essential. The secret is . . . *elimination.*

Make your list of things that no one will care much if you don't do. (Some of these suggestions require the expenditure of money, so they might have to be tucked away at the back of your mind until the piggy bank is feeling better.) No one is forcing you to give up anything, but if something has to go, consider these *timesavers* (some are moneysavers, too).

DON'TS

- *Don't* keep pets.
- *Don't* polish floors. Seal them.
- *Don't* scrub the tub or shower stall. Unless anyone in

your family is allergic to detergent, keep a plastic bottle of liquid detergent and get everyone to pour in a capful before turning on the water. And spray it with colorless silicone furniture polish.

- *Don't* dry dishes. Buy a second drainer and stand it in front of the first, or else spread a towel on a table or utility cart to provide more drip-dry surface.

In fact, if life gets unbearable, *don't* do the dishes at all. Induce the family to eat Elizabethan style. That is, each person has his own mug, plate, knife, fork, and spoon and, after using them, washes them, and resets his own place at the table ready for the next meal.

- *Don't* make beds. Use continental quilts or sleeping bags.*
- *Don't* scrub dirty collars and cuffs. Wet them and dip in a saucerful of detergent; leave for 10 minutes, then wash.
- *Don't* ever buy anything—clothes, sheets, curtains— that needs ironing. (A word of advice: Don't hang drip-dry clothes on metal hangers because they will get rust marks).
- *Don't* sew. Mend sheet tears with press-on tape or iron-on patches, which can be purchased in a five-and-dime store. Iron-on patches come in a variety of weights and colors—there is a pack of all white patches and another of assorted pastel colors.
- *Don't* shop with a friend.
- *Don't* go to sales, with or without a friend, unless it's for something you decided to buy at least 3 months ago.
- *Don't* shop for food when you're hungry.
- *Don't* shop for food with more cash than you intend to spend. I also found I made amazing savings on food when I moved into a tiny apartment for a year (with a dwarf-sized refrigerator) and didn't have space to store extra food.
- *Don't* pay for food by check.
- *Don't* automatically buy the "giant economy" size if the product is also sold in small packages. Bulk-buying saves time but not necessarily money. Check

---

* See page 156. All you ever wanted to know about a continental quilt—Conran's sells them in New York.

per pound prices on all sizes. Also consider if an item is a popular staple in your house or one that is used only rarely. Why stock up on large quantities of goods that are hardly ever used?

- *Don't* pay the manufacturer's recommended retail price without checking around first.
- *Don't* stop "shopping around" at the first lower price you find.
- *Don't* bleach or dye your hair.
- *Don't* wear nail polish. (Sneerers can't deny that this saves time.)
- *Don't* buy any clothes for exotic sports in exotic climates except in those exotic climates.
- *Don't* join a health club. *Do* yoga.

DO'S

- *Do* be carefully inefficient. Start running out of things. (But *never* toilet rolls.)
- *Do* squash toilet rolls so that the center is oval, not round. Then the paper doesn't roll off 10 yds. at a time. This will cut your toilet paper bill.
- *Do* cover kitchen shelves with self-adhesive, wipe-clean plastic wallpaper (such as Con-Tact)—this saves cleaning time.
- *Do* line the grill pan and the tray under the gas burners with aluminum foil.
- *Do* roast in foil, which cuts out basting and oven cleaning; unwrap for the last 15 minutes to brown nicely.
- *Do* use nonstick Teflon pans, which cut out not only the horror of washing up, but a lot of the time as well. (Cheap nonstick pans are as good as the expensive ones, so buy cheap.)
- *Do* close all your store charge accounts . . . or . . .
- *Do* shop by telephone only, if possible—if your weakness is impulse buying. You pay for the call and maybe delivery, but it cuts out those expensive impulsive purchases. (But keep in mind the hidden expenses—shops that allow shopping by phone, such as your neighborhood grocery store, probably charge higher prices for their merchandise than supermarkets, which do not accept phone orders.)
- Do cut your weekly bank withdrawal by 15%. (Makes it more difficult for you to buy unnecessary stuff.)

- *Do* check whether you can join a food cooperative through work, union, or neighborhood association.
- *Do* consider easy maintenance your first requisite when buying anything from flooring (good bets are sealed cork or wood in mid-tones) to lighting fixtures.
- *Do* invest in time switches for electrical equipment, from electrical blankets to immersion heaters, or lights in the back room to ward off burglars when you're away on vacation.
- *Do* get your family to tidy up after themselves or else stand a cardboard box under the kitchen table and dump everything you find in this lost property office. After a bit they will prefer to tidy up their own possessions rather than sort them out of the tangle.

Anyone who has already adapted these shortcuts is to be congratulated—it's surprising how many people haven't. Try to think of just 2 *things* you could add to your elimination list. Be ruthless! Try them!

HOW TO CUT DOWN ON HOUSEWORK

Keep it to a minimum and keep it underfoot. No one's going to strangle you if the mantelpiece is dusty. Your man doesn't love you because you can tell the difference between whitest and whiter-than-white. Your children won't remember you with love in 20 years' time because your floors didn't have a waxy, yellow buildup.

A TV producer and mother of two small children recently asked me, "Now that I can afford some home help, how much cleaner should my home be?" I was astounded. A home should be as clean as you can get away with. On the whole, nobody except you cares how the place looks. If somebody does, always, charmingly, press the critic into service: They either help or stop criticizing, ideally, both.

I don't believe in being too organized. Many women are quite rightly suspicious of Time-and-Motion methods suggested for running the home like a factory. A home is not a factory (thank heaven) and it cannot be organized with the same methods. You are often doing three things at once in a home and it's just when the dog has been sick (because it ate your slipper) that the doorbell rings.

One fairly painless way to cut down on housework is to apply the principle of reverse thinking. Instead of calculating how much there is to do, decide how much time you are prepared to devote to it—and when. I hire myself, like a cleaning lady, on Saturday morning from 9 to 11 A.M. and when my time is up, like the cleaning lady I stop. The work that is left will have to wait until next Saturday morning—or forever. (This is one way of sorting out your priorities, almost without thinking about them.)

I also firmly believe that every mother should have household help and the people who should help are the people who are making the work in the first place—the rest of the family. So in my home we *all* work on Saturday morning (together with my guests). Nine to eleven A.M. is a good time if you have teenagers: get them at it any earlier and they'll complain that you're getting them up at *dawn*; keep them at it any later and they'll howl that you're taking up the *whole weekend*. But most teenagers will work hard for two hours a week, provided that they are not asked to perform extra little chores, simply because, like Mount Everest, they are *there*.

A friend of mine has a variation on this theme. Every morning after her family has charged off, she sets the kitchen timer for one hour and when it pings—she stops.

Try to keep to a routine that starts with getting up at the time you planned. If you get up late, you'll probably do everything late all day and snap at people.

Decide how long your daily schedule will take and realize, if you are running late, that you will either have to abandon the job unfinished or sacrifice whatever other, possibly more enjoyable occupation, you had planned for the afternoon.

If your mother-in-law, or boss or your husband's big sale prospect is about to call at a moment's notice, don't panic and start dusting. Organize some modern luxury such as a crackling log fire or fresh flowers. Serve your unexpected guest a delicious drink as fast as is decent, whether it's homemade lemonade, a cup of tea, or white wine, and plan on serving a cold meal (which you won't worry about).

It's amazing how much better a room can look even if

you *don't actually clean it,* but simply tidy it! Straighten
the cushions, empty the ashtrays, and shove every odd
thing into a large basket or plastic garbage bag. When
tidying the whole house, put items to be shifted from room
to room outside their doors, then deal with replacing all of
them after the tidying is done; otherwise you rush unnecessarily from room to room.

Allow time after breakfast to empty wastepaper baskets
and ashtrays; put everyone's clothes where they ought to
be; throw away dead flowers or freshen the water if necessary; clean sinks; sweep the kitchen floor, and straighten
the beds (you can't tidy a bedroom until you've straight-
ened the bed.)

DAILY LICK AND SPIT

This depends on your situation, work, and life-style. If
you're working outside the home at a full-time job, you
probably won't have time for a daily routine but will rely
on one thorough weekend cleaning swoop. In which case,
still use the basic schedule below, and for further ideas see
How to Be a Working Woman, Wife, and Mother, p. 291.
MONDAY: Clean up the kitchen after the weekend. Defrost
the refrigerator and clean the oven when it's dirty enough.
Scrub out the trash can, empty the plastic bags, and deal
with any other strictly kitchen jobs, plus household desk
work.
WEDNESDAY: If you insist on ironing, do it in the company
of a TV or radio. (If your ironing board is too low causing
you to stoop over, you'll risk a backache, if not a slipped
disc.)
TUESDAY: Do the clothes washing and mending, and all
shopping, including a trip to the dry cleaner's.
THURSDAY: Clean other rooms. Do odd jobs such as cleaning out cupboards, washing woodwork, cleaning ceilings
(lighting fixtures and cobwebs), polishing the silver, if you
have any, and so on. If you can get away with it, this is
the day you can take off with a free conscience—leave the
house at 10 A.M. and do something interesting.

FRIDAY: Clean the entire bathroom thoroughly; clean one room or passages or hell holes such as a basement area or utility room.

The general idea is to do *one* chore (or related chores) each day, rather than a daily smorgasbord of activities.

SPRING-CLEAN FASTER

Spring-cleaning is rarely necessary if you stick to a good weekly schedule. But someday when you are feeling financially flushed, you could run your fingers through the Yellow Pages and get a professional carpet cleaner to give you an estimate. If you have a fireplace that you use a lot, you might consider having the chimney cleaned. Send all the draperies to be cleaned. Look at your list of things to be mended, things to be bought, and things to be overhauled.

I do this the first week in January, just after the holidays. For me it's an anticlimactic time; and since just about everywhere except the Sunbelt the weather is conducive to indoor pursuits, you might as well do the nasty jobs, then chances are you won't have much to do until next January. The rest of the year I just make notes in the back of my appointment book of things to be mended or replaced, as the home inexorably disintegrates around my ears. Don't do *anything* that can be postponed until the annual big cleanup; nobody seems to notice.

Not everyone agrees with me but, temperature permitting, I believe that the best, private, spring cleaning outfit is a leotard. You can always wriggle into a sweater as well if you're not warm enough or the minister drops by.

Spring clean with a friend (who doesn't talk *too* much), to spur you on, cheer you up, patch you up or wipe you down and—ideally—complete the job for you when you get stuck, bored or exhausted. Do the same for her.

WARNING! Mutual help is best done on an hourly basis. Her home might be twice as large and take twice as long.

PLAN A SPRING-CLEANING

Decide what you can afford to do in terms of time, money, and interest.

- Inspect your home, yet another notebook in hand, and list all the things you'd like to see clean. You'll feel so virtuous when you tick them off as each job is finished. In fact, you'll feel virtuous just making the list and doing nothing.
- Decide what to clean and what to renew. It's only a little more trouble to paint a wall than to just scrub it: Paint costs more than water, but achieves more exciting, refreshing results.
- Check if any small jobs—repairing electrical plugs, venetian blind cords, broken windows, leaky faucets —have to be handled by professionals and, if so, arrange for them to be done before anything else. (See Ms. Fixit, p. 170.)
- Check that your ladder is strong and steady, that the first-aid box is well stocked, and that your paint-brushes are not stiff.
- Check your cleaning closets. Are your brooms balding? Is your vacuum cleaner listless? Have you got enough feather dusters and dust cloths, and a ceiling broom?
- Decide in what order the rooms will be cleaned. Clean one room at a time because you can stop right there if time runs out or you get bored. Stop half an hour *before* you had planned, because then you won't be too exhausted to clear up properly.
- Plan the simplest meals for your family, but don't live on sandwiches—broiled chicken or chops and a salad is almost as easy and more nutritious.
- Tell your nearest and dearest—who won't even have noticed that you are spring-cleaning—that you'll expect him to provide a night out, say next Monday, and you'll be having a bubble bath and going to the hairdresser's beforehand.

THE TRUTH ABOUT HOUSEHOLD CLEANSERS*

"Detergent" comes from the Latin for "cleaner," so any cleaner can claim to be a detergent. Soaps and modern detergents both have a similar cleaning effect but soap has an organic base whereas modern detergents are synthetic or man-made.

Nearly every household cleaner—whether soap, scourer, detergent, spray cleaner or floor polish—is based on either soap and sodium carbonate (washing soda), or trisodium phosphate (TSP), or a mixture of both, with a few additions. These additions might be bleach, ammonia, alcohol, caustic soda, vinegar, kerosene, turpentine and paraffin beeswax which are also used in cleaning products. There's not much more to it than that except for packaging and advertising.

If you want to clean with an ecologically clear conscience you should only use a pure soap, such as Ivory. *Any* modern detergent is now thought to provide phosphate food for algae (which choke out the fish), because even biodegradable detergents break down into phosphates.

Household cleaners can work in one of three main ways, or in combinations of the three. They can: (1) dissolve the dirt with a solvent; (2) float off the dirt with oil or soap and then float off the oil or soap with water; (3) use an abrasive or rubbing action to rub off the dirt. This last can be as simple an abrasive action as a washerwoman's rub, or as strong an abrasive action as using steel wool to rub off dirt from cooking pots.

Soaps, detergents and general purpose household cleaners dissolve dirt and float it off the dirty surface, either by themselves or combined with water.

The stronger the chemical, the more likely it is to dissolve the dirt—but also the more likely to damage the surface (such as your antique table) from which the dirt is being removed. So you need some weak cleaners and some strong cleaners and you also need to know which to apply where. Of course, you can buy only one basic,

---

* Basic—soap, washing soda, tsp plus—ammonia, bleach, alcohol, vinegar, turpentine, kerosene, caustic soda (dangerous), paraffin wax.

strong cleaning solution and weaken it yourself for the more delicate jobs (for recipe see p. 36). And incidentally, *nothing* is kind to your hands except rubber gloves. When a manufacturer says "kind to your hands" he means "weak solution."

THE PUREST SOAPS AND DETERGENTS (such as Ivory soap, soap flakes or Dreft powder) have basically nothing added to them, but they are only used for delicate jobs like doing the dishes or handwashing lingerie.

SOAPS AND DETERGENTS FOR LAUNDRY (such as Tide) are basically the same but have added ingredients to improve the cleaning action.

HOUSEHOLD CLEANERS (Such as Spic 'n Span) are composed mainly of TSP or washing soda (sodium carbonate). Whether they are a powder, liquid or spray they are essentially the same, differing in strength and suitable for most washable surfaces.

DISHWASHER DETERGENTS are mainly harsh abrasive TSP with added borax to soften the water.

ABRASIVE POWDER CLEANERS (such as Ajax or Comet) include the same basic ingredients but with a little added abrasive powder. "Abrasive" is Latin for "scraping off," which is what it does, rubbing off the dirt as well as dissolve it off. One of the first historical abrasives was powdered pumice stone. Sometimes bleach is also added.

SOAP PADS (such as Brillo) are basically made of fine steel wool (a *very* strong abrasive) soaked in liquid soap and then dried.

METAL POLISHES also contain a very, very, very fine abrasive and probably some ammonia, which makes glass and non-tarnishable metal shine and sparkle.

LIQUID METAL POLISH is generally a more efficient tarnish remover than a powder polish. Something like Brasso cleans all metals except silver, for which you need a finer abrasive.

WINDOW CLEANING LIQUIDS AND SPRAYS contain ammonia because this makes glass shine and sparkle. When tested (by an Independent Home Economics Division) my home-made recipe was considered to be as good as any on the market so why not use that?

OVEN, TOILET BOWL AND DRAIN CLEANERS such as Lysol are based on a corrosive (a chemical abrasive, or eater-off) called Lye, so always USE RUBBER GLOVES, keep them away from your face and eyes and if the latter accidentally come into contact with one of these cleaners, wash off immediately with lots and lots of cold water rinses.

You really only need five basic household cleaners—a mild soap, a strong detergent, an abrasive cleaning powder, a metal cleaner, and ammonia—but here are the maximum dozen household cleaners, which should save your money as well as your shelf space.

WARNING! Keep all these away from young children.

- Household *soap,* in solid bar or soapflakes. You might acquire a jar to put chopped left-over soap in, topped with boiling water. This results in a soft soap jelly for washing precious objects.
- A dishwasher *detergent* (such as Cascade) which you can use, suitably weakened, for most things that are washed with water.
- *Washing up liquid* (such as Ivory Liquid).
- *An enzyme presoak* (such as Axion) for clothes with protein stains, for soaking off burnt saucepans, washing narrow necked vases and decanters with tidemarks and dingy, unreachable bottoms.
- *A cleansing powder* which contains bleach (such as Comet).
- *Steel wool scouring pads* (cut in half to last twice as long) . . .
- *Household ammonia,* the sparkler of shiny surfaces. Add to water for cleaning windows, pictures, glass, mirror. Also adds a quick sparkle to silver. Also cleans ovens (see p. 56), removes stains and, diluted with water, it makes a heavy duty cleaner.
- *Washing soda* (or sodium carbonate): Add 1 tablespoon to warm water and detergent to wash paintwork. Add 2 tablespoons to water when soaking burnt saucepans or oven racks (or use Bio-Ad). It counteracts oil and grease, softens water, cleans drains and sink. Never use it on aluminum.
- *Household bleach:* Bleach removes color and acts as an antiseptic and deodorizer. It is useful for cleaning any surface that it will not damage (such as the toilet). Store-bought household bleaches (such as Chlorox) are a strong mixture of chlorine bleach and disinfectant and *should not be used for stain removal.*
- *A disinfectant* (such as Lysol).

- *A spray oven cleaner* (such as Easy-Off).
- *Wax-based polish* (such as Klear Paste Wax) for floors and furniture.

As with beauty products, manufacturers of cleaning products sell them by playing on most women's ignorance of chemicals, their feelings of inadequacy and guilt, and their wish for eternal, guaranteed happiness and approval.

They sell you a pretty can of Swipe, implying that if you're insufficiently loved or respected, then it must be because, like Mary Hartman, your floors are yellow with built-up wax and that you're simply not working hard enough at being a good housewife. *Don't* fall for the ads and *do* learn what's in the package so that you don't overbuy.

Cleaners to Make Yourself

Partly out of interest and partly because of the high cost of convenience cleaners, I've included throughout this book quite a lot of simple, cheap "do-it-yourself" ideas as used by Great-Grandmamma.

It's surprising that there hasn't been, as in the beauty business, a move away from slick preparations toward ye olde quainte remedies, made from fresh herbs and real bees' knees plucked at dewy dawn, etc. The beauty business is bending over backwards and spending a fortune trying to persuade you to spend a fortune on their "home-made" products because more and more women are coming to realize that if they make these preparations themselves at home, they can save a lot of money and, in addition, know what's going into the products and onto their bodies.

What goes for beauty cleaners also goes for home cleansers, and, as with the former, there's no reason why you can't make your *own*. Trust me in this *one* matter, please. If you don't trust me, then just peer in that hellhole under the sink and work out what it cost you.

Just try my window-cleaning recipe, which you can make faster than a cup of coffee. To make a good selection of cleansers takes less time than baking a cake. It took me 16 minutes to make my first 6 cleansers. What is tedious is the thought of tripping out to the hardware store for the ingredients, but in fact it's quickly done. Half an hour spent making cleaners every 6 months will save you wads of money and they will also get you an *instant* reputation as a real old-fashioned homemaker. Men step inside the door and say, "Wow! This smells like my grandmother's farmhouse." It's the cleaning equivalent of making your coffee with freshly ground beans—it's the smell that gets you the reputation.

Great-Grandmother's Secret Recipe Home Cleansers

It's no more dangerous to make these cleaners than to use what's under your sink at the moment! Wear rubber gloves of course, but the only recipes to be careful about are the stove cleaners, the toilet bowl cleaner, and the floor bleach. Wash utensils *thoroughly* after use: you don't want the sauce mornay to smell of kerosene.

TO REMOVE A BUILD-UP OF POLISH FROM FURNITURE: Use turpentine applied with an old cloth.

MAKE A DUSTER DOUBLE AS A POLISHING CLOTH by soaking it in a mixture of: 1 tablespoon paraffin and 1 tablespoon vinegar. Leave duster in the mixture for at least an hour then squeeze out and hang to dry. Use it in the *bathroom* for mirrors, as an anti-mist cloth.

ONCE A YEAR WOOD POLISH recipe is: Equal parts linseed oil, turpentine and vinegar. Shake and apply with soft, clean cloth.

LEMON-SCENTED FLOOR POLISH: In a double boiler, melt 1 oz (25 g) paraffin wax and add 1 quart (1 liter) mineral oil and a few drops of lemon essence (optional). Don't leave this mixture on the stove unattended! Bottle when cool. Apply with rag.

WOODEN FLOOR BLEACH (for a really filthy floor): Wear gloves. Thoroughly wash floor, then apply the mixture (following) with a mop. Allow to stand forty minutes. Rinse floor thoroughly with clean water and clean mop.

MIXTURE: Mix 2 lb (900 g) sodium metasilicate with ¼ lb (100 g) sodium perborate. Both are white crystalline powders, soluble in water (buy from drugstore). Dissolve half of this mixture in a gallon (4.5 liters) of very hot water.

CARPET STAIN CLEANER: Add 1 teaspoon **white vinegar** to 1 pint **carpet shampoo.** Lather well with sponge. Rub gently until stain has gone. Douse with clear water, then sponge up as much as possible.

STOVE CLEANER: Fill a cup with undiluted **ammonia** and leave overnight. If possible leave it in a warm stove, i.e. when you've finished cooking and *turned the stove off.* Then clean by wiping interior of oven with the ammonia plus 1 quart (1 liter) water, wiped on with a rag. Alternatively, use the following mixture.

MIXTURE: Dissolve 1 tablespoon **caustic soda** in ½ pint (250 ml) hot water. Separately mix 1 tablespoon **flour** and a little water to a thick cream. Add to soda solution, stir and bottle. Apply to stove with mop.

WARNING. Take great care not to spill mixture. Wear rubber gloves and don't bend over it.

MARBLE CLEANER: Mix 6 oz (170 g) **sodium sulphate** and 2 oz (56 g) **sodium sulphite.** Rub this abrasive on with a damp cloth or sponge. Rinse off with clean, damp sponge. Repolish with wax silicone polish.

TOILET BOWL CLEANER (wear gloves; it's dangerous; if you get it on your hands rinse off immediately in cold water): Mix 5 cups **sodium bicarbonate** and 1 cup **caustic soda.** Store in airtight jar. Sprinkle in toilet bowl, leave for half an hour, then brush with toilet brush and flush toilet.

RECIPE FOR GENERAL CLEANER: ½ cup **ammonia** + ½ cup **washing soda** + 2 quarts (2 liters) warm water. Bottle and, when used, dilute half and half with water, for walls, etc.

ALL-PURPOSE STRONG DETERGENT RECIPE (dilute as necessary): Mix 2 tablespoons of **TSP (Trisodium phosphate,** which you can buy from a drugstore or hardware store) in 1 quart (1 liter) warm water. Apply with sponge and rinse off well. *That is a strong solution for heavy cleaning,* and it's too strong for paintwork. If you want it *for paintwork, dilute it* with 2 quarts (2 liters) warm water and you will not need to rinse off.

METAL CLEANER (not for silver): Dissolve 2 tablespoons **salt** in an equal quantity of **vinegar,** then add **flour** or **baking soda** to make a dry paste. Rub on metal. Afterwards, rub with ammonia if necessary.

WINDOW CLEANER: Mix 1 cup **kerosene,** 1 cup water, and 1 cup **rubbing alcohol.** Shake well and bottle. Rub on glass, polish off when dry. This recipe is a real winner.

POLISH FOR CHROME AND PAINTWORK: Mix 2 cups **kerosene** with 1 cup **rubbing alcohol**. Rub on with damp rag.

NONSLIP LINOLEUM POLISH: (Don't make near a naked flame). Place a wide-necked jar in a bowl of hot water, add 1 pt. **rubbing alcohol** and 3 oz. **brown shellac**, stir until dissolved, then tightly screw on lid. Wash and dry linoleum, then brush on polish and leave to dry.

TO REMOVE GREASE STAINS AND DIRT FROM FURNITURE: Mix ¼ cup **rubbing alcohol**, ½ cup **kerosene**. Bottle and shake. Apply with rag and polish off immediately. Test first on an inconspicuous part of anything old or not valuable.

FURNITURE POLISH: Mix 1 cup **turpentine**, 2 cups **linseed oil**, and 1 cup water. Takes a lot of rubbing, but you get a good shine.

WHITE HOUSE FURNITURE POLISH: 1 cup **turpentine**, 1 cup **linseed oil**, ½ cup **rubbing alcohol**, ½ cup **vinegar**. Mix together and shake well before using. For leather and furniture. Apply with soft rag, then polish.

WOOD ASH: The ash left after a fire makes a good scouring mixture and can remove stains from metal and china. Keep a jar near the sink.

SILVER CLEANER: Mix 1 tbsp. **ammonia**, 1 tbsp. **powdered whitener**, 1 pt. boiling water. Leave for 15 minutes. Don't bend over mixture because it fizzes and fumes. Saturate a piece of old toweling or face cloth in it and let it drip dry. Instead of using an ordinary kitchen towel, dry your silver with this and it will rarely need cleaning.

TIP FROM THE RITZ: The Ritz cloakroom has the most sparkling silver hairbrushes in London. "Use a spot of alcohol by itself on a piece of cotton wool to brighten up silver in a hurry," says the cloakroom lady.

You can decant your cleaning fluids into your own matching jars and bottles bought from the hardware store, along with the ingredients. I have a set of amber glass chemist's bottles in all sizes. Buy pretty, stick-on labels, as used for gifts, and insert your own house brand names.

Be very careful to label these solutions "Poison" and not to keep them with your food or drink. Perhaps you could paint the tops of your cleaning jars with red paint or nail polish. (I can't imagine why red tops on *all* poisons aren't enforced by law). A friend once offered me a liqueur glass of a new, smart, sophisticated French aperitif. I sniffed it gingerly. It smelled horrible. I didn't want to seem bad mannered, *un*smart, and *un*sophisticated, so I held my breath and knocked it down in one swift gulp. The next moment I was literally foaming at the mouth and writhing on the floor. Her husband had decanted the dishwashing liquid into the emptied French aperitif bottle. (In case you wonder what happened next, she phoned the doctor, who instructed her to feed me everything in the refrigerator until I stopped bringing it up. As she was on a jam-making spree, her refrigerator was packed with raspberries and nothing else. She stuffed them down me and I brought them up for 4 hours. Since then, I haven't much cared for raspberry jam, and I always remember to label my poisons.)

GENERAL ADVICE ON CLEANING ROOMS

I can't claim to be a comprehensive cleaner, and I would no more want to read a comprehensive domestic encyclopedia than I would want to write one. For a thorough treatment of idiosyncratic problems with a faint aura of mothballs ("to remove squeak from ladies shoes" . . .), I recommend *The Household Encyclopedia* by N. H. and S. K. Mayer (Pocket Books), which, while a bit out of date, is an excellent, inexpensive, basic little reference book.

I learned most of what follows from a parlormaid named Louise who had been in service after the First World War at Panshanger, one of the great Edwardian houses of England. Her 2 main tips for thorough cleaning are:

- Work at a steady, rather fast pace. Time yourself to work up to it. A steady worker does the work in half the time.
- When you have finished cleaning a room, stand in the doorway and look around the room, slowly and critically from left to right. (Don't knock it till you've tried it.)

Before you begin cleaning, close all doors and windows. If you are lucky enough to have a fireplace, deal with that first. Rake out the wood ash occasionally and save it for your scouring mixture (see Household Cleansers) or for the garden (it's a great phosphate fertilizer). Brush soot from the grate, remove the ash pan, put it on newspaper; carry it to the garden in a trash can. Sweep hearth and wipe with a sponge.

Now tidy and clean. Carry a bucket or basket containing all the things you will need and a screwtop jar to empty ashtrays into (then wipe them with a sponge). Keep the jar in your cleaning basket, and empty it straight into the garbage can. Carry a plastic sack (in your third hand) for old magazines, letters, newspapers, old apple cores, Popsicle sticks, and general trash.

Dust with a soft cloth folded into a pad so that there are no loose corners to catch. Carry a damp sponge in your other hand to remove dirty or sticky marks. Dust from the tops of bookshelves or picture frames. (Check that all the pictures hang straight.) Don't think you can avoid dusting by cleaning. Vacuum, sweep, or dust before cleaning with water and cleanser. Otherwise the dust turns to light mud.

Wash paintwork if necessary. You are supposed to wash paintwork from the bottom up; but I've never understood why, and, gravity being what it is, I've always done it the other way. Use 2 pails: one with warm water and detergent and 2 Handi Wipes, and one with rinsing water. Never fill a bucket more than halfway. It may be too heavy and you risk the water's sloshing over.

Use a soft scrubbing brush for molding and old toothbrushes for problem corners. No matter where you're cleaning, do the floor last. Vacuum or sweep it.

Rinse out cleaning cloths after use and hang them to dry. Don't leave damp cloths in a closet or they will acquire a sinister smell. Hang brushes up on hooks. Never stand brushes on their bristles or they will bend irrevocably sideways.

Most of your cleaning brushes, brooms, buckets, and cloths can be hand washed with warm water and detergent, followed by a rinse in cold water.

Clean a toilet brush after each use by holding it in the toilet bowl while you flush the toilet and, when necessary, leave it overnight in a solution of ¼ cup chlorine bleach to 4 cups water.

Don't wash *cleaning cloths* in the washing machine. Rinse out in a solution of detergent and warm water.

Never leave your *broomheads* on the floor or they will splay sideways. Hang them up or push them in the closet upside down.

Same with *spongemops*. Never leave a wet mop in a wet bucket or it will start to rot and smell terrible.

Finally clean up fast by putting into an empty shopping basket or large plastic garbage bag everything that shouldn't be where it is. Then empty the contents into your Family Sort Out Box.

DOING WINDOWS AND WALLS

WINDOWS: Take down or draw back the curtains. If they're floor length, hitch them over chairs. Clean window frames first: Dust them, then wipe clean with warm water and Spic 'n Span. Wipe once more with clean water. Dry.

If window glass is very dirty, use a little warm water and 1 tbsp. of ammonia or alcohol on a sponge, finishing off with a dry cloth. If not very dirty, use Windex, which also cleans mirrors and picture glass. Better still, make your own! Try Old Mother Conran's amazing window cleaner. (See p. 36)

For luxury window cleaning there's a squeegee with an adjustable handle that lengthens your reach by 2 ft (60 cm.). It has a hinged sponge head that adjusts to clean all size windows.

DRAPES: Dirty drapes will rot, so remove hooks, release gathers. Soak overnight in the bathtub in lukewarm water and biological detergent. Let water out and refill tub with cold water to rinse. Let water out again, gently squeeze surplus water out; then, if necessary, wash in the appropriate way for the fabric.

If, for some reason, you don't want to machine wash drapes, or if they're too big for your machine, you can wash *lined and unlined* washable curtains in the bathtub in a solution of soap powder dissolved in lukewarm water. Kneel down and slosh them around. Leave overnight, slosh around again. Rinse in clean water. Let water out of tub. Squeeze as much water as possible out of drapes. Dry by hanging over shower rod or, if possible, dry in open air, and hang while still damp—the wrinkles will be pulled out by the weight of the drapes.

If you have room enough to run a rod through the bottom of your hems, you can hang the curtains up damp. Sheers and many synthetic fabrics will hang straight and not need ironing.

CLEANING INTERLINED OR VELVET CURTAINS IS A PROFESSIONAL JOB.

WINDOW SHADES: Let's hope that yours are treated with a stain repellent. Wipe both sides with duster. Don't try to vacuum them; it's unnecessarily difficult. Spot-clean with dry-cleaning fluid (for grease) or with a cloth wrung out in soapy water (for dirty fingermarks, etc.). Rinse with a clean cloth wrung out in warm water, then "spot" dry with a towel.

VENETIAN BLINDS: Wear gloves, rubber or otherwise, as you can hurt your hands, especially with metal blinds. Clean with warm soapy water and sponge then rinse with clear water and wipe dry with cloth.

UNPAINTED WOODEN VENETIAN BLINDS: Don't wash them. Wipe with a liquid solvent-based floor wax.

Don't send delicate lace blinds to the laundry. You'll do better washing them gently in lukewarm water, by hand yourself in the bathtub. (That's all the laundry does.) Rinse clean.

WALLPAPER: Rub stains with rye bread or an art gum eraser. It's possible to cover a badly stained part with another piece of the pattern cut to fit and pasted over, but because the wallpaper may have faded the new patch will probably not exactly match, in fact, this is undoubtedly what will happen.

- Take a kitchen knife and smear paste on one corner of a sheet of writing paper or stiff card.
- Quickly blot excess with another sheet of paper. Then prod your pasted paper (sticky side outwards) under the peeling off wallpaper.
- Press wallpaper to your paste paper for a moment.
- Quickly peel wallpaper away from paste paper and push wallpaper smoothly back against wall (starting from the bit that still adheres to the wall and working out to the frayed edges).

GLASS AND PICTURE FRAMES: Use a Handi Wipe dampened with alcohol.

CHIPPED PAINT: To touch up your walls use a small paintbrush and paint.

FINGERMARKS ON WALLS, DOORS, PAINTWORK, PANELING: Wipe the area with a damp, sudsy cloth, then once more with a damp cloth wrung out in hot water. Woodwork should then be rubbed with a dry cloth.

MAINTAINING FLOORS AND CARPETS

FLOOR WAX: There are 2 basic types: solvent-based wax for wood on which you shouldn't use water, and water-based wax for vinyl tiles, asphalt, and rubber.

Solvent-based wax for wood: A wax of this sort smells like cleaning fluid and is self-cleaning: One application removes the previous coat of wax and the dirt, and repolishes. But it only does this if you apply the wax with a clean cloth, mop, or disposable pad on your electric waxer.

Water-based wax: Use on resilient flooring such as asbestos, cork, vinyl, linoleum and rubber. (Never apply a solvent-based wax or one of the new acrylic waxes to this type of floor.) The water-based waxes come in paste, liquid, and liquid self-polishing form. Some serviceable water-solvent pastes are Butcher's Tile Wax and Ultra Gloss Paste Wax; liquid self-polishing waxes include Johnson's Klear and Johnson's Glo-Coat.

Remove a yellow (water-based) waxy buildup with a lot of elbow grease, fine steel wool, and ammonia. Get down on your hands and knees, and with a clean cloth rub ammonia onto the floor (try an inconspicuous check patch first), then rub the wax off carefully with the steel wool. (It takes forever.) Leave 15 minutes. Rinse quickly, dry thoroughly then rewax.

Handling Different Flooring Materials

LINOLEUM: Wash with warm water and detergent. Don't leave soaking wet or it will crack. Rinse well, dry with a mop or cloth, and polish if you want.

CORK: Sweep, vacuum, or damp mop. Occasionally do a quick mop job with warm water and a detergent such as Tide, then rinse off and dry. If it has been sealed, of course you don't wax it. (WARNING! A tough abrasive will rub off the costly sealed layer.)

RUBBER, VINYL, VINYL-ASBESTOS, ASPHALT: Sweep, vacuum, or mop. Avoid coarse abrasives. Avoid rubber solvents (such as dry cleaning fluid) because they will dissolve the surface. Use warm water for washing. For special cleaning use a scrubbing brush or mop with hot water and scouring powder (such as Comet). Carefully remove stubborn stains with steel wool and scouring powder, then repolish. Remove a buildup of wax polish as previously described. On vinyl floors use a water-based wax such as Johnson's Step Saver which cleans and polishes at the same time and doesn't need buffing. On rubber floors use water-based, self polishing waxes.

WOOD OR PARQUET: Sweep, mop, or vacuum. Wash or scrub using detergent with as little warm water as possible. Dry quickly. If *oiled*, sweep or use an oil-impregnated mop, when required. Wax with Preen for wood floors.

If *sealed*, you can sweep or damp mop with water and detergent. Reseal as required. Allow about 2 years for heavy wear (as in a kitchen), longer in a sitting room. Can be sanded by machine. But watch out! It's a fierce beast and can easily take a chunk out of your floor if you sand in one place for a few *seconds* too long.

CERAMIC TILES, TERRAZZO, OR MARBLE: Sweep. If necessary, wash by hand or mop, using hot water and detergent, such as Tide. Remove stubborn marks on quarry tiles and terrazzo with scouring powder (i.e. Comet) or fine steel wool.

SLATE OR QUARRY TILES: Clean with warm water and detergent. When dry, use ordinary mineral oil rubbed very sparingly on a rag. Remove oil with a dry cloth.

Carpet Tips

Use the little vacuum cleaner attachment on the edges of the carpet or they will get exceedingly grubby. You're not supposed to vacuum or carpet sweep new rugs for 2 weeks in order to allow the loose fibers to bed down: Brush it gently, if you feel you must.

SHAMPOOING A CARPET: Test trial patch with shampoo. Move furniture, then:

- Vacuum carpet.
- Buy a proper carpet shampoo or make my recipe for a cleaning solution (see below). Use a rented carpet shampooer; which stops the carpet from getting too wet.
- Start at wall farthest from the door, work toward the door. Don't replace furniture until the carpet has dried.

Making your own shampoo: The formula for this shampoo was given to me by a famous carpet manufacturer. Put a generous amount of soapy detergent into a large bowl of warm water. Add a tablespoonful of ammonia and stir it up to get as much froth as possible. Gently rub froth over the whole carpet. Only the *froth.* Leave to dry, then vacuum. Any stains still remaining can be treated with a dry-cleaning fluid.

An effective carpet cleaner for small carpets or rugs is Johnson's Glory aerosol rug cleaner. It's expensive, but worth it. Turn the can upside down, and spray one small area at a time, then go over it with a damp sponge. Test-cleaning a 10 × 8 ft. oriental rug was a positive pleasure, and I felt like a housewife in a TV commercial as I stroked away years of dirt in 20 minutes.

For bad stains call in a professional carpet cleaner; I've seen them work wonders.

WASHING OLD, VALUABLE CARPETS: Antique shops don't shampoo them. They hang them over a line and beat them. If you have an expensive rug, don't risk washing it yourself. Send it to a real expert (look in the Yellow Pages), who will wash it with baby soap and rinse it in gallons of specially purified water, then dry it on a special rack.

SHAMPOOING LONG-HAIRED RUGS: Handwash in lukewarm water using a mild detergent. Rinse thoroughly with a fabric softener and allow to dry naturally. (It will take ages.) Brush pile gently.

How then do you clean a fur rug like white sheep or goat skin? Same way as you would a white sheep or goat —with lots of warm water and soap, such as Ivory Liquid. Rinse thoroughly (in the bathtub). Add about 2 tablespoons of cooking oil if the skin is dry.

REMOVING STAINS: Remove normal stains with a mild solution of water and detergent, rinse well, then dry by hitting the damp area with your fist wrapped in a towel.

In the case of old oil, paint, polish, or tar stains, soften the soiled area with a little eucalyptus oil left overnight, then try a commercial cleaning fluid. Start at the outside edge of the stain and work inward. If the stain doesn't disappear, try liquid Ajax or my carpet stain cleaner given below, which can be used for alcohol, coffee, tea, wine, food, soot, ink, and fruit stains.

Making carpet stain cleaner: Add 1 tsp. white vinegar to 1 pt. of carpet shampoo. Lather with sponge. Rub gently until stain has gone. Rub gently with clear water.

For owners of unhousebroken puppies or babies who are still at the stage of being amiably sick over your shoulder, there is one thing that will get rid of that rancid smell: soda water. If you take your whiskey neat and don't stock any soda water, just dip your handkerchief in diluted Alka-Seltzer or baking soda and rub in on the spot.

REPAIRING WALL-TO-WALL CARPET: Iron-on rug binding can be used to patch a cut on the back of a carpet or rug. (This product is actually meant to repair the binding on the edge of a carpet.) Mystik Cloth Tape comes in a roll and is adhesive backed. It is available in several colors and widths—the most common is ¾ of an in. wide.

For a big patch job, cut out the square of damaged carpet and remove it. The golden rule is always to work from the back of the carpet. Cut a square the same size as the damaged one, from the ½ yd. (50 cm.) of extra carpet you got when you bought it. Then cut a square of burlap 1 in. (2.5 cm.) larger all around than the carpet square. With a latex fabric adhesive, stick the new carpet centrally on the burlap square and leave it to dry for 5 minutes. Cover the surrounding burlap with the adhesive, lift the fitted carpet square with your finger or a knife blade and slide the square into place. Put a newspaper on top and sit on it for 5 minutes. The patch may look newer than the rest of the carpet, because, of course, it is. You could try rubbing a little dirt around to blur the edges.

TOUCHING UP WORN CARPET: Where color has faded from age or much use—on your stair carpeting or anywhere else—use indelible ink of the same color to restore the dingy spot.

HOW TO CURE CURLING RUGS: Stick a triangle of linoleum under each corner using a fabric adhesive.

CARING FOR FURNITURE AND UPHOLSTERY

Protecting Wood Furniture

If you put antique or modern furniture too near any heat source, it will almost certainly crack or warp unless humidifiers or bowls of water (with flowers in them perhaps) are placed in the room. If you put furniture in a damp atmosphere (such as a bathroom), it may split or swell, making drawers difficult to pull open. Rub soap or candle wax on the runners of any drawers that stick.

Dust furniture and occasionally wipe clean with a damp Handi Wipe followed by a dry duster. To remove stickiness or fingermarks use a damp Handi Wipe or a cloth wrung out in warm water and detergent. Don't polish on a damp surface or white patches will appear.

If you buy a real antique that has a buildup of antique dirt, clean it by dusting, then rub with a hot damp cloth wrung out in soapy hot water. Rinse thoroughly and pat dry immediately until it's dry. In order to make sure it's really dry, wait at least 2 days before putting on any protective polish if necessary.

If you get a grayish haze on your wood furniture, mix 1 tbsp. vinegar in 1 pt. water, wring out a cloth and rub sparingly over wood. If this doesn't work, you'll have to refinish the piece.

Wood Finishes

High-quality modern furniture is made of solid hard-wood, or veneer (plywood), or a combination of the two. Wood is very absorbent and must be treated with a finish that protects it from moisture, grease, and dirt. The protective finish will determine the sheen or luster of the wood, whether it takes on a high gloss, a dull gloss, or a matte look. Wax provides an invisible protective film. Mineral or linseed oil prevents the wood from cracking and drying out.

For mass-produced wood finishes—excepting those having satin, matte, oiled, or French-polished surfaces—occasionally rub with a soft cloth and cream or liquid polish. Johnson's Pledge spray wax is a quick polish for wood (can also be used for leather and vinyl upholstery).

AN OIL FINISH: This is generally achieved by rubbing with linseed oil and turpentine or teak oil rubbed into the wood. To maintain this look, you should dust, then rub with an oily rag. Don't use too much oil. Try not to use any other oil such as cooking oil as it may become horribly sticky. If this should happen, wash with a weak solution of liquid dishwashing detergent and hot water, **rinse thoroughly,** and quickly pat dry. Wait a couple of days before re-oiling.

PERMANENT-SEAL FINISHES: Don't waste your time polishing this finish. You know if it's been treated with a permanent seal if it **looks** as if it never needs polishing so continue to ignore it.

If it's *French-polished*, on no account treat it with anything or you may wreck the finish (layers of shellac dissolved in methylated spirit have been lovingly built up and rubbed down to get the gleaming finish of French polish). If your furniture has a permanent finish (whether French or plasticized), you need only dust it. Never polish a *satin* or *matte* finish or it may become glossy.

To remove polish from furniture use a solution of 1 tablespoon vinegar to 1 pint (500 ml) warm water. Dry and repolish.

How do you clean the *brass inlay on a polished antique* when you don't want to use some vicious modern brass cleaner for fear of what it might do to the surrounding wood? Use a neutral shoe polish.

Cleaning Other Kinds of Furniture

PAINTED: Wash with detergent and warm water. Rinse well, dry fast.

CLEAR PLASTIC: Clean with spray-on Windex and rub as little as possible, or the static you create will only attract more dust.

OTHER PLASTICS: Wash with warm water and detergent, rinse, and pat dry. Remove stains by rubbing with a damp cloth dipped in baking soda.

MARBLE: Marble and tile are very porous, particularly where oil and alcohol are involved. Polish with a colorless wax. Clean with soapy water, or a mild detergent, or try a mild abrasive for removing stains. Whiten by rubbing with vinegar and immediately rinsing off. For bad stains, the International Marble Cleaning Company of Great Neck, Long Island, 39 Water Mill Lane, Great Neck, New York 11021, will, for $6 plus postage, send a ring remover kit that contains a chemical cleaner, a buffer, and a marble polish.

WICKER AND CANE: Wash in hot water and detergent (the bathtub is a good place). Rinse 3 times more than you think necessary, otherwise the cane will quickly split. Do this as quickly as possible and dry fast, so that the water won't hurt a wooden finish (especially if antique).

REMOVING POLISH: Use a solution of 1 tbsp. vinegar to 1 pt. (½ liter) warm water. Dry and repolish.

Cleaning Upholstery

LEATHER AND SUEDE: Remember that these are skin. Leather needs polishing with furniture cream to keep it supple and prevent cracking. Or use saddle soap.

To clean leather, swab with a Handi Wipe wrung out in a solution of lukewarm water and mild soap. Rinse thoroughly several times with another Handi Wipe wrung out in clear water. Dry with cloths.

Treat grease stains on light-colored leather as quickly as possible. When you buy a leather article, get a tube of rubber cement from a hardware store. Spread a thick solution of this over any stain. Peel off when almost dry. It doesn't always remove the stain, but it's well worth a try.

Suede is an almost impossible fabric to clean. You can try to remove grease marks with dry-cleaning solvent, then restore the nap afterward by rubbing *lightly* with an emery board. When suede is very soiled you can use fine sandpaper. Buy suede only if you can afford his 'n' her swimming pools, a Lear jet, a townhouse in New York City, etc.

IMITATION LEATHER UPHOLSTERY: Use a good commercial car upholstery cleaner such as Nu-Vinyl.

Don't use abrasive cleaners on any plastics as they may scratch. Never wash with strong soap or the upholstery will crack. Reinforced plastics can be repaired with car body-repair kits, then repainted with polyurethane paint.

FABRIC-COVERED UPHOLSTERY: Clean by taking off the cushions and vacuuming or brushing out the corners of the furniture. Shampoo periodically with a foam carpet cleaner applied with a cloth, not a brush. Do not use a liquid cleaner because moisture can seep through to the filling and rot it. Work on one area at a time and be careful to overlap each area with the next. If you have a real problem, call in a professional upholstery cleaner. You will be happily amazed at the results he can get—often retrieving what would appear to be a lost cause. Never try to clean velvet upholstery; it's a professional job.

SLIPCOVERS: Every few months you might tumble them in the dryer without heat, just to get the dust out. When really dirty, dry clean if possible, as they are less likely to shrink. Otherwise machine wash in lukewarm water. Make sure the detergent has dissolved before putting in the fabric. Treat gently. Squeeze or spin damp-dry. Don't twist or wring. Replace on chair while the seams are still slightly damp; they will then stretch out to fit neatly.

Removing Furniture Stains

CIGARETTE BURNS, INK, OR PAINT STAINS: You can eliminate light marks as follows. (I do it myself, but you might prefer to get professional help, or first practice on something of little value.) Rub with fine dry steel wool or sandpaper. As you have now removed the color as well as the polish, rub in linseed oil to darken. Leave to soak in, then the next day or so give it a coat of polish and buff well. It's best to try this out first on a bit of the wood that doesn't show.

ALCOHOL SPOTS AND RINGS: You can rarely remove these if they have been left on a table too long. But try rubbing on cigar ash with a wet finger or rub the surface with mineral oil; dry and apply paste wax. In the future wipe fast after parties. You can, of course, rub down the *whole* surface of the table, then repolish, as above.

RUST STAINS: Remove by rubbing with petroleum jelly.

WHITE RINGS AND HEAT MARKS ON A FRENCH-POLISHED SURFACE: Try a very little alcohol rubbed on with a soft cloth. Repolish with brown shoe polish while the surface is still soft.

SCRATCHES: On deeply scratched light woodwork, fill the scars with beeswax, otherwise neutral shoe polish can hide scratches. On deeply scratched dark wooden furniture, drip on matching colored sealing wax to fill, smooth evenly and polish. For minor scratches on dark wood, try touching up with iodine, shoe polish, or olive oil on a cotton swab. Try to eliminate bad marks by rubbing down gently with finest steel wool, then refinishing. (I've always had success with this.) Fine furniture, if badly scratched, should be professionally sanded and refinished.

REPAIRING TINY HOLES (SMALLER THAN PEPPERCORNS): Sounds as if you have termites. You can either apply a special insecticide or holler for help from an antique expert. I wouldn't take any chances here as termites spread exceedingly fast to other wood—window frames, floorboards, beams. Never import any pieces of furniture into your home without checking it for those sinister tiny holes, although much fake antique furniture has phony holes, cunningly inserted in the factory. If you're dubious, stand the item on newspaper for a month. Tiny piles of sawdust mean you've got termites.

CANDLEWAX: Scrape off as much as possible with a blunt knife. If the wax is on a carpet or upholstery, cover it with tissue or blotting paper and hold a hot steam iron just clear of the paper, so that it warms the wax, which you then blot, using a fresh bit of tissue each time. If it is on fabric, place the fabric between two bits of blotting paper and iron. Then clean with dry-cleaning fluid. Work from the middle of the stain to the edge.

GREASE MARKS: On sofas, chair backs and arms or bed headboards. Rub gently with a cloth and dry-cleaning fluid. Work from outer edge of stain inward. Then, if necessary, repeat with another cloth wrung out in a solution of warm water and liquid detergent. Rinse well.

LIGHT FITTINGS AND PICTURES

If possible, remove fittings to clean. Alternatively, get a steady stool or ladder if they are at ceiling level. Wear rubber gloves. Turn off switch. Wipe bulb. (You can lose 25 percent of your light with a grimy bulb.) Dust with a feather duster, especially paper shades. Try to remove dirt marks with a gum eraser, or try a (just) damp cloth. Wash acrylic shades with warm soapy water (I wash them in the bath). Let them drain on a towel: don't rub them or you will increase static, which attracts dirt. (It's worth telling you this twice.)

Clean glass and frames of pictures with a Handi Wipe damped with alcohol.

TACKLING INDIVIDUAL ROOMS

Bedrooms

MATTRESSES: Take the polyethylene wrapping off mattresses and pillows or they may eventually mildew. A kapok, feather or hair mattress should be turned from end to end daily (thought I'd let you know). A spring interior needs turning only once a month. You need do nothing to a rubber mattress.

CLEANING MATTRESS STAINS. For these, as well as stuffed toys, use upholstery shampoo, rinse, then thump with towel until damp dry. URINE STAINS, "spot" with solution of ½ cup white vinegar and ½ cup cold water. Blot dry. Apply solution of ½ cup liquid detergent mixed well with lukewarm water. Leave 10 minutes. Blot dry, rinse liberally with cool water. Buy a cotton mattress cover if your mattress is clean but you can't get the stains out.

SHEETS: With indelible ink, mark each corner of every sheet "S" for single, "D" for double, "K" for king size, and so on. Although you can feel the difference in weight, one has days when one isn't certain of anything, and they certainly aren't improved by unfolding and folding clean sheets for half the morning. Permanently pressed sheets never seem to wear, but the middle of a sheet is nevertheless the part that somebody puts his foot through first when it's wearing thin (the sheet, that is). When sheets are showing signs of wear but before they get too thin, you can convert the less worn sides into middles by cutting the sheets down the middle and joining the 2 outside edges together with a flat seam. Then hem the 2 outside edges. You can also make new pillowcases from old sheets.

Mend holes in sheets by sewing a square patch on either side, considerably bigger than the hole, or apply a stick-on patch (see p. 82).

If stored in too warm a place, sheets can yellow. Send them to the laundry with a note or wash them yourself using a mild bleach, not a strong household bleach that might rot the fibers.

If you're tired of your permanent press sheets, why not swap your roses for someone else's lilacs? Whatever you do, don't try to dye these no-iron sheets, or they'll go blotchy (the dye people say they won't, but mine always do); and don't ever dye *anything* flower patterned; they end up looking really tacky.

BLANKETS: Before washing, soak really dirty blankets in the bathtub in cold water with a softener such as Calgon. Cotton blanket covers are easier to clean than blankets.

To clean spots on a blanket, put a thick towel underneath the dirty area and "spot" with a damp cloth dipped in baking soda. Rinse by squeezing a wet washcloth over the spot and blot dry with a towel.

Blankets can be turned sides to middle like sheets, when they have become thin and worn, then covered with a blanket cover. Another use for aged blankets is this old campers' trick: Use 3 thin blankets underneath the bottom sheet for warmth.

CLOSETS AND DRAWERS: Empty closets, wipe with a sponge wrung out in detergent and warm water. Don't get the wood too wet. When dry, line closets and drawers with self-adhesive Con-Tact to prevent bottoms from getting dirty again; wallpaper or lining paper is often prettier.

I find the best way to keep a closet dry, and therefore mildew-free, is to fill a cloth bag with 12 oz. (350 g.) of diatomaceous earth granules (available for a few cents from a drugstore). Hang it in the lower half of the closet. When the bag is about double its original weight through absorption of moisture, empty the granules into an aluminum pan and bake in a 400°F (200°C) oven for an hour or so. Then you refill the bag. For less than a couple of dollars buy a commercial variant of the above called De-Moist.

So that it doesn't get grubby looking, I paint the inside of the closet a dark but dramatic color—last year it was plum, this year it's cigar—so that the clothes look more dramatic against it. Try keeping your closets in apple-pie order: You will enjoy picking out your clothes just as you do when you select from a store rack.

To encourage this self-deception, I hang clothes not in *logical* order—all skirts, all blouses—but in the enticing, inviting way in which they're displayed in some shops: in *color* order. It's just as easy to remember that you want the *pink* blouse as to remember that you want the blouse.

I use shoe boxes and stacking wicker baskets for belts, jewelry, and similar fiddly items which I keep on the closet shelf or in a drawer.

Because I have to travel a lot, and much of it is at short notice, I use the back of the closet door for my current checklist of traveling clothes, and can quite truly pack to travel halfway around the world in 10 minutes.

A tip I got a long time ago from Shirley Lord, vice-president of Helena Rubinstein, is to keep a separate makeup case for traveling. Even if you aren't (as she then was) married to a millionaire, you can make your own *instant travel kit* by saving up little empty bottles and decanting a little of your everyday makeup into them. Also, try not quite finishing your blusher or eye shadow, then popping the old one into your travel bag when you buy a new one. I also keep an emergency first-aid kit in a small plastic bag because a Band-Aid in time can save trotting out to hunt for a drugstore in a foreign place.

I never buy anything from a store to help tidy the closet. Such items are very expensive and make the clothes that much more difficult to get at. There are 2 exceptions: (1)

simple metal or plastic-coated-wire shoe racks, which I think are great space savers and (2) hang-up shoe bags, in which you can keep shoes and/or to use, as I do, for storing my hair dryer, mending equipment, and so forth. This also hangs on the back of the closet door.

To keep my drawers neat, and garments accessible, I file all my underwear in clear plastic bags (2 sizes, big ones and little sandwich baggies).

It seems only sensible to keep shoe-cleaning equipment where the shoes are cleaned, which is by the sink, and I keep a towel in the bag for spreading out on the counter before I get to work on them.

To CLEAN HAIR BRUSHES: Wash in warm water with detergent. Expensive wooden-backed teak, rosewood or ebony hair brushes, with natural bristle, shouldn't be *immersed* in water. Rinse in clear warm water then finally slosh in cold water to harden the bristles, and wave fiercely and quickly to flick the water out, before laying on their backs to dry, away from direct heat.

Bathroom

AN OVERALL ROUTINE: Owners of small children might find it worthwhile to keep a brush, dustpan, and wastepaper basket in, and exclusively for, the bathroom, so you can deal with those candy wrappers, discarded toilet paper rolls, and empty bottles, talcum powder cans, and tissue boxes.

Remove hair spray from mirrors with a Handi Wipe soaked in alcohol.

To solve the sleazy soap problem there are lots of nasty plastic devices. Instead I use a saucer and cut a circle to fit into it from a ½-in.-thick foam plastic cloth (choosing pale blue to match the bathroom). The soap stands on that. No sludge, no slime, just rinse the foam pad occasionally.

THE BATH: I find a hand shower invaluable for bathing tots, getting kids to wash themselves, for rinsing hair, but *especially* for cleaning the tub. More backs may have been put out cleaning bathtubs than in any other activity.

If you have serious stain problems that just won't yield to elbow grease, these tips may help. Use a cleanser that contains a *mild* abrasive, such as Soft Scrub, on the bathtub (harsh abrasives may scratch the tub surface), or try dry detergent powder (Tide). Never use toilet bowl cleaner for the tub; it's too harsh. For general grime and dinge, run a full hot bath and pour in detergent. Let the foamy mess soak for at least 6 hours; then rinse out with cold water.

Removing stains from bathtub. Rub stain hard with cloth dipped in vinegar. If that doesn't work, try a mild abrasive. For coppery green and tan stains, cut a lemon and smear the juice (citric acid) on the offending areas. Leave overnight, then wash off thoroughly. Or try equal quantities of hydrogen peroxide and baking powder, mixed to a paste and left overnight. Or apply "Janitor in a Drum" which removes even lime stains as well as scum and rust. For really nasty brown stains use oxalic acid (wear rubber gloves), and rinse thoroughly.

Clean chrome bath taps with a cloth and soapy water. Polish with a soft cloth. If stains persist, rub on dry baking soda with a damp cloth. Don't use abrasive scourers on chrome or in time they will rub away the finish. Polish with automobile chrome cleaner, if you must. Clean dirty tap bases with an old toothbrush. (Also good for wooden carving.)

THE SHOWER: If your shower starts losing power, it may be because you're in a hard water area and a lime deposit is building up in the shower head and blocking the water exits. Remove head, soak for 10 minutes in vinegar, then rub off the deposit with an old toothbrush. Wash shower-head in warm soapy water, rinse, dry, and replace. After showering, pull the curtain *outside* the tub and spread it to dry. Then you won't get mildew on the bottom. Avoid black scum marks on shower tiles by cleaning them thoroughly with Tide or Softscrub then when dry, spraying with a colorless, silicone furniture spray and allowing to dry.

THE TOILET: Keep your toilet brush in water with a little disinfectant. You don't have to buy a smart holder. I keep mine in a hand-decorated paint can or an earthenware flower pot on matching base.

Clean the toilet bowl by lifting the seat and pouring in a bucket of hot water with bleach or detergent and a disinfectant such as Lysol. Scrub with a long-handled toilet brush. Swab the outside of the bowl and seat with a sponge.

A dirty toilet bowl can be cleaned with Vanish or

chlorine bleach (never both because the combination produces chlorine gas vapors). Alternately, for very bad stains, use Old Mother Conran's toilet cleaner (p. 00).

Toilets are meant for human waste and nothing else. Anything else is likely to block it, including large wedges of toilet paper or tissue, cotton swabs, newspaper, sanitary napkins, or tea bags. If your toilet gets blocked, see Maintenance, p. 170, or holler for a plumber (see the Yellow Pages).

Kitchen

CLEANING-UP ROUTINE: Put food away and straighten up cabinets; clean windows, ledges, and working surfaces, then the equipment, in that order.

STOVE: Turn off the electricity or the pilot lights. Be sure the burners are switched off and remove any pots and pans. Half fill the sink with hot water and detergent. Remove grill pan, burners, shelves, and trays and put in the sink to soak if there is room, preferably overnight in hot water with ½ cup of Axion (an enzyme solution works best). Wipe enameled parts with a warm damp sponge. Use a mild abrasive for stubborn dirt on stove enamel (or sinks). You're not supposed to use a harsh abrasive or a caustic cleaner on enamel areas or on the inside of an oven, but if you are faced with a filthy oven buy a spray cleaner, such as Easy-Off, or make your own (see below). Otherwise clean the oven with hot water and detergent. Scrub burners, grill pan, shelves, trays (gas and electric ovens vary somewhat in their elements). Rinse, dry, then replace. Remember to light the gas pilot lights and test, or turn on the electricity.

If you don't mind having an oven with pale gray streaks (and who's going to look in it?), you can make your oven self-cleaning (sort of). Dissolve ½ oz. baking soda in ½ pt. warm water. Wipe over interior oven surface, and the next time you clean it, the muck will come off easily. Then reapply solution.

Grill pan. Unable to find out how to clean the exterior of a really filthy oven and grill pan, I eventually telephoned the manufacturer. "You shouldn't have let it get filthy," they chided me severely. Apart from its being none of their business, it wasn't a helpful answer, because I had bought the filthy oven along with the filthy apartment.

If it has a handle and it's plastic, remove it. (You may need a Phillips screwdriver.) Remember, they hitched it on somehow; all you have to do is find out what they did and reverse it. Now attack with an abrasive cleanser such as Comet and vicious little scouring pads or Brillo, and to hell with those gentle warm water instructions.

SINK: Clean the sink, whether porcelain or stainless steel, with hot water and dishwashing liquid.

Porcelain sink. Sprinkle detergent, then fill with a few inches of warm water and 4 tbsp. of chlorine bleach. Rub, leave 10 minutes, rub again. Rinse well. For stubborn stains: Mix 2 tbsp. baking powder with enough hydrogen peroxide to make a paste. Apply with a rag. Leave overnight.

Stainless steel sink. Never use an abrasive or scourer or you may scratch it. Try one of the special stainless steel cleansers. If dull, wipe with vinegar on a sponge, then dry.

Sink outlet. To clean the outlet pour 4 tbsp. of washing soda down the drain (aim for the first of every month, then you might remember), and flush with hot soapy water. Alternately you can use a cup of bleach.

Anything, except water, is likely to block a sink (unless you have a fitted electrical waste disposer). That includes coffee grounds, matchsticks, tea bags, and vegetable peelings. So use a sink drainer and keep a plunger handy. (This is a stick with a rubber, hollow breast shape on the end of it. Buy the "C" cup size.) If the sink does stop up, turn to Maintenance, p. 170, How to Unblock a Sink Drain.

REFRIGERATOR: A refrigerator won't do its job of keeping food fresh if you leave the door open or jam in so much food that the cold air can't circulate around it. If the cooling unit gets clogged up with ice it can't do its job efficiently. Always leave a refrigerator open if you turn off the gas or electricity when you go on vacation, otherwise the inside may become spotted with nasty green mold.

Wrap all food in plastic bags or keep in covered boxes or bowls, or cellophane wrap or aluminum foil. Otherwise the liederkranz may impart its flavor to the raspberry mousse which may in turn add an interesting bouquet to the milk and butter. Don't refrigerate dripping jars or cans. Clean really dirty shelves with a sponge dampened with a solution of warm water and strong detergent. Close the tops or fold the inner seals of packages before putting them away. An open package of bicarbonate of soda prevents smells. Regularly wipe out bread, cake, and cookie bin.

If you don't have an automatic defrosting refrigerator, you should defrost it once every 2 weeks to save operating costs. A frosted refrigerator is expensive to run. Turn off the refrigerator. Take all the food out and throw away anything from the back that is growing whiskers or looks too small to survive. A good place to store things (while you're cleaning the refrigerator) is in the empty dishwasher or on a utility cart or worktable. Take out the shelves and empty the ice trays. Wash the shelves and plastic boxes and bowls with warm water and a little baking soda. (You shouldn't use detergent because it can leave a soapy smell if not rinsed off thoroughly.)

Wait for the ice to melt. *On no account dig at it with a knife or any sharp instrument* or you may have to buy a new refrigerator. You can speed up defrosting by leaving the door open and putting a pot of hot water in the middle of the refrigerator. An even better tip: If you have an old-fashioned hair dryer with a hose attachment, plug the dryer into the nearest socket and put the hose end into the freezer. Better put a tray or folded towel or both on the bottom shelf to prevent the melted ice from running all over the kitchen floor.

CARE OF SMALL ELECTRICAL APPLIANCES: Never immerse one in water unless the manufacturer says you can; don't overload; don't use metal scouring pads to clean them; keep them clean and dry; have them serviced regularly. Unplug small appliances before cleaning. Never poke with hairpins, paper clips, or *anything*.

Dishwasher. Clean as you would a stainless steel sink, with hot water and dishwashing liquid. Do not put cast iron, pewter, bone-handled or other hollow-handled knives, anything gilded or antique or hand-painted, in your dishwasher.

Blender. Fill it two-thirds full with hot soapy water, put the lid on, and switch it on for 30 seconds. Then rinse out under the tap.

Electric fan. Wipe the blades, base, and grill with a damp cloth. Then wipe with a cloth wrung out in soapy water, and finally, with a cloth wrung out in clean water. Towel dry.

Air-conditioner. Wash or change the filter every month, or even more often. Reusable filters can be washed in soapy water, rinsed in clean water, then dried, and replaced.

POTS, PANS, AND DISHES: If you are left with a nasty burnt mess in your pans, try soaking them overnight in lukewarm water and a handful of enzyme presoak, such as Axion. Sometimes you may have to leave them several days, but this advice has saved many pots for many ladies, and, in fact, this is the *only* way I clean saucepans.

Before using a pot for the first time, wash it in hot soapy water. Rinse and dry thoroughly. Wipe with cooking oil, then wash, wipe, and oil again. Don't put a pot directly onto a very hot burner; start it on a low flame and then turn it up to a higher heat. Don't leave empty pots and pans on the burners or in the oven.

If Teflon discolors, try mixing 2 tbsp. baking soda, ¼ cup household bleach, and 1 cup water. Boil this solution in the stained pan for 5 minutes. Wash, rinse, and dry. Wipe with oil before using.

Nonstick pans. Don't use abrasives and scourers or you may remove the nonstick surface. Don't use metal implements; use wooden spoons, (plastic spoons melt). Don't store nonstick pans inside one another or they may scratch. When they stick, clean the pans and repeat the wash-wipe-oil treatment twice.

Aluminum pans. Don't scrape them with metal spoons as they scratch the surface. Don't use washing soda, which is bad for aluminum. Don't use a harsh scouring pad. If you shove a hot aluminum frying pan into water, it will hiss and perhaps buckle; cool it first.

Clean aluminum pots that have gone dark by filling them with water and boiling up some rhubarb or a sliced lemon or some other acid food. If food has been burned or fish has been cooked in it, boil a little water in the pan and squirt in some dishwashing liquid *before* you take it off the stove.

Stainless steel pans (such as Revere Ware) and enamelware. Don't use abrasives or harsh scouring pads or silver or brass cleaner, as they can pit the surface. Use hot water and detergent to clean. (Dishwasher detergent, if necessary).

If the inside discolors, fill with hot water and 2 tbsp. bleach. Leave overnight, then wash thoroughly. To remove stains from enamelware you can also try a solution of 1 tablespoon baking soda to ½ pt. warm water.

To clean *stainless steel cutlery*, put neat bleach in a bowl and dunk cutlery for about an hour or longer. Then rinse. They will sparkle like new.

Cast-iron cookware. If vitreous-lined, use *only hot water* and detergent. If not vitreous-lined, clean as quickly as possible after using with warm water and detergent. Dry, then rub with oil on a paper towel to discourage rusting.

Clean rusting cast iron by drying it thoroughly and rubbing an oiled rag over it. If your cast iron is really rusty, scour thoroughly with fine steel wool, then wash with dishwashing liquid and hot water. Dry thoroughly by popping into the oven for a minute. Oil thoroughly with a rag. Then bake (empty) on lowest possible oven temperature for an hour. On no account use this method to treat cast-iron pots that have enameled interiors.

Ovenproof dishes. These are not necessarily flameproof. Unless they are stamped "flame-proof" assume they are not (however "ovenish" they look), and don't use them on top of the stove. I lost a beautiful and expensive Royal Worcester fish dish that way. Play it safe and always use an asbestos mat on an *electric* burner, but don't try this trick on a naked gas flame because the stove could be damaged.

Don't put anything plastic or with a plastic handle in the oven or the plastic will probably melt.

As with enamelware, never clean with abrasives or harsh scouring pads.

Hot dishes and plates straight from the oven can mark wood, plastic, tablecloths, painted surfaces. Don't ever risk it. (Plastics aren't magic and can scratch, burn and chip.) Buy cheap, natural cork table mats. Never stand a hot dish on china or it will crack if not shatter.

Corning Ware. Not nonstick, but you can freeze food in it and then take it straight from the freezer to a hot oven and the dish won't crack—that's why they make rocket nosecones of the stuff. There's a hook-on handle that enables the dishes to be used directly on the flame as saucepans. Get the stains off by soaking overnight in water and 1 tbsp. of Axion.

TRAYS: Don't use abrasive powders on trays with a printed pattern (especially tin trays) or you risk scratching the pattern off. Wash with hot water and dishwasher liquid.

HANDLING ORNAMENTAL FINISHES, CUTLERY, AND CHINA, GLASS, AND WOOD WARE

Metal Utensils

BRASS, COPPER, AND BRONZE: If it's lacquered it doesn't need cleaning, only dusting. If it isn't lacquered and not used for cooking, why not lacquer it? You can buy cellulose clear lacquer in your local hardware store. It dries very quickly (in about 10 minutes) and hardens in an hour.

PEWTER: It shouldn't be necessary to clean modern pewter with anything but detergent and water. For heavy stains try cleaning with a brass polish, such as Brasso, or a metal polish, such as Noxon. Don't use silver polish—it isn't coarse enough. Neglected antique pewter can be cleaned in caustic soda, but as it's dangerous, wear gloves. In a vitreous enamel pail, dissolve a cup of caustic soda in 2 gal. (9 liters) warm water. Put pewter in and boil for 2 hours. Allow to cool, fish out pewter, and try Comet or Ajax (gently), then wash in hot water. Rub with brass polish. Whew!

SILVER: Goddard's is an excellent, fast silver cleaner. Alternately, make your own.

If possible, keep in a silver bag to prevent scratching and tarnishing. Good stores sell yard-long baize bags with divisions for each different set of implements. This also means that silver is stored in the minimum space. You might make your own bag.

Keep a bag of alum or camphor in the drawer to prevent its going black.

Never let bleach get near silver; the result is a disastrous stain impossible to remove. Brides have been known to burst into tears as yet another wedding gift, a thinly silver-plated gravy boat, turns irrevocably black before the first anniversary. Having had the same trouble myself I won't bother you with pages of tedious chemical reasoning, but the main offenders are lemon, white vinegar, fruit juice, alcohol, anything acid. Egg and salt can also stain silver. (Eventually, after rubbing my gravy boat with all sorts of never-fail "quick clean" preparations, I had it replated.)

If you want your gravy boat to gleam when its donor comes to dinner, you should wash it as soon as possible after each use. Never leave sauces, nor gravy, nor mayonnaise, nor vinaigrette in any silver container, *never*. Similarly, never leave sauces in any other silver container, such as a bowl, nor on spoons. I lost a lovely rat-tail teaspoon through leaving it in a jar of chutney. The silver was eaten away.

Get egg tarnish off silver by rubbing it with salt and lemon juice. Vinegar, lemon juice, egg and salt can also stain silver cutlery, so wash as fast as possible. Incidentally, don't use silverdip on stainless steel because it pits it.

For general silver cleaning, try Goddard's. Or use my silver cleaning cloth (p. 61).

STORING AND MAINTAINING KNIVES: Keep them in a compartment or jar (blade upright) by themselves because you will be less likely to cut yourself and you'll keep the knives from scratching other implements. Don't leave ivory- or plastic-handled knives in hot water or put them in the dishwasher. (The glue will melt.) Carbon steel knives should be wiped clean after use and rubbed with cooking oil before putting away. Remove stains with emery paper. Sharpen on carborundum stone.

China

Don't pile china in a cupboard unless it is designed to stack. China is at risk if stored too high, too low, or too far back in a cupboard. Things that are difficult to reach are more likely to get broken.

TEA STAINS: Remove tea stains from china by soaking overnight in a solution of denture cleaner. If you don't use the stuff, rub china with a damp cloth dipped in baking soda or Borax, or pour in a solution of 1/2 cup bleach to 2 qt. water. Rinse and dry.

Tea stains inside the teapot. Fill the teapot with boiling water, add 1 tsp. denture cleaning powder, and stir. Leave overnight, rinse thoroughly. Alternately, don't let anyone look inside your teapot.

Glass and Crystal

Natural materials are not static. They expand with heat and contract with cold and damp. If you hold a glass under the hot tap it may expand too fast and crack. If you pour hot water into a glass, put in a spoon to absorb the heat.

Wash with soapy water. Rinse. Then rinse again in a bowl containing 1 cup vinegar to 6 cups water. Air dry, don't rub.

GLASS DECANTERS AND NARROW-NECKED VASES: The Vanderbilt butlers cleaned these by swilling them around with brandy and lead gunshot pellets. *You* can soak them overnight in an enzyme presoak (Axion) and warm water. Best to avoid stains by rinsing out the decanter as soon as possible after use.

Wood

BOWLS, PLATES, CHOPPING BOARDS: Don't leave in too warm a place. Don't dry near direct heat as they may split. Don't use abrasive powders or steel wool. Don't leave damp. Never leave to soak or the wood will quickly split. Dry immediately. When dry, rub lightly with oil on a paper towel. If a salad bowl gets smelly, wash quickly in warm, soapy water, rinse thoroughly, and dry immediately. Don't put it in the dishwasher. Scrub chopping boards with dishwashing liquid and hot water and dry immediately.

NATURAL, UNTREATED WOOD SURFACES: To clean your table or chopping block, wipe with a cloth sprinkled with dishwashing liquid. *Rinse well, repeatedly.* With a cloth, apply a half-and-half solution of chlorine bleach and water. Rinse well, repeatedly. If there are knife cuts or other marks, rub down the surface with steel wool or sandpaper (first use a heavy grade, finishing with a light one), then rub with a rag dipped in mineral oil, and wipe dry.

GETTING RID OF THE GARBAGE

ELECTRIC WASTE DISPOSALS: These sink units eliminate the sludgy smelly stuff. If your community allows you to use one, get the sort that unclogs itself when you push a button, otherwise you may be sending out frequent SOS's to a repairman. Whatever make you have and however careful you are, you will need 4 times as many teaspoons as before. Disposal units seem to ensnare them, like insect-eating orchids.

TRASH CANS: A pedal can drives me crazy because it generally has an inadequate base balance and is therefore unsteady and tips drunkenly toward me every time I tread on the pedal. And it doesn't take enough of my trash. I use plastic waist-high garbage cans (lined with plastic bags), which stack when empty. I also use these in the bathroom for dirty laundry.

WALL-MOUNTED LITTER SACKS: I haven't the patience to push each one into place. Also, everyone in the family, except me, invariably overfills them so that the bags fall downwards out of their holder, and then there's a mess on the floor to clean up.

GARBAGE CANS: Metal ones make noise and get bent; the large plastic ones split; hence my choice of smaller size plastic kitchen receptacles. I wash mine in the bathtub with warm water and detergent and a stiff brush. Rinse with clear water and disinfectant. Tip them upside down in the tub to dry.

Keep extra plastic garbage bags in your kitchen paper drawer for those moments when all your trash bins are full and you need additional receptacles for rubbish. Good for cleaning up after parties and Christmas.

A trashmasher electric garbage compactor is invaluable if you live in the country and have to get rid of your own garbage, although the sacks are very expensive. Depending on what you dump in it, it can reduce 8 sacks of garbage to one sack; it's quiet (except when crushing bottles) and will eat almost anything. Hide the key so that baby can't compact whatever it cares to throw in.

GETTING RID OF NASTY SMELLS

How do you get rid of a *persistent* nasty smell, such as in a rented apartment that seems previously to have housed a dozen cats? It's amazing to think that our ancestors dealt with this problem before anyone thought of disguising the odor with synthetic daffodil spray. They would open windows and doors to create a draft, and you can continue this tradition.

Other, more sophisticated, ways to disguise smells are by using Airwick, or by burning incense, scented candles, or the special perfumes from Mary Chess. You can also place jars of potpourri on your radiators—the heat diffuses the aroma of the dried flowers and spices.

In a bathroom use Lysol spray. In a kitchen, boil cloves in a cup of vinegar.

If you install a ventilating fan in your kitchen, either in the window or over the oven, **buy a strong one.** Your oven fan should be hooded.

Common Household Odors

COOKING OR TOBACCO: To rid clothes of these odors hang them in the open air for several hours. To get rid of the smell of *perspiration*, wash, rinse thoroughly in warm water with a little added vinegar, then rinse in clear luke-warm water, and dry, if possible, in the open air.

ONION OR FISH: To remove either of these smells from *knives*, push them up to the hilt in earth (e.g., your kitchen window box of herbs). Add 1 tsp. mustard powder to the dishwater to get the smell of fish off *silver*. Add 1 tsp. of vinegar to dishwater to remove a fishy smell from *china*. If you can't get rid of a smell in a *saucepan*, try boiling a little vinegar in it for a minute.

PAINT: When you're painting, cut an onion in half and put it cut sides up in the room. Afterwards, throw it away fast so you don't accidentally use it for cooking.

SMOKE: After a party or poker session, place a cup of vinegar in the room.

CAT OR DOG: Air the place. Open all doors and windows. Turn on all fans. If the animals are still resident, bathe them. Then wash whatever rugs they lie on, and swab all upholstered surfaces with a cloth wrung out in warm, soapy water. Dry with a clean cloth. Train your animal to sleep in its own place (basket and/or rug). Wash this *at least* once a week. Change the cat litter box daily and sprinkle 1 tbsp. of baking soda on the bottom of the box before adding new litter.

DRAIN: Every time you use the sink, flush out the drain with hot water and, once a week, put ½ cup of baking soda down it, then flush again with hot water. If you think something malodorous is stuck in the U bend, or trap, try using a plunger, then flush with hot water. If that doesn't work, unscrew the bolt in the U bend in the same way as if you'd lost your diamond ring down it (see Maintenance, p. 170).

GARBAGE: Empty the kitchen trash can every day (after dinner is best). To avoid the can or pail getting dirty, line it with a paper sack (including the ones in which you bring the food home) or with a plastic garbage sack (many sanitation departments require that trash be securely bagged). When dirty, clean can or pail by squirting dishwashing liquid into it, adding ½ cup chlorine bleach, and half filling with water. Sponge sides; pour dirty water down the sink, then rinse the sink.

HOW TO WASH THE DISHES

NOTE: *With* a dishwasher never put in antique or precious glass, hand-painted or valuable china or bone-handled knives or wood or plastic anything. It's worth telling you this twice. Probably the manufacturers are cautiously covering themselves because I have heard of a family which eats entirely from plastics and uses a dishwasher for it. You might risk a trial run with a plastic article, if it is not valuable.

Read the instructions book *before* using the dishwasher for the first time.

WASHING WITHOUT A DISHWASHER AND SAVING ENERGY: With two sinks, or a sink and a rinsing bowl and two washing up racks, you rarely need to dry up, although you might need to polish glass and cutlery. Breakages happen if too many things are crowded into the bowl or piled up to drain. If you are right-handed and planning a kitchen from scratch, remember that you will wash up from right to left, so plan to have the draining surface on the left.

If there's only one drainer and not much space around the sink use a nearby table to stack and then to drain, or pull up a utility cart behind you (or to one side) on which to stack the dishes. (Glasses and cutlery, plates and cups on top, serving dishes on lower shelf and cooking pots beneath.) As you clear one surface into the sink—use it for draining. Spread a towel on any drying surface which doesn't drain into the sink, or the china won't drain dry.

If you say "but utility carts are the sort of thing my *grandmother* had," I would say "with good reason." If you can get hers, grab it fast. Use it as a push-around extra work and stowing space. I use one when I'm painting (pictures), when cooking in tiny areas with little storage space, when sewing, and sometimes when doing a repair job.

Washing up starts with *proper stacking*. Some would-be male helpers tend to pile things into a sink, higgledy-piggledy, run warm water on them and then leave them. These men probably never have to reach into the greasy cold water to remove the dishes in order to put in hot water to start actually doing the washing. I may be a female chauvinist, but I find that men also tend to ignore the goo on the undersides of plates and they think that saucepans, baking tins and vegetable dishes don't count or get done by leprechauns . . .

Empty coffee grounds or tea leaves. Scrape bits off plates and stack crockery and utensils according to size and greasiness.

Put cutlery and table silver to soak in a jug or saucepan of hot water and detergent. Keep bone or wooden handles out of water.

Wash articles in this order: glass, silver, cutlery, non-greasy china, non-greasy serving pans, greasy china, greasy serving pans, cooking pans.

Wash glass in warm water and detergent and rinse in clear warm water. Use a soft nail brush or old toothbrush for cut glass.

Keep party china or rarely used china in plastic bags, so that you don't have to wash it again before using it.

Clean sink outlet. Wipe stove and grill pan, drainer, sink. Rinse dishcloth and spread to dry.

What to do with the time you've SAVED

First, take stock of yourself (body, soul, and mind). Decide which areas could stand some improvement. Decide what changes would improve your quality of life. New friends? Fewer friends? Less weight? More curves? More fun? Less distractions? Once you've decided what you want, stand up, take a deep breath, and START!

WHAT YOU CAN DO INSIDE YOUR HOME

Make yourself more beautiful: This basically entails taking better care of yourself, encouraging healthy narcissism, learning to love and take care of your body, conditioning your skin and hair. Learn to relax. Take care of your clothes.

IMPROVE YOUR HEALTH: Do some exercises every day—find the particular ones that work best for you. Grope your way out of bed and do them right away. Take up jogging. Choose a well-balanced diet and stick to it.

FURTHER YOUR EDUCATION: Do you want to know more about anything? Did you get a high school diploma? Do you need an advanced degree in order to get out there and work at something that is fulfilling and lucrative? (Some people have 3 degrees and still take courses.) Arrange to take extension courses from a state university branch or local college. You can take many courses at home, which can be the best place to study.

WHAT YOU CAN DO OUTSIDE YOUR HOME

ATTEND DAYTIME OR EVENING CLASSES: Do you realize the many areas you can explore? Wouldn't you like to be better informed about one of the following: antiques, art history, astronomy, beauty culture, boat building, ceramics, chamber music, chess, citizens' rights, cooking on a shoestring, decorating, dramatic arts, dressmaking, French, German, Greek, Italian, Spanish, Russian, guitar-making, jewelry designing, model engineering, painting, photography, psychology, sculpture, toy making, weaving, wine making, woodworking, or (heaven help you!) writing?

If you can't locally find the class you want, you and enough interested people may be able to persuade your local school board to run an evening class on anything— it's likely to operate quite a selection anyway.

PREPARE FOR A NEW CAREER: If you have enough time, you could sign up for a course in a subject that especially interests you and may eventually lead to a well-paying job. Many companies will pay all or part of the employees' cost for serious self-improvement courses in language, law, economics, history, sociology, philosophy, business administration, real estate, nursing, teaching, or other work-related subjects. I know a young man who, while an office boy at a large New York corporation, earned his law degree this way and wound up a company vice-president.

ENJOY SOME PHYSICAL ACTIVITY: By which I don't necessarily mean play softball unless you really like softball. Visit your local schools, YWCA, YWHA to find out what's being offered. If you were always hopeless at sports at school, go in for something gentle and uncompetitive like yoga or dancing (classical, modern, ballet, ballroom, Latin American, or folk). A sure way to get exercise is to join a gym, or golf or tennis club. We should all jog for 15 minutes 3 times a week. This supposedly adds up to 6 miles, according to experts, who haven't timed *me*.

If you live near a lake or river, get out on it! You can row a boat, paddle a canoe, or sail a rented Sunfish—you may even get hooked on all water sports from scuba diving to sailing around the world. Half the battle is taking the initiative. Do it now!

HELP SOMEBODY WHO NEEDS YOU: All charities are begging for your help. Working for others can be the most rewarding of all out-of-home activities—it can also be the most demanding. Most good causes are well advertised. All you have to do is turn up or telephone to offer your services. If you would like to do charitable work and really don't know where you might best be of service, ask a minister or rabbi for advice. You needn't be a churchgoer.

MEET MEN: If this is your specific aim in your free time, go about it methodically and intelligently, like any other project. The celebrated Lady Docker of England, who was once a salesclerk, said that she married millionaires because she mixed with them. Go where the men are: to educational courses likely to attract men—accounting, law, science, math or participate in unisex sports that men prefer—sailing, skiing, canoeing, golfing, backpacking, skindiving, or tennis. Do not allow yourself to be conned into any amateur dramatic group, tennis club, charity work, artistic evening class, or above all, singles club if your main purpose is to meet men. Such snake pits are full of beady-eyed man chasers (not like you, of course) and generally unchaseworthy men.

CONFESSIONS OF A DRY
CLEANER'S DAUGHTER,
or How to Keep Clothes and Remove Stains

In the last decade there's been a 10 percent decline in the number of dry-cleaning stores in the United States. Speaking traitorously as a dry cleaner's daughter, I would say a lot more of you would save even more on cleaning bills if you would equip yourself with my stain removal kit (see p. 76). Keep it in a drawer out of the reach of children, and remember to clearly label all bottles. If possible, order the chemicals by their generic names from the hardware store (e.g., trichloroethylene, instead of dry-cleaning fluid) because it's much cheaper. (It costs less than $3 a qt. at a hardware store.)

Whatever the stain, if there's nothing available with which to treat it, act immediately by soaking in lots of *cold water*. If cold water doesn't remove the stain, try using lukewarm water and ordinary soap, followed by lots of rinsing in clear water. *Never use hot water or you may permanently set the stain.* The 7 golden rules of stain removal are:

- Treat stains as quickly as possible.
- Never use hot water.
- Treat from the wrong side of the fabric, if possible, so that the dirt needn't be pushed right through it.
- If the fabric is colored, first check the effect of any chemical remover on an inconspicuous area.
- After using a chemical, rinse well in lukewarm water.
- Use a weak solution several times, rather than a strong solution once.
- Avoid leaving a ring in place of the stain by this old trick I learned at my daddy's knee known in the trade as "spotting." When using a chemical always make a ring larger than the stained area, then gradually work in toward the stain, never vice versa. Treat potential water rings in the same way. After treatment, place the still-wet article on a towel and thump the fabric dry with another towel, *working around the edge* of the treated area, and toward the middle.

For the stain remover there are 2 SORTS OF FABRICS: nonwashable and washable (if in doubt treat as nonwashable). There are 3 KINDS OF STAINS: greasy (cooking oil), nongreasy (vinegar), and a combination of both (vinaigrette dressing).

The theory of stain removal is to either dissolve the stain or wash it out. If you don't know a specific treatment, choose one of these main methods.

TREATING DIFFERENT TYPES OF FABRIC

Nonwashable Fabrics

NONGREASE STAINS:

Procedure A: Sponge with lots of cool water. Work liquid detergent into the stain then rinse off well with lukewarm water (*not* hot water). If stain remains, try Procedure D (see further on).

GREASE STAINS:

Procedure B: Dab with a wad of absorbent cotton (tissues are no good) soaked in a grease solvent such as trichloroethylene (which is a grease solvent) or any old brand name cleaning fluid. Repeat until the stain disappears. If it doesn't disappear, it isn't a grease stain. Trico (as it's called in the trade) dissolves rubber, so don't use it on rubberbacked items, such as rainwear or sports clothes. Work near an open window so that the slightly toxic fumes evaporate quickly. Don't smoke.

COMBINATION STAINS:

Procedure C: First try *Procedure B*. If stain remains, then it isn't grease. Allow to dry thoroughly and try *Procedure A*. If the dratted stain is still there, try *Procedure D* (see further on).

Procedure D: If the stain disappears but you are left with a yellowish spot, apply a *mild* bleach solution.

(Mild bleach solution: Buy 20 vol 4 percent hydrogen peroxide, from a drugstore, and dilute 50/50 with water.)

Apply to stain with a Q-tip. Leave for 5 to 15 minutes. Watch it: don't walk away. Snatch it up as soon as the stain goes and rinse thoroughly.

WARNING: Store-bought household bleaches (such as Clorox) are a strong mixture of chlorine bleach and disinfectant and should not be used for stain removal on fabric.

Procedure E: Do not use chlorine bleach on silk, wool, acetate, rayon, polyurethane foam, mohair, leather, or special finish fabrics such as spandex. Instead, try a solution of 4 tbsp. ammonia to 4 tbsp. water. Dampen stain with solution until stain disappears. Then rinse off in cold water, followed by another rinse in cold water and vinegar (1 quart water and 1 tbsp. vinegar) followed by a final rinse in clear water.

ANONYMOUS STAINS AND HARDENED OLD STAINS: Perhaps you want to tackle a hardened old stain, like ice cream on a child's dress, that you didn't notice last summer. Or perhaps you've no idea what the stain is. A friend of mine, who runs a hotel, and whose life is filled with anonymous stains, always uses:

Procedure F: Dab eucalyptus oil with a Q-tip or cotton

swab on the hard, dried-out stain and leave overnight to float off the stain. The next morning, remove the eucalyptus oil with Trico or dry-cleaning solvent. Then, if the stain is still there, try Procedure A, then Procedure D.

Washable Fabrics

NONGREASE STAINS: Try *Procedure A.* If stain remains, try *Procedure D.*

GREASE STAINS: Try *Procedure B.*

COMBINATION STAINS and ANONYMOUS STAINS: Try *Procedure C,* as for nonwashables.

PROTEIN STAINS:

Procedure G: Soak for several hours in warm water, or overnight in cold water in which has been carefully and completely dissolved a little enzyme presoak such as Axion. (About 1 tbsp. Axion to 1 quart water.) This breaks down the protein molecules in stains for urine, sweat, blood, milk, egg, tea, coffee, fruit, wine, and vegetable matter.

Warning 1: Enzymes don't work in water that's too hot for your hand.

Warning 2: If you don't dissolve the powder completely, you risk having little white spots all over the garment.

SCORCH, MILDEW OR MAKEUP STAINS: Test fabric on a hidden seam, then use *Procedure D.* It's always worth trying. I once scorched a beautiful pink suit, gave it to a friend for charity, and, much to my chagrin, saw her wearing it the next week without the scorch mark. She had used *Procedure D.*

My Daddy taught me NEVER to buy white wool or white crepe or white garments of questionable repute. After dry cleaning, it will never regain its virgin bloom, any more than a white dinner jacket will.

STAIN SURVIVAL KIT—A Real Moneysaver

General Supplies

You will need a bucket and a box containing the following: packet of tissues, 2 small sponges, 2 old handkerchiefs, Q-tips, cotton wool, ordinary clothesbrush, wire clothesbrush (use gently, it's a ruthless weapon), Scotch tape (for wrapping around knuckles, sticky side out, then dabbing at lint on a dark suit), can of dry-cleaning spray (removes spots without leaving a ring, and especially good for ties), small, heavy mixing basin (not plastic), enzyme presoak such as Axion, chlorine bleach, alcohol, ammonia, vinegar.

FOR WATER-SOLUBLE STAINS: baking soda, washing soda, Borax, small jar of liquid dishwashing detergent.

FOR FAT, OIL, AND GREASE STAINS: rubbing alcohol, benzine, turpentine, eucalyptus oil (to soften hard paint and old stiff stains). Commercial oil-paint remover or thinner, grease solvent such as trichloroethylene (use near open window and don't smoke).

FOR OTHER ASSORTED PROBLEMS: You may also need an eraser (for wallpaper), blotting paper (for candle wax), acetone (for nail polish), powdered denture cleaner (for stained teapots).

HOW TO REMOVE THE STAINS IN YOUR LIFE

A Garden-Variety Selection of Common Stains

Please forgive some repetitions; I want to give you a concise, comprehensive reference list.

ALCOHOL: To remove drink stains after a party, "spot" with rubbing alcohol. For acetate fabric, dilute 1 part alcohol and 2 parts water.

ANIMAL MESSES: Sponge with Borax solution (1 pt. water to

1 tbsp. Borax). Rugs especially won't smell so much if you squirt the area with soda water. Even the Queen of England resorts to this when her corgis misbehave.

ANTIPERSPIRANTS: Sponge with mixture of 50/50 liquid detergent and warm water. Try sponging with ammonia. For silk and wool, dilute ammonia with water 50/50.

BALLPOINT PEN: Soak with alcohol.

BEER: Sponge immediately with plenty of clear cold water.

BIRD DROPPINGS: Dissolve a handful of washing soda and 1 tbsp. of a soapless detergent in half a bucket of warm water. Scrub gently.

BLOOD, MEAT JUICE, AND GRAVY: Once dried, especially by heat, blood is very difficult to remove. A carpet cleaner once told me of an emergency call he received: A guy had had a spat with his wife; in fact, he had smashed a hammer across her head. As the carpet was white wall-to-wall, he had the presence of mind to immediately call the carpet cleaner as well as the ambulance. That's what I call sangfroid. But he could have tried a strong enzyme presoak solution, then sponged lavishly with cold water, and finally tried cold water plus a tbsp. of ammonia.

CANDLE WAX: Although any manicurist or Latin lover will tell you never to use them as weapons, scrape as much wax as possible off with your fingernails. If the wax is on wood, do the best you can by rubbing with fingernail and ball of finger. If the wax is on cloth, place blotting paper over the stain and iron with a hot iron. Attack any remaining stain with trichloroethylene.

CANDY AND CHOCOLATE: Treat as a combination stain. (Procedure C.)

CARBON PAPER: On fingers or clothing, use dry-cleaning fluid or trichloroethylene.

CHEWING GUM: To freeze-harden the gum, rub with a cube of ice (in a plastic bag to prevent wetting the material), scrape as much as possible off with a fingernail, then use dry-cleaning fluid.

COFFEE, TEA (and, I discovered recently, curry on a pink dressing gown): Instant action essential. Sponge with Borax and warm water. If stain persists, treat as a combination stain. (Procedure C.)

COSMETICS: Mostly colored grease. Remove even the powder around your neckline by "spotting" with trichloroethylene, followed by the procedure for nongrease stains and then Procedure D for yellowish spots.

FELT-TIP PEN: Water-soluble. Soak immediately, then use soap and warm water.

FRUIT: Wash out immediately in cold water, then warm water with an enzyme presoak. Wash delicate fabrics in cold water, then work eucalyptus oil into stain and leave for 1 hour to "float" the stain off. Then wash out with detergent and warm water. On nonwashable fabrics leave the oil for several hours, then sponge with liquid detergent and water. Better still, always tuck your napkin in your collar when eating spaghetti or peaches, regardless of the company, because a fruit stain is a potential fast disaster.

GRASS OR SEAWEED: Spot with alcohol, then wash thoroughly.

GREASE: Try Procedure B, then, if necessary, Procedures F and D.

HAIR SPRAY: To remove this sticky substance from mirrors, wipe them with alcohol.

HUMAN BEINGS: For stains you can't get off your skin, such as Band-Aid marks, enamel paint, or tar on feet, try clear acetone.

ICE CREAM: Use trichloroethylene, then wash.

JELLY AND JAM: Soak in warm Borax solution (1 pt. water to 1 oz. Borax), then wash.

LATEX ADHESIVE: Can be removed with rubber solvent (trichloroethylene).

LIPSTICK: See Cosmetics.

MAKEUP: See Cosmetics.

MILDEW: Brush off as much as possible, then employ Procedure D.

MOLD: Brush off mold, wash garment with soap and water (if garment is washable), rinse well, and dry in the sun.

NECKTIES: Treat as appropriate, but treat whole tie, not just the stain. Regularly clean neckties by swabbing with trichloroethylene. Then, after thumping dry with a towel, press into shape by hand or under a damp cloth. Never send ties to the cleaner's, especially not an expensive lined one. The more expensive a tie, the easier a dry cleaner can ruin it.

PAINT: If you are painting, buy 2 pt. oil-paint remover or 2 pt. rubbing alcohol—when you need it you need it quickly and plentifully (as when you've upset a can of paint on the oriental rug).

A pool of paint. First spoon up all you can of the free

liquid, working from the edge inward so as not to enlarge the area affected. Mop with newspaper, then with tissues.

Latex water-based paint. Wash immediately with lots of cold water. If stain has set, try rubbing alcohol, but I don't hold out much hope for an old stain. You could pick at it with a comb, or thumb and forefinger.

Oil paint on natural fibers. Mop up. Soak immediately and liberally with commercial paint remover, then wash with lots and lots of cold water. If you have no remover, remember the way an artist cleans oil brushes: Wipe well with newspaper, rub with a rag soaked in turpentine, then wash in warm soapy water.

Oil paint on artificial fabrics and most plastics (including vinyl floor tiles). Soak with rubbing alcohol until all traces of paint are gone. Wash with lukewarm water and detergent.

Oil or emulsion paint that has set. Cross your fingers, and apply a little paint thinner. This will quickly soften the paint. It may soften everything else as well, so stand by with lots of water to stop the rot. Once softened, old paint stains can be treated as fresh paint stains. Paint thinner is wonderful for taming oil paint (and varnish, polyurethane sealers, etc.). The only snag is that it dissolves any plastics and adhesives, so if you don't watch out you can really come unstuck. It is also good for cleaning paintbrushes—just dunk thoroughly in paint thinner for 5 minutes, then hold under the cold water faucet.

PET MESSES: Mop or wipe up. Either squirt with soda water or else make a paste of 2 tablespoons baking soda with lukewarm water. Apply to area, allow to dry and vacuum off.

PERSPIRATION: See "Antiperspirant." If yellowish stain remains, try Procedure D.

RUST: I know of no commercial preparation that removes rust stain from fabrics more efficiently than this do-it-yourself formula: Mix ¾ oz. potassium persulfate in 1 pt. of water. Soak the spot with it. Rinse and repeat the treatment if necessary.

For mild stains, stretch the stained area over (not in) a basin full of boiling water (you need the steam action), and squeeze fresh lemon juice on it. If unsuccessful, it won't hurt to then try a commercial rust remover or the above recipe.

SCORCH MARKS: Rinse immediately in cold running water,

sponge with Borax and water. If this gives no results, try Procedure D.

SEAWATER:

On fabrics. Sponge with warm water to dissolve salt. If stain persists, spot with rubbing alcohol, then launder or dry clean.

On shoes. Try 2 tsp. rubbing alcohol to 1 tbsp. milk. Rub on, leave to dry, then repolish. If unsuccessful, apply shoe dye of the same color on the entire shoe.

SHOE POLISH: Difficult. Try Procedures B, then A, then D.

SOOT: Brush off excess and sponge with trichloroethylene.

TAR: Scrape off with back of a knife or with thumbnail. Swab with turpentine, then trichloroethylene. If you get *tar in your hair* after swimming in the ocean, get someone else to wash it off, a hank at a time, patiently, with detergent, then give hair an oil treatment. Douse it with cooking oil and leave on overnight (put towel over pillow); shampoo in the morning. Float tar off a dog or cat's paw by rubbing in eucalyptus oil, leave for half an hour, then wash off with warm water and detergent. Repeat until tar is completely removed.

URINE: Sponge or wash in lukewarm water. Sponge remaining stain with a solution of vinegar and water (1 tbsp. vinegar to 1 pt. water).

YELLOWISH, VAGUE STAINS: Launder, then try Procedure D.

VOMIT: Sponge with Borax solution. If on a carpet, remove vomit with a cloth, then squirt soda water to get rid of the smell. Rinse cloth, then boil in saucepan of water with 1 tbsp. of vinegar to remove the smell. (Also good for sleazy washcloths.)

WALLPAPER MARKS: Try to avoid cleaning wallpaper—nobody minds a spot here or there (could you hang something over it?). If the paper is not washable, you'd risk leaving a large, obvious "clean" patch that will show how grubby the rest of the wallpaper is. If washable, as many wallpapers today are, wipe with a damp cloth or sponge. Otherwise, try a soft eraser or a piece of soft bread. For grease marks try a proprietary dry cleaner.

WAX CRAYON: Try procedure A, and then Procedure D.

WINE: Stretch the stained bit of fabric over a basin, keeping it in position with a rubber band or string. Push material down into a solution of one teaspoon borax to one cup warm water for half an hour. Then launder or dry clean.

WORD OF WARNING: Do not mix the following combinations:
- *Acetate* + acetone (or nail polish remover) or chlorine bleach.
- *Modacrylic* + acetone or hydrogen peroxide.
- *Polyester* + chlorine bleach or acetone or trichloroethylene.
- *Silk* or *wool* + chlorine bleach or hydrogen peroxide
- *Permanent press cotton, spandex, rayon, mohair, leather, polyurethane* + chlorine bleach.

HOW TO GIVE YOUR CLOTHES A REST

Sorting Out Clothes

Twice a year I file my clothes into 2 piles. To accomplish this requires some ruthless weeding out.

PILE 1: (This first pile is contributed to charity or to thrift shops.)
- Clothes that I never felt comfortable in after leaving the shop. (Speaking as an ex-fashion editor, I don't think you can aim at being really stunning unless you're prepared for a 15 percent mistake-allowance in your clothes budget.)
- Last year's cheap passing fashions.
- Anything that's too small.
- Anything bought on sale and never worn. (Do not buy at sales unless *you'd planned to buy it anyway*.)

PILE 2: (Do not sell, give away, or throw away this pile; rather, give these clothes a rest.)
- Anything I once loved dearly but haven't worn for a year.
- Any fashion that has *just* passed (which is when it looks its worst).
- Anything I feel everyone has seen me in too often.

I keep an old 1920s cabin-trunk, beautifully fitted, for filing these clothes. By storing instead of discarding you will not experience the pain of awaking the following day regretting your commendable job of sorting out. And next year, what a joy to see once again that classic navy and white striped silk scarf you'd forgotten about, that low-cut black number that makes you look a size smaller, and that high-necked angora dress that looks quite different now that you've had your hair cut short—and they all fit you. All clothes should be cleaned before filing, but not necessarily pressed. Add moth repellant.

Staying slim, or at least the same size, is the biggest economy you can make. Nevertheless, I keep a few clothes handy for when I'm a larger size—I hang these at the far end of the closet. This way, during those months when there's more of me to love, the extra is not visible through bursting seams.

Sorting Out Makeup

I also file old makeup. I never throw out anything I've stopped using, but keep it all sorted out in plastic bags in a big cardboard box. It takes up hardly any room, and on those days when I feel I badly need a new face I don't rush out and spend a fortune. Rather, I have a happy dip in my beauty box, experiment with products I'd forgotten about (all of which, amazingly, are in the correct color range for me), and emerge with several products that feel new to me. If some of the creams have separated, I mix them up again with my finger; if some of the water-based products have dried up, I add a little water or skin freshener; and if the nail polish has gone thick, it can be made to run again by adding a drop or 2 of nail polish remover.

SWIFT SEWING BOX

I used to have a great big efficient grandmother-type sewing box with pretty rows of different colored threads and so forth. I used to have a basket grandly labeled SEWING, which was generally overflowing with school clothes that I couldn't summon up the energy to attack.

Then I realized that when traveling on business, I could take a tiny travel sewing kit and immediately repair anything that needed it. I put this kit on the television set in the sitting room and pointed it out to the men in the family. Now anyone who has anything that needs sewing does it himself. I never asked them to. I just don't sew for anyone over 7, but I *do* see that the sewing kit is stocked up. If the men in your life travel, get them cheap pocket sewing books (from the five-and-dime), smaller than a passport. I've just given one to each of the men in my life and you'd thought I was dishing out gold cufflinks; they seemed pathetically grateful. I almost felt guilty.

BASIC SEWING KIT

- Needles, large and small.
- Pins.
- Small scissors.
- Thimble.
- Tape measure.
- Spools of thread: black, white, beige, brown, pale blue.
- Black button thread.
- Elastic.
- Trouser-band hooks.
- Hooks and eyes.
- Snaps.
- Seam ripper.
- Transparent plastic button bag.
- Odd sock bag.
- A pair of old jeans to cut up to use for patches.

When my children were small I kept a little emergency box by the front door containing 2 needles, threaded (black and white thread) and knotted (I rethreaded them on Sunday mornings); a few shirt buttons; and change for bus fares.

ZIPPER TIP: Zippers are less likely to stick if you close them before cleaning the garment. If your zipper sticks, it might be because a thread has caught in it. On the other hand, it might need lubrication: Try a light touch of cooking oil or grease—even your face cream might unstick it. If your zipper won't stay up and it's not because the garment is too small for you, pull it up, then slap a piece of Scotch transparent tape horizontally across it, or vertically up the zipper as a temporary measure.

SEWING TIP: I once worked with Charlotte Altmann, an exquisitely dressed architect who made all her own clothes (including tailoring) and her own furnishings. She only ever used one stitch—a running stitch with three stitches, then she over-sewed the third stitch. I had no confidence in her method but I tried it—and have used no other stitch for all sewing jobs for the past fifteen years.

SUPERWASH

Which Washing Product?

They really ought to print the washing powder instructions on the cornflakes pack because everybody *reads* the cornflakes pack. For washerwomen who are bewildered by manufacturers' claims, descriptions and instructions, here are the encapsulated facts about washing products.

As I've said, the word "detergent" is derived from the Latin for "cleaner." Pure soap was the original detergent for washing people, clothes and homes. Synthetic detergents are a mixture of chemicals, each one with a different purpose, such as scum-inhibiting.

You would use a soft, good quality solid soap on your face rather than a harsh, household soap which you might use on the tougher, dirtier floor. Similarly, you should use two sorts of synthetic detergents for your laundry: *strong* (such as Tide) for heavy-duty cleaning of fabrics such as cotton, and *weak* for more delicate materials like silk.

To make a weak laundry detergent, simply weaken a strong detergent dissolving 1 cup strong detergent with 1 cup warm water. Bottle it. And use as you need it.

There are three *textures* of cleaner: (1) solid, (2) powder or flake and (3) liquid. A liquid detergent does the same job as a light-duty powder or flakes. It is liquid merely for convenience.

How much to use: Whatever you use, it is important when washing clothes to maintain a good lather throughout the wash, except for special, low-lather products used with front-loading automatic washing machines. On no account use high-lather products in these or the machine may leak.

Enzyme presoaks (such as Axion) break down proteins by chemical action during soaking, so that the garment can then be washed by detergents in the normal way.

Natural body proteins include blood, sweat and urine as well as most food stains, such as egg yolk and cocoa. (Stubborn old stains may need several soakings.)

NEVER presoak wool, silk, fabrics which are not colorfast or specially finished fabrics, such as permanent-press, in anything at all.

It is important to remember that the enzymes need time to act. I find it easiest to soak in the bath overnight.

The longer the soak, the cooler the water can be. Generally speaking, soak garments overnight, eight hours in cold water with enzyme presoak, or an hour in hand-hot water (50°C or 122°F to be precise). If the water is too hot the enzymes will not act. So don't add presoak to a hot water machine wash.

Whether you do it once or twice a week (don't do it more often: save energy), don't do it on a Monday when you have all the clearing up from the weekend. Use gloves to protect your hands when laundering—a must if your skin is sensitive to washing powders.

Before Washing

Empty pockets, mend tears, remove stains. (Remember never to use *hot* water.) Sort clothes into the following piles and wash each pile separately:

- White cotton and linen.
- Colored cotton and linen.
- Nylon and other synthetics.
- Rayon and silk.
- Woolens.
- Items whose color you suspect might run.

Taking the Worry out of Washing

Always read the care instruction label on a garment. Use
very hot water for white and colorfast cottons (cheap
cottons are not always fast). Use hand-hot water for
synthetics, warm water for woolens and anything you're
dubious about.

FASTNESS: Wash all black things separately, it then won't
really matter if they're not fast. Never wash pale colors
with dark colors in case the colors bleed. Never wash
white with any other color. Colored sheets and towels
should be washed separately for the first few times as
surplus dye may come out. (It doesn't mean that they will
get paler.)

You can tell whether or not a color will run by wetting
a corner of it in hot water and squeezing it in a white
towel. Anything brightly colored or printed might run.
Graceful ethnic fabrics don't only run, *they gallop*.

I used to be very mean with water when handwashing.
Then an Italian laundrymaid saw me in action and told me
that you can never get anything clean if you wash it in
grubby water. Simple, really. She told me to keep on
rinsing until the water is clear, otherwise you risk a
grubby wash, a soapy smell and a sticky feel.

WOOLENS AND DELICATE FABRICS SUCH AS LACE: Always hand
wash unless such garments are definitely marked otherwise. Wash in cold water with Woolite. Do everything
gently. Rinse in cold water, squeeze gently, then press
damp-dry in a towel. Damp-dry an item by gently squeezing the water out of it (wringing can ruin the shape),
spreading it on a towel and rolling the towel up. Stand
on it barefoot for a moment. Repeat the process with a
dry towel.

Don't hang up woolens: lay them out on a towel, pull
into shape and leave to dry over the back of a sofa, or on
the table or somewhere else flat, and warm, but not hot.

Many garment manufacturers now produce treated wool
garments. You can wash such an item in a washing
machine and spin-dry it and it will still retain its shape.
Be careful to obey the manufacturer's washing instructions.

GIRDLES: Wash in lukewarm water, never boil. Don't iron.
Don't let it get too dirty. Don't wring it out: pat dry in a
towel and proceed as for woolens. Remember that the

average male does not consider it glamorous to see such items drying on the back of a sofa.

FABRIC SOFTENERS: Fabric softeners can be a lot of extra bother. If you use them, follow the manufacturer's instructions to add to the wash water, the final rinse, or the dryer. They work by coating the fibers with a thin, invisible layer, which includes silicones and thereby prevents the fibers from adhering to one another. This tends to make each item feel soft and fluffy as opposed to thick, compressed, and "felted" (a bit like blotting paper). They now come in both liquid (Downy) and sheet (Bounce) form. Good for blankets.

DON'T WASH

The rule is: If in doubt, dry clean.
- Angora or cashmere sweaters unless you have a tumble dryer. *Dry clean.*
- Anything cheap in crepe, satin, or corduroy, or acetate or rayon (unless the label says you can). You risk the garment's losing shape. *Dry clean.*
- A pleated skirt (unless the label says you can). *Dry clean.*
- Neckties. Best to try cleaning with your home dry-cleaning kit (see p. 76).

WHEN TO USE BLEACH

- To disinfect both the wash and the washing machine.
- To lift off heavy soil, stains, and residues of stains.
- To whiten and brighten fabrics.
- To remove stains from sinks or bathtubs, deodorize sinks and toilet bowls, remove stains from china, coffeepots, teapots and cups, disinfect chopping blocks, wells and swimming pools, and remove mildew, etc.

HOW TO USE BLEACH

- Use bleach carefully according to directions, but remember that bleach shortens the life of any fabric.
- Don't mix bleach with any other chemical or cleaner. It could be dangerous.
- When bleaching permanent-press garments, use *chlorine bleach* (such as Purex) for whites and an

oxygen bleach (such as Snowy) for colors (this is a preventive bleach that stops colors looking dingy rather than making them white).

- *Don't* add liquid chlorine bleach directly to the water at the beginning of the washing machine cycle or it may cancel out the optical brightener in the detergent. Dilute the bleach (½ pt. [250 ml] chlorine bleach mixed with 2 qt. [2 liters] water is the amount to add to 8 gal. [36 liters] of water), stop the machine, and add it halfway through the washing cycle.
- If you want *to restore whiteness to cotton and nylon* in 20 extra minutes in a washing machine: Use hottest possible water; dissolve twice as much soap or detergent as normal; wash clothes for 5 minutes; stop washer and add a strong bleach solution (1 cup chlorine bleach diluted in 1 qt. [1 liter] of water); run washing machine for 5 minutes; stop washer for 10 minutes; start washer and go through complete cycle.
- Chlorine bleach in granule form (such as Action) doesn't have to be diluted before being added to wash. It acts slower than liquid bleach.
- *Don't* use chlorine bleach on silk, wool, permanently treated clothes, spandex, mohair, leather, acetate, or rayon. Remember to check the labels on garments made from these fabrics to see if they specify "dry clean only."

COLD WATER DETERGENTS:

Advantages. Permanent pleats stay pleated, wool doesn't shrink, colors don't run, white nylon stays white, and you can save a substantial amount a year on your fuel bill (maybe up to $60).

So try cold water laundering unless you are in a hard-water area or using a public laundromat (where there is a bacteria risk) or where cold water is less than 32°F in winter.

Disadvantages. They can leave a residue on fabric and washing machine unless used in *cold* water.

When flame-resistant garments are washed in soap or nonphosphate detergents they lose their resistance.

WASHING IN SOFT-WATER AREAS

- Try a cold water wash.
- Use soap powder.

- Clean whites with a 10 minute presoak in bleach water. (¼ cup for 4 gal. [18 liters] of water).

WASHING IN HARD-WATER AREAS

- You can use Calgon powder to soften the water, or install an expensive water softener. Otherwise
- If soap is used in a hard-water area, a limestone scum will form.
- Synthetic detergents generally work very well in hard water.
- Try a *cold water* wash with a non-phosphate detergent and rinse very well (¼ cup Purex to 4 gal. [18 liters] of water for ten minutes.)
- **Warning: Non-phosphate detergents can clog your machine with calcium deposits if used with hot water.**
- If a *new washing machine* isn't giving as good results as hand washing, and you are in a hard-water area, try checking the washing instructions on the package. Check to be sure you're using the right washing agent for your machine and your local water, and if you are, then try using a lot more of it.

TIPS TO INCREASE EFFICIENCY:

Always thoroughly dissolve soap or detergent powder before adding clothes. Too much soap powder or synthetic detergent cannot harm a fabric, so long as it has been properly dissolved before the washing starts. (Except for some fully automatic washing machines and then the manufacturer tells you to put the dry powder in the machine before the clothes).

If the detergent hasn't been properly dissolved you risk a patchy-looking garment, so never sprinkle powdered detergent on clothes.

To hand wash. Use liquid dishwashing detergent, which is as mild as and cheaper than special soap powders.

Treasured or fragile items. Wash them by hand in a sink or bathtub. You are wildly optimistic if you wash a treasured garment in a washing machine.

Children's sleepwear. They have been flame-resistant since a 1976 law, and must be washed with a phosphate detergent in order to retain their resistance. If you use nonphosphate detergents, soak clothes afterward for an hour in a bucket of cold water and 1 cup vinegar; then rinse in clear water and dry. (Word of Warning: "Tris," a flame-resistant treatment, has been banned by the federal government as a suspected carcinogen. Make sure the package clearly states No "Tris.")

If your permanent-press clothes wrinkle. Pretreat spots by rubbing in dishwashing liquid; don't wash heavy and light items together; don't overload washing machine or dryer; give garments a final rinse in cold water. Take out of dryer immediately on stopping or (if you don't want to be hanging around the dryer waiting for it to stop), drip-dry the garments over the shower rod, squeezing the bottoms, and gently pulling into shape.

Loading a washing machine. Don't put more things in the machine than will comfortably fit. Don't pack it like a suitcase. If you don't feel like, or don't have a scale for, weighing the sheets, fill the machine two-thirds full, as a rough guide. Always put stockings and underwear in a pillowcase so they don't catch in the machine.

For scummy-looking wash. Once a month try putting it through the washing machine as usual, only without adding soap or detergent to the water.

Eliminating wash-day blues. Do what I was taught by my father the dry cleaner: However desirable and alluring a garment looks or makes you look, if it is going to be a cleaning problem DON'T BUY IT. Don't buy anything that isn't colorfast, shrink-resistant, and no-iron. It is an amazingly easy rule to follow, once you've made up your mind to do it.

For dirt rings around collars and cuffs. Rub on liquid detergent or shampoo and leave for an hour, then wash.

For really dirty, grease-stained overalls. (Such as axle grease on a mechanic's overalls): Soak the stains liberally in kerosene. Then add one cup kerosene to the dishwasher and wash overalls alone.

Tumbler Driers: A good tumbler dryer can also reduce ironing by 90 percent. Don't fill it too full, half capacity at most or the clothes will wrinkle and take far longer to dry. For permanent-press items remove articles, shake out and hang or fold immediately they have finished tumbling. Pillows and other feather-filled objects can be washed whole and tumble-dried. Clean out the lint filter every time you load it and check the exhaust duct once a year or the engine will seize up.

Tips on Ironing

The secret of ironing is to avoid it. Don't think that you can't avoid it: I learned by accident when, fifteen years ago, I ironed a shirt. It took two tearsodden hours and I scorched it (some say, carefully). Since then it has been understood in my family that Mother Doesn't Iron (like Mother Doesn't Speak German or Mother Doesn't Play the Guitar or Mother Isn't Blonde.) In my family we are all allowed a couple of idiosyncrasies per person, we choose our own and respect everyone else's. Anyone who wants his shirts ironed does them himself and this is regarded by me as idiosyncratic.

If you like ironing (my mother finds it very soothing), put the iron on something flameproof, such as the asbestos pad on the end of the ironing board. Any old ironing board will do. My mother uses a cheap wooden one, which she covers with pretty materials at intervals, sticking it on with drawing pins.

Get a sleeve board: you can't iron a sleeve without it unless you mess around folding clean teatowels into arm-shaped pads.

If you're going to iron, do so while the clothes are still damp. If you can't iron at once, either roll up the clothes while still damp (I once accidentally left some sheets like this for a week and they went grey-green in parts) or else, just before you iron, wet with a flour shaker filled with water; the very best thing for damping-as-you-iron is a pressure sprayer, or, of course, a steam iron.

It is important to know what you're ironing. Read the label first. Silk, or any of the synthetics, can fall apart under your eyes if you use too hot an iron. If you know it's cotton or linen, use a hot iron. If you don't know, take it gently. Start ironing on a part that won't show in case you're about to burn it.

Always try to iron clothes through a damp cloth (you can buy a pressing cloth in the housewares department for this). Many cheap fabrics, such as boutique crepe and satin, should always be ironed through a damp cloth so the iron marks won't show.

The point of ironing on the wrong side is that ironing makes the material shiny. On the other hand, it's fiddly to turn things inside out and back again, and you risk creasing them more than they were in the beginning.

Never iron velvet; steam it. Put on your electric kettle to boil, and point the steam at the area you wish to de-crease. Wear rubber gloves so you won't steam-scald yourself. If you don't have a kettle, hang the velvet in the bathroom over the hottest possible bath. (This is also a good quick way to de-crease suits when traveling.) If that doesn't work, take it to the dry cleaner's.

Pressing is the same as ironing only you do it over a damp cloth and push hard.

WARNING: If you put ironed things away when warm but still a little damp (which is very easy), mildew will sprout.

FOOD

HOW TO SAVE TIME AND MONEY ON FOOD SHOPPING

Jeer if you must, but I've used the following grocery checklist for 12 years. I always write out my shopping list from my grocery checklist because otherwise I impulse buy.

Add to this list or draw up your own by writing down what's in your cupboards *now*. Star weekly necessities like this, *, and divide the list into supermarket, bakery, butcher, delicatessen, greengrocer, pet store, or whatever your taste and needs dictate.

Fix your checklist on the back of the kitchen door (I also tape one in the back of my address book). Or use the list in this book crossing out what you never use, and filling in your preferences. Before shopping, run your eye over your grocery list to check what you might need. Jot down grape jelly just *before* the jar is finished.

Get the family to write in the notebook if they finish

anything, or are about to do so. After a few peanut butter famines, they'll learn. Consider crossing off all junk food and substituting fresh fruit and vegetables, which can be crunched raw.

GROCERY CHECKLIST

For your weekly shopping list keep a spiral notebook, with an attached pencil, in the kitchen. You can also use this notebook for planning meals. Work out menus on the left-hand page; on the facing page write down what you need to buy in order to make them. You can then tear out the shopping list on the day you go to market. The ambitious might find that an office desk calendar makes a great, year-round menu planner (and you can then use it, painlessly, *next* year).

Bakery Products

Baking powder - bread - cakes and pies (fresh, frozen, mix) - cookies (fresh, frozen, mix) - cornmeal - crackers - croissants - doughnuts - flour - muffins and rolls (fresh, frozen, mix) - piecrust (mix, ready-made) - yeast

....

....

....

Cleansers and Household Items

(Some suggested brand names are noted in parentheses.) Aluminum foil - baking soda - bar soap, mild (Ivory), liquid detergent (Dawn) - basin/tub cleaner (Lysol) - bleach, chlorine (Purex) - bleach, non-chlorine (Snowy) - Borax - bug killer (in summer) - charcoal (in summer) - copper and brass polish (Brasso. You can use Brasso for any metal except silver, for which it is a bit coarse.) - detergent for delicate hand wash (Ivory Flakes, Lux) cold water detergent (Woolite) - detergent for washing machine (Tide) - dishwasher detergent (Cascade) - disinfectant (Lysol) - drain cleaner (Drano) - dustcloths - wood floor wax polish (Preen, liquid and spray wax)

- floor polish for linoleum, vinyl, or cork (Glo-Coat) - furniture polish (Pledge) - Handi Wipes - laundry presoak (Axion) - light bulbs - mop heads - nonscratch pads for Teflon - oven cleaner (Easy-Off) - paper napkins - paper towels - plastic bags - plastic trash can liners - plastic wrap (Saran) - rubber gloves - scouring pads - scouring powder (Comet) - shoe polish - silver polish (Goddard's, Noxon Quick-Dip) - soap pads (Brillo) - sponges - toilet bowl cleaner (Vanish) - washing soda (Arm and Hammer) - wax paper - window and glass cleaner (ammonia, Windex)

Dairy Products

Butter - buttermilk - cheese - cottage cheese - cream cheese - cream, sour and sweet - eggs - margarine - milk - yogurt

....

....

....

Drug Items

After-shave lotion - aspirin - Band-Aids - deodorant - hairspray - makeup - medicines - razor and blades - rubbing alcohol - sanitary napkins - shampoo - shaving cream or foam - soap - tampons - tissues - toilet paper - toothbrushes - toothpaste - vitamins

....

....

....

Fruit

FRESH:
Apples - apricots - bananas - blackberries - blueberries - cherries - cranberries - dates - figs - grapefruit - grapes - lemons - limes - melons (cantaloupe, casaba, cranshaw, honeydew, watermelon) - nectarines - oranges - peaches - pears - pineapple - plums - raspberries - rhubarb - strawberries - tangerines

CANNED OR IN JARS:

Applesauce - apricots - blackberries - blueberries - cherries (pitted, nonpitted) - cranberry sauce (whole, jellied) - figs - fruit cocktail - fruit pie fillings - grapefruit sections - oranges (juice) - peaches (slices, halves) - pear halves - pineapple (chunks, crushed, juice) - plums - raspberries - spiced apples

FROZEN:

Fruit (nonsweetened, mixed) - fruit salad - fruit in syrup (raspberries, strawberries) - peaches

....

....

....

Groceries

Beans - bouillon cubes - breakfast cereal - candy - canned goods - chocolate - coffee (beans, ground, instant) - desserts - dried fruits - dried milk - evaporated milk - frozen foods - herbs and spices - honey - ice cream - jam - jelly - juices (fresh, frozen, canned) - maple syrup - noodles - nuts (cocktail, almonds, cashews, peanuts, pecans, walnuts) - oil (corn, olive, peanut, polyunsaturated, sunflower) - olives - onions - pasta - peanut butter - pickles and relish - potato chips - rice - rolled oats - sauces - snacks - soft drinks - soups (canned, dried) - sugar - tea - tomatoes (canned, whole, puree) - vinegar

....

....

....

Baby Department

Canned baby food - cereals - cotton balls - disposable diapers - formula - juices - medicines - powder - Q-tips - shampoo - soap - viatmins

....

....

....

Liquor Store

Beer - bourbon - brandy - gin - liqueurs - rum - rye - scotch - vodka - wine (red, rosé, sherry, white)

....

....

....

Meat

FRESH OR FROZEN:
Roasts (boneless beef) - rump, bottom, top, eye round, shoulder, sirloin - boned beef - rib roast - lamb - cook-before-eating ham - fresh pork (butt, leg, loin, picnic shoulder) - cured pork shoulder - veal (leg, loin, shoulder, rib)
OTHER CUTS:
Beef or calves' liver - beef, lamb, pork, or veal cubes (stewmeat) - ground meat - lamb, pork, veal, loin, rib, or shoulder chops - brisket - short ribs - spare ribs - steaks (T-bone, filet mignon, porterhouse, club) - steaks (round, London broil, skirt, strip, flank) - steaks (cubed, minute) - veal cutlets (scaloppine) - veal breast
CANNED:
Corned beef - ham - deviled ham - hash (roast beef, corned beef) - liver paté - Spam - stew - Vienna sausage

....

....

....

Poultry

FRESH OR FROZEN:
Chicken (backs, breasts, drumsticks, thighs, wings, whole) - duck - goose - rock Cornish hen - turkey (backs, boneless roast, breasts, drumsticks, thighs, wings, whole)
CANNED:
Chicken or turkey, boned

....

....

....

Miscellaneous

Bacon - brains - cold cuts - corned beef - frankfurters -
kidneys - sausage - sweetbreads - tongue

....

....

....

Pet Department

Bird seed - cat food - cat litter - dog food - fish food - flea
powder - shampoo

....

....

....

Seafood

FRESH OR FROZEN:
Breaded fish (sticks, cakes, fillets, portions) - clams - crabs
- lobster (whole, tails) - oysters (shucked) - scallops -
shrimp (in shell, unshelled) - unbreaded fish (portions,
fillets) - whole fish (dressed)
CANNED:
Clams - crab - lobster - mackerel - salmon - shrimp - tuna

....

....

....

Vegetables

FRESH:
Acorn squash - artichokes - asparagus - avocados - beets -
broccoli - brussels sprouts - cabbage - carrots - cauliflower
- celery - chives - collards - corn - cucumber - eggplant -
garlic - green beans - kale - lettuce (iceberg, leaf, Boston,
romaine) - mint - mushrooms - onions - parsley - peas -

peppers - potatoes (white, sweet) - radishes - scallions - shallots - spinach - summer squash - tomatoes - turnips - watercress - wax beans - zucchini

CANNED:

Artichoke hearts - asparagus - beans (green, kidney, lima) - bean sprouts - beets - carrots - greens - mixed vegetables - mushrooms - okra- onions - peas - potatoes - sauerkraut - tomatoes - whole kernel corn - yams

FROZEN:

Asparagus - beans (green, lima) - broccoli - brussels sprouts - carrots - cauliflower - french fried potatoes - kale - mixed vegetables - okra - peas - spinach - summer squash - whole kernel corn

....

....

....

SEASONAL FOOD CHART

FRUITS:	WHEN AVAILABLE
Bananas	- *all year*
Lemons	- *all year*
Grapefruit	- *all year*, most plentiful January through May
Rhubarb	- *January to June*
Pineapples	- *March to June,* most plentiful April and May
Strawberries	- *peak May and June*
Cherries	- *May through August*
Cantaloupe	- *May through September*
Limes	- *all year*, peak June and July
Apricots	- *June and July*
Raspberries and blackberries	- *June through August*
Watermelon	- *peak June through August*
Blueberries	- *June through September*
Nectarines	- *June through September*
Peaches	- *June through September*
Plums	- *June to September*
Grapes	- *July through October*
Cranshaw melon	- *July through October*
Honeyball and honeydew melons	- *all year*, best July to October
Casaba melon	- *July to November*
Persian melon	- *August and September*
Pears, Bartlett	- *August through November*
Cranberries	- *September through January*
Apples	- *all year*, peak October through March (look for best local varieties early) summer through early winter)
Pears, other than Bartlett	- *November through May*
Tangerines	- *peak November through January*
Avocados	- *all year*, peak December through June
Oranges	- *all year* (depending on variety), peak December through June
Apricots	- some imports available December and January
VEGETABLES:	
Beans, lima	- *all year*, (pole beans, very locally)
Cabbage	- *all year*

Carrots	– *all year*
Celery	– *all year*
Potatoes	– *all year*
Sweet potatoes and yams	– *all year*, low May through July
Mushrooms	– *all year*, low in August
Asparagus	– *Mid-February* through June
Tomatoes	– most plentiful early spring *(March)* to fall
Peas	– most plentiful in spring *(March onward)*
Summer squash	– most plentiful in spring *(March)* through fall
Spinach	– best in early spring *(March)*
Lettuce	– *all year*, most plentiful in spring *(March* onward)
Artichokes	– *peak April* and May
Radishes	– most plentiful *May* through July
Cucumber	– most plentiful all summer *(May* onward)
Corn	– most plentiful *early May* through mid-September
Beans, green and wax	– May through October, best *June and July*
Beets	– *all year*, peak June through August
Onions	– *all year*, peak June through September
Peppers	– most plentiful late summer *(July* onward)
Broccoli	– *all year*, peak October to May (least abundant July and August)
Eggplant	– most plentiful late summer *(July* onward)
Cauliflower	– most plentiful *September* through January
Winter squash	– early fall *(October)* through late winter
Brussels sprouts	– peak *October* through February
Spinach	– late fall *(November* onward)

Making money is not easy; spending it is very easy; not wasting it is an art. But it's an art that anyone can learn, and although it requires a little discipline at first, you don't need nearly as much willpower as when following a diet . . . and the reward is real money . . . your unspent money—tax paid.

Considering the amount of time, money, and energy you spend in the supermarket, selecting a store should be undertaken with as much care as choosing a mate. In cities and suburbs, rival chains fight for your hand and the purse it clutches. If your dream emporium is only a few minutes away, you're in luck; but too often, nearest is dearest, especially if it's a quaint little place that's conveniently open at the odd hours when you invariably run out of something.

Start by investing a little time in choosing your store, taking into consideration distance from home, good management, quality, price, variety, layout, checkout traffic, and jam potential. This is the priority order advised by Jim McDonald, head of Safeway Stores. (When he took me to one of his stores to show me how to shop, the check-out girl nearly fainted when she recognized him: I couldn't have made a bigger impact had I been with Steve McQueen.)

To Shop Better

Your one aim is to get in and out as fast as possible. Try to beat your own best time on every trip. This way you'll not only save time but also money.

- *Set aside a specific time for marketing.* If possible at an hour when the store is apt to be uncrowded. It should be at the end of the week, and NEVER on Monday, when the produce is senile and the shelves depleted.

- *Always make a shopping list.* Try to stick to it. (That means leaving ravenous kids at home.) Don't be inflexible. If you see an amazingly cheap treat, such as a special on minced clams, which isn't on your list, buy it. But knock something else off.

- *Plan your shopping.* Remember that practice is what counts, not theory. So take your personal weaknesses into account as well as the limitations of your situation. For instance, if you overspend wildly when you're stuck with unanticipated guests, then planning ahead and stocking your cupboard with special items for these events can be regarded as a wise investment rather than as extravagance.

- *A working woman doesn't have time to comparison shop.* Nor does she have time to shop all the different markets for their advertised specials. Office-lunch-hour shopping or last-minute shopping can be very expensive and unsoothing. Face the fact that if you're working, it might be an overall saving to buy a little more food than you need each week.

- *Preplan the menus for an entire week.* At least preplan the main meal, putting down on your shopping list something vague like "2 fish dishes, 3 meat meals." You can then zero in on the week's supermarket specials. This flexibility also allows you to use leftovers. Cooking some of your main dishes ahead of time is a good, painless way to build up your freezer stock, cooking twice the amount needed for one meal.
- *Resist impulse buying.* But be flexible. If you'd planned on beef and the quality turns out to be poor, make a fast switch and substitute lamb, pork, or poultry. If the fresh vegetables are not so fresh, buy frozen.
- *Shop methodically.* Buy cans and dry goods first, then produce, then meat and dairy products, and frozen foods last. Make sure the perishables are put into the freezer and refrigerator as soon as you get home.

What Labels Mean

Labeling regulations in the United States are the envy of housekeepers throughout the rest of the Western world. You may get eyestrain just *thinking* about peering at all the fine print on package labels, but before settling on a favorite brand for a particular product, those labels should be read.

All that federal regulations require on the label are: the common or usual *name* of the food, the *form* (sliced, whole, cut, halves), the *liquid* in which it is packed, *net weight* (which includes the weight of the liquid), *added ingredients* (such as seasoning, flavoring, preservatives, coloring, or special sweeteners), *any special treatment*, and *the packer's or distributor's name and address.*

Beyond that, labels vary widely and wildly. Foods are graded for the benefit of the wholesaler, not the retail customer, so some packers put grades on their labels and others do not. Grade terminology is confusing because it is not uniform. With packaged foods, that are prepared or precooked, like spaghetti and meatballs or chicken pot pie, the ingredients must be listed, and the wording should be carefully observed. For example, "orange drink" means there is more water than orange juice in the drink; "gravy and meatballs" means more gravy than meat, while the reverse "meatballs and gravy" requires a fixed amount of meat, and more of it than gravy.

USDA GRADES: Meat and poultry are inspected federally (or by the state if the state system is equal to or stricter than the federal one) for wholesomeness, but the grades refer to *quality*.

Meat. All meat is graded, and you should look out for the U. S. Department of Agriculture stamp denoting Prime, Choice, or Good. In practice, most supermarket meat is Choice or Good. New federal beef grading standards that went into effect February 23, 1976, lowered the marbling requirements.

The designation *Choice* means that the meat is "very high quality, quite tender, juicy and flavorful," according to USDA standards, but has slightly less "marbling" (an intermixture of fat within the lean, which enhances both flavor and juiciness) than *Prime*. *Good* is leaner and not as juicy or flavorful, but is often a good buy. The grades apply to beef, veal, pork, and lamb.

Poultry. The only grade you are likely to see is USDA Grade A, meaning that the bird is meatier than lower grades. The overall best buy in poultry is generally a brand name, like Perdue or Paramount, though it's apt to be a bit more expensive.

Eggs. They are graded AA, A, or B, and sized—*extra large,* 27 oz. per dozen; *large,* 24 oz. per dozen; *medium,* 21 oz. per dozen; and *small,* 18 oz. per dozen. If there is less than a 7 cents spread in the price of a dozen eggs between 2 sizes, the *larger* size is the better buy. Grade A or AA is best for poaching or frying, Grade B for baking.

Milk and cheese. These are also graded. Milk should be Grade A.

Dating. On canned and packaged goods this is optional, as is nutrition labeling. For this reason it is difficult to compare brands. With regard to fresh produce such as milk and bread, the USDA points out, the quality of most items depends much more on how they have been stored and handled than on the dates.

Unit Pricing

This refers to the price per unit of food, as opposed to the price per package. Package sizes in supermarkets seem to be calculated to baffle the consumer. In 2 New York City area stores owned by the same chain, 9 brands of canned tuna were available in 6 different sizes. It takes an MIT graduate to figure whether an 18-oz. package of something for 69 cents is more or less expensive than a 16-oz. package for 66 cents (not to mention that 15½-oz. package).

Under the unit-pricing system the 18-oz. can should have a clearly visible label on the shelf—not on the can—saying that the contents cost $.038 per oz. Though shelf labels under the stacked products are mandatory in only a handful of states and some cities, thousands of chain stores voluntarily label their shelves with the name of the item, the size, and the unit price. If the unit price information is misleading, hard to read, or missing, complain to the manager! (This is one of the reasons you should shop at a well-managed store.)

What's in a Name

Not much. The reason that you will probably never see a TV commercial for those Kounty Kist canned beans or Aunt Nellie's soup is because they are private-label or "house" brands, which generally cost less than nationally advertised products, partly because they are not nationally advertised. Specifications for supermarkets' own brands are not necessarily higher, lower, or the same as for, say, Campbell's or General Foods products. But the chain's brands do generally cost less than their TV superstar equivalents. A Washington *Post* sampling of 26 A & P house-brand items (they have various names, including A & P, Ann Page, Superfine, and Jane Parker) showed that they cost $14.92 versus $17.38 for a comparable basket of nationally advertised foods.

Buying name-brand orange juice is particularly wasteful, because the Food and Drug Administration largely determines the standards and characteristics of all brands.

Don't be brainwashed by the commercials. Taste-test for yourself house v. national brands. Those ladies who "can't tell the difference" must have had their taste buds torn out at birth. Big-name manufacturers, who are naturally intent on pushing their own brands, will almost never reveal what products they put out under lower-priced chain-store labels. However, it helps to know that Heinz makes the soups for such chains as A & P, Grand Union, Giant, and Pantry Pride; Morton's, Diamond, and International make salt for a number of chains. A & P canned pineapple and fruit salad are made by Dole and Del Monte. Borden and Sealtest provide ice cream for several chains. And so forth.

HOW TO TELL IF FOOD IS FRESH

FRUIT: Most newspapers tell you what fruits are in good supply and well priced. Handle a fruit gently to decide if it's ripe; don't judge solely by appearance. A slightly bruised or speckled fruit, say, a peach, can be otherwise perfect, and you should be able to get it cheaper. Never buy more fresh fruit than you can eat, cook, preserve, or freeze within a day or so, otherwise it won't be fresh. Check your area for a good farmer's market or roadside produce stand.

FISH: Almost anywhere in the United States fresh fish is available at any time of the year. This includes shellfish, fish from lakes or streams, and saltwater *poisson*. However, though you can pick out your own live Maine lobster in Dallas or Chicago, you'll do much better with the prize that some hardy soul plucked out of local waters that morning. Since supermarket fish counters generally, and often literally, stink, it pays to cultivate a local fish market, who will tell you exactly what varieties are available when. To save time, have him prepare the fish as fillets or steaks, or pan-dress them (a whole fish scaled, eviscerated, and usually with the head and tail removed).

The scales and flesh must glisten, even the cuts should be bright. This shine applies not only to whole fish but also to fillets, chunks, and scallops. If dull, the fish has been around too long. Flesh should be firm, springy, and cling to the bone.

HOW TO TEST FOR FRESH FISH

- Try pressing the flesh with your finger; if the mark remains indented, the fish has started to go bad.
- Pick it up by the head or tail; the fish should be firm, not limp and floppy.
- The eyes should be bright, clear, full, bulging, and without traces of blood.
- Gills should be reddish pink and free of slime and odor.
- If a fish looks at all slimy (especially a boned fillet), it is deteriorating.
- If a fishtail is broken or brittle, it may mean that the fish is not fresh but has been frozen and defrosted, so pass it up.

Scallops. Check for shininess and firmness as well as color. Fresh scallops are pinkish white or soft yellow or orange; if they're gray and milky they're old.

Shrimp. They are usually available fresh only in July, August, and September. The rest of the year they're frozen and defrosted as the fish dealer needs them. Watch out for the shrimp if it has a carbolic odor (pick it up to sniff).

Crab. If you're buying soft-shelled crabs, remember they should be alive (so should lobsters), the shell should be brown and shiny, not dull.

HOW TO TEST GOOD MEAT

Fresh—that is refrigerated, not frozen—beef, lamb, pork, and poultry are in abundance everywhere at all seasons. If you have friends who hunt, it's always a treat to get gifts of game such as venison, hare, and pheasant that are generally unobtainable. Otherwise, getting meat that's really fresh is not much of a problem. More important is getting good-quality meat. At most supermarkets you can phone a butcher and get him to cut and dress meat exactly as you like.

In the long run, I find that it's not a wild extravagance to go to a small local butcher for *important* meat: the veal or leg of lamb for a big party, a rib roast for an anniversary.

Superorganized people who stock up on meat only twice a year, and eat out of the freezer, usually depend on a butcher shop to fill their special orders for such large quantities of meat. You can sometimes get a wholesale price if you buy meat this way.

Each variety of meat has different indications as to its age and quality. Generally speaking, it should be neither dark nor pale. It should be firm and elastic to the touch. It should not be unduly flabby or moist, and it certainly shouldn't smell. Cheaper cuts are as nutritious as the more costly cuts, but you have to spend a longer time preparing and cooking them.

Beef. Choosing good beef isn't easy, because so much depends on how it has been treated before it reaches the counter. The best beef comes from young animals, which after slaughtering are hung, head downward, for a few days in order to tenderize the meat with minimum loss of weight. Properly hung lean meat is moist and red with a brownish tinge, marbled—the fat between the lean should be firm and cream or pale yellow. Quality meat should include little or no gristle. Bones should be shiny and pink with perhaps a bluish tinge. With imported beef, the fat is nearer to white and the meat is pink.

Bright red meat hasn't been hung long enough. Brownish dry-looking meat could well come from an older, tougher animal, but is suitable for slow crockpot casserole cooking or braising.

Pork. It should not be excessively fat. The fat should be firm and milky white, not soft or oily. The meat should be pale pink, firm, and smooth, with little gristle. A fresh cut looks slightly moist, not dry. Bones are pinkish, tinged with pale blue. The skin should be thin, pliant, smooth, and hairless, not thick and coarse.

Bacon. Should have firm, moist flesh and white or creamy fat, untinged with yellow or green. It comes from the body of the pig; ham comes from either the side or underbelly (the bacon usually sold in packages), or the back.

Both are cured and soaked in brine for four days, then left to mature for up to ten days. At this point bacon is called *cured bacon,* with pale rind, pink flesh and a delicate flavor. Subsequent smoking results in *smoked cured bacon,* which is darker pink and has a golden rind.

Veal. Look for soft, moist, fine-grained delicate pale pink flesh with little, if any, fat. Young veal has bubbles on the surface. Avoid flabby, wet, dry brown, blue-tinged, or mottled veal. There should be gelatinous tissue around the meat. Bones should be soft. Imported veal is a creamy color.

Lamb. Is a sheep under fifteen months old. Meat from young animals is rosy pink, although hill lambs are darker. An older animal has dark red meat. Fat should be creamy white, never yellow, which indicates a rather ancient animal. With frozen lamb the lean is paler and the fat is white and crumbly. Blue-tinged, glistening bones come from a young animal.

Mutton (which generally means a sheep over a year old). Has white flinty bones.

Variety meats. Are what's left of the carcass after it has been cut up; head, feet, tail, sweetbreads, tongue, liver, kidney, brains, heart. These meats are often cheaper compared to popular cuts. They contain little wastage in bone or gristle and seldom require long preparation or cooking. Much of this is delicious and excellent nutrition and as it's easily digestible is good for children and invalids. Depending upon which country you're in, variety meats are classified as gourmet delicacies (France) or low-status scraps (Britain).

Liver. Calf's liver is the most delicate in flavor (and expensive), followed by lamb, pig and ox liver (the most pungent and cheapest). Fresh liver is wobbly and moist, not hard and dry. Calf liver is creamy brown, ox liver is dark.

Kidneys. Lamb's kidney's are best, then calf's kidneys (scarce), pig's kidneys and ox's kidneys, which are largest and coarsest and probably tough, suitable only for slow cooking, casseroles and pies. Always remember to snip out the cores before cooking or you may sniff an ammonia-like smell.

Tongue. Generally ox or lamb; pig's tongue is always sold with the head and calves don't seem to have tongues, or perhaps they're so delicious that the butchers eat them. Tongue should be soaked overnight in slightly salted water before boiling, and skinned before serving.

Brains. Calf's, lamb's, or pig's brains should be soaked in cold water for a couple of hours to remove blood before cooking.

Hearts. There's no such thing as a tender heart at the meat counter. They require long slow cooking and are delicious.

Sweetbreads. Are not what is sometimes rumored but glands from the throat and chest cavity. Lamb's sweetbreads are considered most delicate, then calf's; ox sweetbreads are larger, tougher and stronger and taste very different.

THE COLD FACTS ABOUT FREEZING

How to Freeze Food

Place food in the freezer in meal-sized packages and wrap in moisture-proof nontoxic pliable material: aluminum foil, plastic wrap, laminated paper, waxed cartons, (including milk cartons), plastic refrigerator cartons. Or you can freeze food in Corning Ware dishes (food goes directly from freezer to oven in these). There is also the convenient Seal-a-Meal, a device that heat-seals portion-size meals in plastic pouches.

However, I don't use any of these. I just use old ice cream cartons or polythene sandwich baggies closed with rubber bands.

Make sure all packages of food are airtight; leave room for expansion. Date and label each package.

There's as much unnecessary mystique about freezing fruit and vegetables as there is about the containers in which to freeze them. Basically, the method of freezing depends on the fruit or vegetable *and its size*. The quicker you freeze after picking home-grown produce, the better it is for retaining crispness and flavor. As a general rule eat within 6 months, although the produce may last longer.

SOFT FRUIT: To dry-freeze, wash quickly in cold water, drain, and dry. Remove stalks, peel or slice as necessary, spread on trays lined with wax paper, freeze for about an hour (until firm), then pack in containers.

VEGETABLES: For *short-term storage* (up to 3 months), you

can freeze most vegetables without blanching, but after that time they will deteriorate as fast and dramatically as Cinderella.

The very few vegetables that can be frozen for longer periods of time without blanching include tomatoes and mushrooms (washed and dried) and herbs. A few vegetables should be completely cooked before freezing, including red cabbage, squash, and old (as opposed to new) potatoes. All other vegetables should be *blanched* for a short time in order to retard the enzyme action that causes loss of color, flavor, and nutritive value.

How to Blanch

You will need one large pot of at least 3 qt. capacity with a lid, and a strainer that fits into the pot and allows the lid to sit on top.

1. Clean, trim, and grade vegetables to uniform size so the pieces will be equally processed. Blanch only 1 lb. of vegetables at a time so the heat will penetrate evenly.

2. Boil 3 qt. of water. Put vegetables into the strainer, then the strainer into the pot, and pop on the lid. Turn up the heat and bring water back to boiling as quickly as possible (within a minute).

3. As soon as the boiling point is reached, time according to the following instructions (shorter times for small vegetables, longer times for large vegetables.)

4. When blanching time is up, tip the vegetables into a large bowl of iced-chilled water (running water from the faucet isn't cold enough), and chill for the same length of time as for blanching. Drain. Open freeze or pack and freeze immediately.

BLANCHING TIMES FOR VEGETABLES

1 to 2 minutes: Asparagus (thin), cabbage, leeks, peas, spinach, summer squash.

3 to 4 minutes: Asparagus (thick), aubergines (eggplants), beans, broccoli, brussels sprouts, carrots, cauliflower, celery, corn, onions, peppers, potatoes (small, new).

5 to 7 minutes: Artichokes (globe), corn on the cob.

When freezing, place the package in contact with the refrigerated surface of the freezer for quick freezing, leaving space on the other side of the package for air to circulate. After the temperature of the food has been lowered to proper storage temperature, it should be packed close together with other packages. The tighter you pack a freezer, the better it functions.

But beware: Freezers cannot freeze too large a quantity at one time. Various manufacturers make different suggestions. One says that the load frozen at one time should not exceed one-tenth of the total capacity of the freezer; another says not to freeze more than 3 lb. per cu. ft. of freezer capacity. In any case, the food should freeze within 24 hours.

Refreezing

It is safe to refreeze partially defrosted food if it still contains ice crystals and no part of it is warm. If thawing is complete, you can refreeze fruits as long as they smell and taste good. If beef, veal, and lamb show no sign of spoilage, they can be refrozen, too. However, if the color or odor of any thawed food is poor or questionable, *get rid of it*. Don't taste it—you could poison yourself. *Don't refreeze ice cream, completely thawed vegetables, seafoods, or commercially prepared frozen dishes.*

Foods Not to Freeze

Milk, hard-boiled or fresh eggs, bananas, mayonnaise (pity), cooked rice, potatoes (except for uncooked chips, which seem to freeze well), tomatoes, anything juicy like pears, melons, salad greens, cucumbers (a drooping cucumber looks particularly despondent when defrosted).

Pasta can be frozen, but should be undercooked to allow for the reheating. It is never as good as when freshly made.

A simple, graphic guide, *Freezing Meat and Fish in the Home*, is available for 35 cents from the U.S. Department of Agriculture, Washington, D.C. 20250.

SUGGESTED HOME STORAGE PERIODS TO MAINTAIN HIGH-QUALITY FROZEN FOOD STORED AT 0°F (−19°C) OR LOWER

Fresh Meats

	MONTHS
Beef and lamb roasts and steaks	8 to 12
Veal and pork roasts	4 to 8
Chops, cutlets	3 to 6
Variety meats	3 to 4
Ground beef, veal, or lamb, and stew meats	3 to 4
Ground pork	1 to 3
Sausage	1 to 2

Cured, Smoked, and Ready-to-Serve Meats

Ham (whole, half, sliced)	1 to 2
Bacon, corned beef, frankfurters	Less than 1
Ready-to-eat luncheon meats	Freezing not recommended

Cooked Meat

Cooked meat and meat dishes	2 to 3

Fresh Poultry

Chicken and turkey	12
Duck and goose	6
Giblets	3

Cooked Poultry

Cooked poultry dishes and slices, pieces covered with gravy or broth	6
Fried chicken	4

Sandwiches of poultry meat and cooked   1
   slices or pieces not covered with gravy
   or broth

Fresh Fish

Lean: cod, flounder, haddock, sole	6
Fatty: blue, mackerel, perch, salmon	3
Breaded	3

Commercially Frozen Fish

Shrimp and fillets of lean-type fish	3 to 4
Clams (shucked), cooked fish, fish cakes	3
Fillets of fatty-type fish and crab meat	2 to 3
Oysters (shucked)	1

Fruits and Vegetables

Most	8 to 12
Home-frozen citrus fruits and juices	4 to 6

Milk Products

Cheddar-type cheese (1 lb. or less, not thicker than 1 in.)	6 or less
Butter and margarine	2
Commercial frozen milk desserts	1

Prepared Foods

Cookies	6
Cakes, prebaked	4 to 9
Combination main dishes, such as chicken pie and fruit pies	3 to 6
Breads, prebaked and cake batters	3
Yeast bread dough and pie shells	1 to 2

- *For economy* use your freezer to capacity. A well-filled freezer operates more efficiently than one that is partly filled.
- *For quality* keep foods moving in and out of the freezer. Take food out regularly within the recommended storage period. Add food regularly. Don't go over the recommended storage period.
- *For convenience and efficiency* date and keep a record of frozen foods in storage.

When you remove the food, cross out entry. Place the record near the freezer for easy reference (hang on the door). This is much less trouble than it sounds and it means that you don't count on preparing food which was eaten last month.

I list freezer contents in the back of my menu book. It's easy to write it all in the book as it goes in because I generally do that in big batches, but it's more difficult to remember to tick them off as you remove them, unless you tape your list on the freezer door. I use the freezer list as a menu book. But "Would you like salmon soufflé or venison this evening?" can be embarrassing if you're out of venison and haven't ticked it off.

Using Your Freezer Economically

A 12 cu. ft (0.3 cu. m) freezer costs around 50 cents a week to run. See it costs no more by doing the following:

- *Check* that the thermostat isn't set too low.
- *Choose* a cool site, if possible, and certainly insulate if placed near any hot appliance, such as a stove.
- Ensure adequate ventilation both around and beneath the unit.
- Keep motor unit and condenser grill free from dust.
- Never overstock with warm food.
- Keep the freezer full: freezing air is expensive.
- Never leave the fast freeze switch on for more than 24 hours.
- Open door as little as possible.

Preparing Frozen Food for Eating

PRECOOKED VEGETABLES: Don't thaw. Cook in a little boiling salted water. How long? A frozen food king once told me to take no notice of whatever time the manufacturer puts on the pack. They tend to over-time them. Cook them until *you* reckon they are done, just as you would cook any other vegetable.

MEAT AND POULTRY: Unless you have a microwave oven, when defrosting it's best to leave these in the refrigerator overnight. The meat must be completely thawed before cooking. Fast thawing destroys the taste.

BAKED GOODS: Unwrap and then thaw overnight—anywhere, not necessarily in fridge—although frozen croissants can go straight into a very low oven for ten minutes. Baked goods freeze extremely well.

SAUCES AND CASSEROLES may be heated from the frozen state in a double boiler.

SQUIRRELING

I like to have squirrellike reserves of food and other supplies on hand in case of emergency or (more likely) exhaustion: Friends could descend on me in droves on a winter weekend and be snowed in *chez nous* for several weeks. Natural disaster, such as hurricanes and floods, can turn a comfortable country home into a beleaguered frontier fort, cut off from civilization and resupply. In the event of earthquake, an ever-present possibility in some areas, a city apartment dweller could be left without means of sustenance from outside sources. (See Emergency Planning, p. 261.)

In any sense, the idea of "putting by," an old English phrase, appeals to me as a way to be thrifty, feel secure, and honor ancient rituals of preservation. In strictly practical, contemporary terms, you save money when you stock up on food because in our lifetime supermarket prices will defy Newton by going up without ever coming down.

What Reserves to Stock

VITAMINS: In setting up your store of canned and bottled food, don't forget your vitamin needs. (The vitamin content won't be so high as in fresh food.)

For *vitamin C*, store canned mandarin oranges, grapefruit, tomatoes and berries; *for vitamin A and iron*, apricots; *for vitamins A and C*, peaches, carrots, broccoli, squash and pumpkin. For *vitamin E*, and essential fatty acids, put by various nuts, peanut butter and soft pressed vegetable oil. Fresh potatoes and onions can be stored for several months in a cool, dry, dark place; potatoes are rich in *vitamin C and iron*. Wheatgerm is a useful supplement; it contains *iron*, high quality protein, *B vitamins, vitamin E and essential fatty acids.*

The thing to remember about storing food, all food, is that you must rotate it—so mark your cans. There are many ways to stock up on food, mostly thrifty, mostly easy, all rewarding.

Always try to keep a reserve supply of the following foods: sugar, honey, molasses, preserves, whole wheat flour, salt, pepper, baking powder, baking soda, yeast, coffee and tea, rice, beans, shortening, oil, herbs and spices, vanilla, mayonnaise and/or salad dressing, prepared mustard, pickles, Worcestershire sauce, catsup, bread, eggs, meat, canned tuna fish, canned ham, frankfurters, canned chicken and turkey, sardines, corned beef, liverwurst, and stew as well as a few costly delicacies such as pâté and crabmeat.

Also stock vegetables, fruits, juices as well as reconstituted lemon or lime juice, or powdered instant juice drink (which also provides vitamin C), canned or powdered milk, and canned soups. For flavoring and for easing troubled spirits, keep some alcohol on hand—brandy and wine, for example.

Some things aren't worth giving shelf space to, for example, instant sauces, because making your own with storage cupboard ingredients is almost as quick and the results taste better.

Foods such as flour, rice, beans, and sugar should be stored in airtight, screw-top jars. It's also a good idea to store some water, in plastic containers, in case of emergency.

Store a can: You should always have a store of canned soups, juices, fruit and vegetables. Not only for emergencies, but also to widen your options whenever you need a quick, nutritious meal; a good supply of canned food is like a perpetual feast. Canned tuna is always a good hedge against meat shortages (and will last up to twenty years).

CAUTION: Never buy dented, swollen, leaky or rusted cans—or you may be buying your last meal. (There was a Las Vegas eccentric who always bought cut-rate dented cans and left $85 million, but died of botulism, not old age. Do not follow his example.) Canned food lasts longer and more safely than any other stored food.

Freeze-dried foods: These are perfect for storage, last 20 years or more, and take up the least space of any stored food. They are expensive, but worth it, as I can testify from taking them on sailing and camping trips. Most sporting goods stores stock freeze-dried foods.

Soybeans: A few words about the soybean (a great source of protein). It is difficult to see why this is so often regarded as fake meat simply because the protein content is as high as steak, although the beans are, of course, far cheaper. The fact that soybeans are the basis of the hamburger "stretchers" available at the supermarket probably contributes to this misconception. But I prefer my burgers unstretched and my soybeans undisguised. I treat them as genuine biteable beans. Soak overnight and boil for 25 to 30 minutes in salted water. *Serve hot* with traditional Italian pasta sauces—tomato, Bolognese, or marinara. *Serve cold* with French dressing, black olives, onion rings, chopped hard-boiled eggs, and (optional) a can of tuna.

One pound of beans costing 60 cents provided 7 meals for 3 people while this book was being written. And others on whom I experimented for over 2 weeks in order to discover the human soybean tolerance clamored for more.

You can also use soybeans in the hearty "peasant" country dishes that are so easy to prepare, especially for guests (because they are ready when you are). Try them in a French cassoulet, or beans and bacon, or add them to a basic casserole.

The following *basic casserole recipe* has been used in my home for years, and because it's based on what is actually *there*, it tastes different each time:

In a little butter or oil, lightly fry about ½ lb. (200 g) peeled, sliced onion, 2 cloves of chopped garlic, and 1 to 2 lb. (½ to 1 kilo) of any chopped stewing meat or chicken pieces. When this is browned, add 1 lb. (½ kilo) of soybeans (soaked overnight), a bayleaf or 2, some herbs (preferably thyme), about one pint of stock (½ liter) (or chicken bouillon cube equivalent), a mug of wine (preferably red), and a pound of real peeled tomatoes, *or* a can of tomato paste, or a can of tomatoes. Stew gently for at least an hour. Serves from 4 to 8, depending on ingredients and appetites.

Canning Cans and Can'ts

For one thing, numerous studies have shown that families who grow and preserve their own food are better nourished than those who do not. Home-preserved food tastes and looks better than mass-canned products. Home canning also saves money. It is essentially a safe method of preserving food so long as you remember that the main function of canning is to sterilize both food and jar in order to kill all bacteria and other micro-organisms. If improperly canned, low-acid foods such as fish may nourish *Clostridium botulinum*—the botulism bacteria—which can be fatal.

POINTERS:
- *Know what you're doing.* Since canning methods have changed greatly in recent years, don't follow Grandma's hazily remembered precepts. Get a book!
- *Remember the acid test.* Raw foods are classified as either low-acid or high-acid. *Low-acid* foods, including vegetables (except tomatoes), meats, poultry and fish must be prepared in a pressure canner to prevent botulism. *That means that they must* be processed at a higher temperature than boiling water, which a pressure cooker can provide. A pressure of 10 lb. (4.5 kg) yielding a temperature of 240°F (116°C) is recommended for safety. *Never* lower the temperature

or shorten the recommended processing time. Prices for medium- to large-sized pressure canners range from around $40 to $75. The kind with the weighted gauge are more apt to give you reliable readings. Though tomatoes traditionally were considered a high-acid fruit, some new varieties are less acid, so pressure-can them to be on the safe side.

- *High-acid* foods may be safely preserved by the traditional *boiling water bath method*. By this method, preserves, relishes, pickles, jams, jellies, marmalades, etc. are packed hot in hot sterilized jars, which are properly sealed and submerged in a covered container of water which must boil for at least ten minutes at about 200°F (95°C). The water must be kept an inch or two over the tops of the jars the entire time, so add more boiling water if necessary.

- *Check your equipment.* I always shop for jars and lids in the off-season, when they are often marked down but—more important—available. (Despite the manufacturers' promises to provide plenty, there seems to be a dearth of jars or lids or both each spring.) Never re-use lids because the rubber washer will only work once. Never use cheap, badly designed lids by an unknown manufacturer. Never use old mayonnaise or peanut butter jars which may break at high temperatures. Have the dial pressure on your canner checked before each canning season. A jelly bag or fruit press is necessary for extracting juice from fruit for jellies. For jellies you will also need an 8- (8-) to 10-quart (10-liter) kettle with a broad, flat bottom. A jelly thermometer comes in handy if you don't add pectin to jams and jellies.

- *Other useful equipment for canning:* A quart measure, measuring cup and spoons, paring and utility knives, food chopper, masher, reamer, grater, bowls, wire basket, colander, long-handled spoon, ladle, clock with second hand, and household scale.

Most canned food should not be kept for more than a year or so. If you spot any sign of spoilage—a bad smell, foam, mould—throw the food away. Don't taste it! A spoonful of botulin-infected food can kill you.

THE CUPBOARD COOK

Reserve-Supply Cookery

When, unexpectedly, you have to produce a hostess-type meal, it's generally the challenge and the panic that dismay you. But you are perfectly capable. *Looking* serene and prepared is half the secret of being prepared—let no boy scout tell you otherwise.

The emergencies that send you reeling will fall into 2 categories. There are the *emergencies of quality,* when, for instance, the man in your life telephones from the office to say he's bringing Mr. Big home to sample your culinary splendors; and there are the *emergencies of quantity,* when, for example, all the family invite their friends in at the same time and expect you to perform the miracle of the loaves and fishes all over again.

You can easily cope with both emergencies from your squirrel supply.

In an emergency, dress first, then set the table (shows that the guests are obviously expected—you can keep them waiting for food), then start cooking. The worst part of the evening will be the stomach rumbling interlude before dinner, so plan to keep your audience interested. Get your man to bring the boss home via a classy bar; get the famished friends to help out in the kitchen—they'll enjoy it as long as you pretend it's "such great fun" and do not bustle.

It helps with emergency cooking if you keep a stock-pot. I kept a stockpot last winter and boiled it up every day (the only necessary discipline, because it otherwise goes sour), then threw the remains away in the spring. Don't, however, confuse your stockpot with your garbage can. The only ingredients that you throw into a stockpot are bones (any old *animal* bones), the odd vegetable, herbs, and chopped onions. Bones can smell nauseatingly funereal; disguise the odor by adding chopped garlic and a tbsp. of vinegar or a slosh of white wine.

The most important aspect of cooking is knowing what you can get away with and what you can't. What I have found I *must* have fresh are: coffee beans, potatoes, onions, cream, lemons, wine vinegar, cooking wine, butter or margarine in which to toss vegetables, and freshly ground black pepper, not that beige dust. Nonetheless, do keep emergency jars of instant coffee and cream substitute buried in the depths of your storage cupboard.

CAMOUFLAGE COOKERY

Golden Rule

Monique Guillaume, the famous French cookery writer, told me that whenever she serves anything frozen she tries to add *something* fresh, e.g., a lump of butter on peas, a grating of nutmeg on spinach, cream to a white sauce, lemon juice and a little grated peel on fish dishes, and a dash of red wine or cooking sherry to any meat stew (well, she's French).

Camouflage is the secret of successful storage-cupboard cookery. The principle is simple: Use available fresh window dressing to disguise the unappetizing look, feel, or taste of stored food. A few tips:

- For a fresh touch try to have a bit of *greenery* to chop finely and sprinkle onto whatever you're serving. If you leave onions long enough, they will generally sprout. For a chive taste, snip the ends onto soups or omelettes. Or grow your own chives.
- A fresh *red or green pepper* lasts about 3 weeks and tastes delicious shredded into salad. However shriveled, when chopped into almost any stew dish it imparts a gourmet flavor.
- A piece of grated *lemon peel* gives a fresh flavor to almost anything from soup to fruit.
- Almost any fresh *fruit*, from oranges to grapes, tastes delicious when peeled, chopped up, sprinkled with a little white wine, then served in individual wine glasses (any old shape or size) with a dab of sugar sprinkled on and topped with fresh or sour cream. If you whip the cream, stir in a dash of something alcoholic.

How to Acquire an Instant Gourmet Reputation

Don't try to compete; don't try to do what good cooks with the necessary time can do. Instead, do what even *they* can rarely find time for. I make my own bread, my own yogurt, and use a black-pepper grinder.

COFFEE: I grind my coffee beans fresh in a little electric grinder. It takes 30 seconds; there's nothing to wash up and everyone always falls about, praising the coffee, in a way that they never do about a normal meal, however good. I get away with culinary murder. If you want to establish a reputation as a gourmet cook, just do this and practically nothing else. Incidentally, *whole coffee beans* generally cost less than comparable vacuum-packed or instant coffee, and they also keep their flavor longer. Since escalating coffee prices are not likely to go down, an electric grinder, which can be bought for under $20, will probably pay for itself in less than a year.

BREAD: Nothing smells as good as *fresh baked bread,* but I make mine only once a month and freeze it (half loaf, half sliced). Homemade bread costs half as much to produce as the presliced, superenriched, deflavorized belly wadding sold at the supermarket.

The Duchess of Devonshire's home-made brown bread

This is the family recipe. All the famous 1920s beautiful Mitford sisters, including the Duchess, were brought up on it.

It is not only delicious, but easy to make. Use 100 percent stone-ground whole-wheat flour.

INGREDIENTS
1½ lb. (650 g) whole-wheat flour
½ oz. (12 g) salt
½ oz. (12 g) dried yeast
1½ cups water (warm)
½ oz. (12 g) sugar

METHOD
1. Warm a mixing bowl.
2. Put half of the flour into mixing bowl.
3. Add sugar and salt.

4. Cream yeast with 2 tablespoons warm water and add to mixture.
5. Cover the basin with a clean cloth and leave in a warm place for fifteen minutes.
6. Add remaining flour to make a soft dough, using a little more water if necessary.
7. Knead dough on a well floured surface for five to ten minutes.
8. Cut dough in half, shape each piece and place in two warmed, greased and floured 1-lb. (450-g) loaf tins.
9. Place tins in a warm place, covered with a damp cloth. Leave until dough has risen to about double its size—approximately thirty minutes.
10. Bake at 400°F (200°C) for forty-five minutes.
11. Turn out on to cooling rack.

Baking can be habit forming. Gourmet James Beard, whose *Beard on Bread* (Alfred A. Knopf) is a classic in its field, says: "Once you are hooked by the miracle of yeast, you'll be a breadmaker for life."

JAMS AND JELLIES: You might make *preserves* your specialty. In many areas there are acres of wild berries—blackberries, blueberries, raspberries, even strawberries—to be had for the picking. These make the most elegant preserves of all. Make plenty and preserve the fragrance and taste of summer for year-round delight. Be generous: There are few gifts that give greater pleasure than a jar of homemade jam, jelly, or chutney.

NOTES OF A JADED COOK

There eventually comes a time in the affairs of a woman when your mind blanks out, you feel resentful, apologetic, apathetic, and mutinous, and you simply can't concentrate on food. Don't worry. *You are a jaded cook.* It was a jaded cook who once said that the best thing about Christmas was that you never had to think "What shall I give them for dinner?" It was a jaded cook who pointed out that the main advantage of spaghetti is that you don't have to peel it. You could deal with this feeling as calmly as Ethel

Kennedy, who has a 14-day family menu plan for her 11 children. It is based on simple roasts and broiled meats, omelettes, and salads. When she comes to the fifteenth day, she simply starts over again.

The Kennedy secret is . . . ORGANIZATION. You, too, can have a food plan.

WORD OF WARNING: Keep quiet about it. Don't tell anyone, or someone might complain. Keep your plan for . . .

   . . . when the housework is getting on top of you

   . . . or when you're spring cleaning

   . . . or studying

   . . . or simply lazing, i.e. with your feet up on the sofa reading a bad book (my ideal position).

If anyone *does* notice and upbraids you, make it quite clear that you are no longer the entertaining cook that once you were when newly wed and showing off. Life is too short to stuff a mushroom.

So when you have a spare half hour, jot down your basic 14-day plan and *stick to it*. Don't plan anything that isn't basic. The menu is simply to stop you from going out of your mind and to cut preparation time to a minimum.

ARE YOU EATING POISON?

Processed Food

Many people are becoming increasingly worried about today's polluted and degraded foods. It has been calculated that nearly half the people in this country are overweight and undernourished. The United States is apparently fast becoming a nation fed entirely on factory canned, instant-mixed, synthetic, dehydrated, freeze-dried, chemically processed pap.

There is said to be a potential danger, both physical and mental, in modern processed food, especially those that use the refined carbohydrates (white flour and white sugar). Some people think that this is linked with the increased incidence of coronary thrombosis, obesity, constipation, ulcers, and other twentieth-century diseases.

Additives

There is reported to be an alarming amount of lead in corned beef, sardines, butter, cheese, and apples. Other possible poisons on our plate include chemical additives such as sodium nitrites used in bacon, mercury waste in fish, flour bleach, cyclamates, saccharin, monosodium glutamate, and the chemicals added to cattle feed. Apart from chemical additives you can also be poisoned by agricultural and industrial wastes, defoliates, pesticides, detergents, DDT and anything on which it has been sprayed.

In addition to the known effects of these, it is also suspected that there are unknown effects on the body and brain of biologically active substances such as the afore-mentioned insecticide residue. (If you really care what lurks behind the label, consult *A Consumer's Dictionary of Food Additives*, rev. ed., by Ruth Winter, Crown Publishers.)

What Do You Do About It?

What health food experts advise you to eat is compost-grown vegetables and fruit. If you can't manage that, try to stick to fresh meat, fish, dairy foods, eggs, cheese, butter, honey, fresh and dried fruit, fresh vegetables, wheat grains, and raw foods such as salad.

Steam vegetables or cook them quickly with their skins on so that the water-soluble vitamins and minerals aren't lost in the cooking water. They also taste better that way. Don't cook them until they become soggy—serve crunchy vegetables.

The Semantics of Junk

We all eat a lot of junk, from breakfast cereal to midnight snacks. Too often, though, I hear people dismissing as *junk* foods many quite nutritious fast-food items. I'd certainly rather lunch in style at 21 or the Ritz (the Paris one) if I had the time and someone to foot the bill. But as I often have to eat lunch in a hurry, I enjoy a hotdog, a cheeseburger, a ham sandwich with lettuce and tomato, a roast beef on rye, or I pick up a sausage, pizza, or shish kebab. This is *convenience* food, not very esthetic, but nutritionally adequate.

By contrast, *junk* food is just what the term implies: nutritionally valueless garbage that you might as well deposit directly in the toilet and thus spare your intestines the trouble of processing it. Junk means doughnuts and french fries and potato chips and pretzels and fish sticks and most breakfast cereals (whose packages may be more nourishing than their contents).

Quack Health Foods (the new consumer con)

"Organic," "health," or "natural" foods that have supposedly been grown without chemical fertilizers, fungicides, or pesticides are called organic. Some chemists call some fertilizers "organic" even though they are chemical because they are made out of natural minerals, such as lime. However, when you get fertilizers made from byproducts of petrochemicals, obviously you are straying a long way from nature.

There's nothing intrinsically wrong with organic food—indeed, the fewer chemicals we ingest the healthier we will be. But the move toward what I can only call the "foods of innocence" has spawned a worldwide racket. Any old dusty packet of nuts and raisins, essentially identical to the same product available at a supermarket, often sells for twice as much under the magic label "organic food." A USDA check on fifty-five common processed food items at a "natural" store and at a supermarket showed that the cost at the former was as much as 190% higher than at the latter!

The protein equivalent of some cheaper plant food combinations compared with steak:*

Combination in best proportions		Steak protein equivalent
2 cups rice + ¾ cup peas or beans	=	9.50 oz (270 g)
2½ cups rice + ¼ cup soybeans	=	9.25 oz (262 g)
1½ cups rice + 2 cups skim milk	=	7.75 oz (219 g)

* Source: Lappé, *Diet for a Small Planet*, Ballantine Books, New York, 1975, $1.95.

1½ cups rice + 2½ oz (70 g) cheese	=	7.75 oz (219 g)
4 slices whole-wheat bread + 1 oz (25 g) cheese	=	2.50 oz (70 g)
1 cup whole-wheat flour + 1 tbsp non-fat dry milk	=	3.00 oz (85 g)
1½ cups whole-wheat flour + ¼ cup beans	=	4.60 oz (130 g)
1 cup whole-wheat flour + ¼ cup soy flour	=	4.10 oz (115 g)
6–7 cornmeal tortillas + ¼ cup beans	=	2.60 oz (75 g)
½ cup non-fat dry milk + 1 cup beans	=	8.33 oz (235 g)
⅓ cup peanut butter + ½ cup skim milk + 6 slices whole-wheat bread	=	10.10 oz (285 g)

Some good food items, such as stone-ground, whole wheat flour, obviously costs more than the mass-manufactured, bleached supermarket product. But don't forget that (1) a dried apricot is a dried apricot, whatever the label, and (2) the best way to procure *real* organic food is to grow your own, an admirable undertaking that will, so to speak, weed out the believers from the do-ers.

If you really care about what lurks behind the label, consult *NutriScore* by Ruth Fremes and Dr. Zak Sabry (Methuen Ltd., $6.95). A truly terrific book.

LET HIM DO IT!

The greatest untapped reservoir of culinary skill (and elbow grease) is possibly The Male—husband, mate, or son(s). Cooking is creative and most males are as creative as most females. (If not more so, if you pay attention to people who draw up huge lists of male composers/writers/artists as opposed to skimpy little lists of female composers/writers/artists.) Weekends are the ideal time to put them, instead of yourself, in charge of the kitchen. Male chefs do not like the idea of being snickered at, and prefer to close the kitchen door while they concoct their masterpieces. Great! Lie back on the sofa, sip a glass of sherry, and listen to some Mozart.

In summer, there's nothing better than an outdoor meal when the male can don full plumage of apron and chef's hat and grill steak, chicken, or (like Jimmy Carter) breaded catfish. On a summer vacation at the beach, the males cannot only dig and catch dinner (mussels, clams) but cap piscatorial triumph with culinary laurels by cooking the stuff *(moules marinières)*, or organizing a clambake. But watch out for the *one-menu male* (it's usually baked potato, steak, and salad, followed by cheese).

ENCOURAGING THE KIDS: With boys I have the experience of my own highly successful system. The extension of teaching them to cook for themselves was to teach them to cook for me. My youngest, unaided and unsupervised, began by doing the marketing, cooking, and cleaning up for my business lunches (at home) when he was 12. I paid him and we were both pleased with the system. I kept the meals simple, with dishes that I knew he could put together correctly.

This also had a hidden benefit: It stopped the finicky habits he and his brother had before the pay system was put into operation. (One son wouldn't eat meat, the other son said he was allergic to eggs, and they both refused to touch fish. I used to live from one cauliflower with cheese sauce to the next, because neither of them complained about that.)

If, in however small a way, you can involve the people you cook for in the actual preparation of the meals (fetching and carrying if not cooking), you will be amazed at the swiftness by which their standards fall.

FRIENDLY PERSUASION: What are some practical ways to encourage your man to cook? How do you get him to try it? We must remember that men have to counter centuries of indoctrination before they pick up a wooden spoon. It is therefore *our duty* to encourage and help our underprivileged menfolk to cook for us, to realize how glamorous and exciting this pastime is, and that it is not just women's work. You must vary your methods according to the man, but before he starts always make it clear that a good cook cleans up after himself, or the whole performance will turn into a charade as far as saving *you* work is concerned.

One method of avoiding the cooking from time to time is to praise every single burnt offering he produces. Don't tell lies, just notice the good bits, as you wish he did for you. Remember, it is easier to praise than to cook.

Plan some exotic dish that is assembled rather than cooked. Ask him to help you, and praise, praise, praise. Next week, ask him to make it while you do some nasty essential job. (So you can't be asked to help.)

Indulge in Positive Encouragement for your man's Sunday barbecue effort, or whatever his specialty develops into, and tell all his friends about it. Get it *firmly labeled* as his specialty. Buy him the special equipment for making this dish. Then, gently suggest that as he is so marvelous at barbecues, or whatever, would he like to try (you name it—something dramatic that he loves to eat). You buy the ingredients, you lay them out, you lead him to them, then head back to the sofa.

THE ONE PARENT COOK

I personally can never never understand anyone who sees cooking as a refreshing hobby. I wish I could. I see it as something that keeps on coming at you three times a day, if you've been dishing up a thousand meals a year for years and years.

Cooking for a family is the most time-consuming chore in the whole home routine, and one of the advantages of *not* having a spouse around the house is that, suddenly, it isn't. You cook for kids, and they're easily satisfied: you're satisfied even easier.

When I stopped doing a full-time job (so stopped being able to afford home help) in order to Be With The Children More, what I found most irksome was that they were invariably late to the midday meal. But, as they pointed out, I had always said that if they were doing something productive (such as inventing the square wheel or finishing a puppet, *not* such as watching television) then they shouldn't drop everything to focus on the stomach.

Eventually we reorganized meals to suit what we all wanted, not what we were supposed to do. I cooked a hot breakfast early in the morning and they were expected to be on time. I saw that there was always plenty of fresh fruit, cheese, salads and homebaked bread (and home-made soup in winter). When they decided it was mealtime, they helped themselves. They did *not* snack (I've always discouraged this habit, which leads to incessant eating and unhealthy thick waistlines).

I still did the cooking and when they wanted a traditional evening meal, they ordered one from me, as if they were in a restaurant, booking it in advance and inviting friends. They felt deliriously grand, placing their orders with me, and I got away with very little cooking. I could check that they were eating properly at lunchtime simply by checking my shopping list against what remained in the refrigerator. (At first, they immediately ate all the fruit, so we didn't have any until next shopping day!)

So, if you're a single-parent cook, try working out your own, personal, *simple* routine.

HOW TO BUY THE BEST AND CHEAPEST

Caveat Emptor

Always read the contract and/or warranty that accompanies a purchase. The time to read the boring fine print is BEFORE you buy—not when something goes wrong. Remember that there is no such thing as an unconditional guarantee. Find out what is *not* covered by a warranty or contract. Ask the seller if you have doubts. Ask him for it in writing. Is the entire product covered, or only some of the parts? Who pays for the labor costs during the warranty or contract period? Is there an authorized service representative nearby? Will a product in need of repair have to be shipped to the manufacturer? If so, who pays the return postage?

Never buy anything from a stranger who appears unsolicited at your door. Above all, never give that glib salesman a deposit, except perhaps the verbal equivalent of a well-placed boot. This may seem simplistic, but it is very important advice, and I urge all starry-eyed consumers, such as myself, not to ignore it.

ARMCHAIR SHOPPING— THE MAIL-ORDER CATALOG

Pros

Buying Mail Order saves time and trouble in choosing the goods—you can study the catalogue in the quiet of your armchair, and ask other opinions; if you have ever stood on one leg and agonized in a store before buying what your husband turned out to hate, you will appreciate the advantage.

Mail Order saves the frustrating length of time spent in catching the assistant's eye and completing the purchase in a shop. Today I sometimes feel a store assistant's job is to prevent you from buying the goods and unless you're built on the lines of a gorilla you might strain your back, armpits and temper in getting the goods to your home.

You can return mail-order goods if you're dissatisfied— with reputable firms this is an honest-to-goodness offer. They figure that only someone with good reason would go to the bother of getting the goods back to them; for instance, if after being unpacked, the merchandise looked as if some burly longshoreman had tap danced on it. (We all know that these things can happen.)

Mail-order goods can be cheaper than store bought, because the savings on expensive retail operations (all those indolent salesclerks with insolent eyelashes) can be passed on to the customer. Stores in posh city districts usually have higher overheads than a functional mail-order warehouse in a cheap-rent area where labor is plentiful. Then too, while you do have to know your family's right sizes for everything, shopping the catalogs can save money, hours, and many, many gallons of expensive Arabian gas! You can also get reasonable credit terms if you establish a mail-order account.

Cons

It can be difficult to judge from a photograph what the goods really look like and whether the quality is up to standard. However, there are reputable firms who sell direct-mail furniture and who try to deliver merchandise that is *better* than it looks in the catalog, rightly reckoning that then they'll have a delighted customer who'll come back for more, rather than a disappointed one who won't. Needless to say, this does not always hold true; and there is the possibility of a computer goof that can send you some totally unwanted object.

If you hate putting pen to paper, it can be a drag to write for a few catalogs in the first place. Then when you want to order you have to list item numbers, descriptions, sizes, colors, mailing cost computed by weight of item and distance from nearest mailing center to your postal zone, plus sales tax (if applicable) . . . suggesting that the most valuable product a mail-order house has to offer is a pocket calculator. . . . Still, it may be nothing compared with the agony of bus waits, subways, parking, and lining up in crowded, overheated stores.

There might possibly be a delay in the arrival of the goods, except around Christmas when you can expect to get fairly rapid delivery. But try getting instant delivery of even the most mundane item from stores these days. . . .

If the goods fail to give satisfaction it's even more bother to pack them up again and send them back. Well, in my experience that applies equally to retail stores. I have waited 6 weeks for a store to collect something they delivered to me that had not been ordered. If the goods are returned there could be a delay in returning your money if the company is not a reputable one, so I emphasize: CHOOSE YOUR COMPANY WITH CARE

Ads for special direct-mail items in major newspapers or magazines are usually a safe bet, because most self-respecting newspapers keep a careful eye on their advertisers—they don't want dissatisfied readers. They may even have "hot line" consumer complaint columns.

The most satisfactory single-shot mail order in my experience has been not from mail-order houses but from big city department stores advertising in metropolitan dailies. They generally advertise only a few items at a time, but these are usually on sale. For "white sale" linens and towels, or glassware, they are unbeatable. *But* you have to wait for these sales.

You can also safely buy almost anything you will ever need, and a whole lot you want, from the catalogs of Messrs. Sears Roebuck, J. C. Penney, and Montgomery Ward.

HOME EQUIPMENT: WHAT AND HOW TO BUY

If God had wanted women to stay in the kitchen he would have given them aluminum hands.
                                    —BETTY FRIEDAN

What You Need

You need all the mechanical help you can get. Thank heaven (and Thomas Edison, and all the inspirers, inventors, and manufacturers of household appliances), the modern home has the equivalent of at least a dozen "slaves." The slaves, of course, are the appliances that allow you to turn over most mind-numbing household chores to these many "aluminum hands"—and get the hell out of the kitchen.

But, even if money is no obstacle, manufacturers don't make a sensible choice of appliances easy. They bewilder you with visions of supermachines that do everything but change the baby's diaper. Actually, you can get along surprisingly well *without* a lot of equipment that the Joneses may consider essential. In fact, you can often get along without even those things *you* consider essential. For instance, I think a washing machine is a necessity. But to my surprise, during a 6 months' stretch without one, I didn't even notice the loss; I simply soaked everything in detergent in the bathtub and sink overnight, then rinsed them out the next morning.

INDISPENSABLES: Every household needs a refrigerator—99.9 percent of all homes with electricity have one. Also, of course, a stove, (or separate burners and an oven). Next in importance are a washing machine, a dryer, a vacuum cleaner, and a transistor radio to keep you cheery and informed. Also a dishwasher, if there are more than 3 in the family.

My biased list of useful, if not vital, appliances would also include an electric blender, a Cuisinart food processor, and a freezer. A steam iron (and adjustable ironing board to suit your height) is still sometimes necessary, although not for me, because Mother Doesn't Iron.

OPTIONAL EXTRAS: Whether or not to have a broiler-rotisserie, a range hood with exhaust fan, a garbage disposal, a trashmasher, a waffle iron, water softener, knife sharpener, floor polisher, a toaster, a toaster oven, coffee grinder, or electric carving knife depends entirely on your life-style and particular needs (though some of these and other major appliances are often thrown in "free" when you buy a home, and even in some rentals. Such electrical extras include microwave ovens, mixers, coffee-makers, crockpots, and fondue pots).

ENERGY WASTERS: To my mind, electrical contraptions such as kettles, frying pans, skillets, can openers, griddles, juice extractors, meat grinders, hot trays, corn poppers, and drying racks are *not necessary*. They save hardly any time and will simply add to dust-attracting clutter and energy consumption (see Maintenance, p. 163).

If you ever build a house, though you may be tempted, *don't* lump together those lovely appliances as part of your home mortgage. It means that you will pay for them over the entire period of the mortgage, maybe 20 or 30 years. As you will be aware from the table on p. 151, few appliances last anywhere near that long. Thus, due to the extended period of interest payments, the total cost of the built-in appliance will be more than twice its actual price if separately purchased and installed. A $400 appliance purchased on a 25-year, 8 percent mortgage would cost the buyer more than $900. If the appliance lasts as long as 15 years, the buyer is paying for a deceased horse for those last 10 years.

Of course, if you buy a new, ready-built house, you can probably do nothing about that little piece of contractor-banker usury except holler. In fact, you may even be lured into buying the house by the thousands of dollars' worth of appliances, which is exactly what the builder intended in the first place.

Features to Look For in Various Appliances

REFRIGERATORS: The average family needs at least 12 cu. ft. of space, with the freezer and the chilling section each having a separate door. It should have adjustable shelves, as well as inside-the-door racks with compartments for butter, cheese, and eggs. You may also want such extras as a "crisper" drawer for storing fresh vegetables (at 40°F), an ice-maker, an ice-water dispenser, but these are expensive and unnecessary luxuries. The extra cost of a frost-free or self-defrosting refrigerator (about $50) may be a worthwhile investment over the appliance's 10–15-year lifetime (with my memory, it certainly is). Otherwise, a refrigerator should be defrosted manually every 2 weeks.

Handling hot foods. Meat should be kept in the coldest part of the refrigerator at 29° to 31°F; milk at 32° to 35°F. Before placing them in your refrigerator, cool hot foods fast to slow down chemical changes that affect vitamin retention and edibility. Cool foods quickly by placing them in shallow pans in ice or cold water to start the cooling, or use the refrigerator. Contrary to common belief, refrigerating warm food doesn't spoil it. But do not put so much warm food in the refrigerator that it raises the temperature above 45°F, and do not put large containers of hot food in the refrigerator.

COOKING RANGES: Choose a stove with care; you'll probably be spending more than 500 hours a year at it. Whether you buy a gas or an electric stove may depend on the cost and availability of either fuel in your area.

Gas versus electricity. Gas is sometimes cheaper than electricity. However, only about 40 percent of a gas burner's heat reaches a utensil on top of it, versus about 75 percent of an electric burner's energy. Electric elements take longer to heat up than gas burners, and they also take longer to cool off, so you can switch off an electric stove before it has finished cooking. A drawback is that the element on an electric range stays so hot even after it's turned off (and doesn't *look* hot) that it can easily melt a plastic dish or burn a hand.

I prefer a gas range for 3 reasons: (1) It can be used during a blackout, (2) a gas burner can be finely tuned to provide the exact amount of heat needed for what's cooking. (3) All the professional cooks that I see cooking use gas burners. The top part of a gas oven gets hotter than the bottom, but this need not be a culinary disadvantage, because you can fill the oven accordingly with different foods and cook economically.

Most stoves come with built-in ovens and broilers, and some electric models have eye-level ovens (provided your eye is on that level). One popular extra is a motorized roasting spit, which can be attached inside either gas or electric ovens: It ensures evenly cooked meat.

Self-cleaning ovens. The biggest advance in "rangeology" is the self-cleaning oven. The cleaning takes place at very high temperatures, up to 1,000°F (500°C), turning cooking residues into gas and vapor that go out the vent, leaving only some fine ash that can easily be wiped out. The cycle takes 2–4 hours and costs about 12 cents, far less than a can of oven cleaner. Another new advance is the continuous cleaning oven, which requires no heat for the cleaning to take place. You simply wipe the interior of the oven with a damp cloth whenever you want. As you may expect, ovens with their own cleaning capacities cost more than standard ranges.

An energy-saving tip. Many people still believe the propaganda that a pilot light on a gas range costs nothing to run. In fact, it can account for one-third of the monthly cost of cooking with gas. However, many new gas ranges come equipped with electric-coil starters that cost far less to run, though the initial cost of the range is higher. Each time you start a burner with an electric-coil starter, your electrical consumption is equivalent to running a 25-watt light bulb for 2 to 3 seconds. Assuming very frequent use of the stove, that works out to be about 40 cents a year. (For other energy-saving suggestions see Heat & Cool, p. 155, and Money Money Money, p. 234.)

Range hoods. Every kitchen should have an exhaust fan, preferably with a ducted-range hood. Apart from the not-necessarily delightful odors of cookery, a range can put out as much as 200 lb. of grease-laden moisture a year. A ducted hood relieves the load on your air-conditioning system as well. Much cheaper to buy and install is a ductless hood, which does not expel the air but only filters and recirculates it. Grease and odor filters trap a lot of kitchen smog, but, of course, do not cool the atmosphere.

QUICK-COOKING OVENS, TOASTERS, ROTISSERIES, SLOW COOKERS:

Microwave ovens. Now used by more than 2 million Americans, and most owners swear by them as great timesavers—the kitchen complement to a freezer. Unlike gas or electric ovens, which cook by the direct application of heat, microwave (radar) ovens generate electromagnetic waves that cause food molecules to vibrate far faster than the eye can see. This friction process heats food far faster than conventional methods. The cooking can be done on paper plates, plastic, glass, and ceramic, anything but metal, and does not mess up the oven. The fast-cooking process helps preserve the natural flavor and color of food, and, according to the industry, saves a median 62 percent in kilowatt hours. Against this savings you should measure the cost, from $300 to $600 for the average unit, and the space it occupies. Despite some bad publicity a few years ago, brand-name micros are now safe if used strictly according to instructions. However, they don't give the food a lovely brown color—it comes out the same color it goes in—but you can always brown it in your conventional oven or buy an optional browning skillet for your microwave.

You really have to reeducate yourself to use a microwave oven. You can't just make your Aunt Sarah's casserole recipe and blithely stick it in, but you can totter home at night after a hard day over a hot typewriter and defrost a frozen steak in 15 minutes or bake a potato (very comforting) in 3 minutes. Be prepared to experiment, and for one or two failures. Don't show off your microwave to visitors until you've really tamed it. Be sure to use the special cookbook that accompanies each oven. You should also buy a specialized book such as *Mastering Microwave Cooking* by Jack Denton Scott and Maria Louisa Scott (Bantam Books).

Toasters. I prefer *toaster ovens* to ordinary toasters because they can also be used (when meals are only for one or two people) to bake potatoes and frozen dinners, reheat cooked food, make grilled cheese sandwiches, and to warm fresh or frozen rolls, muffins, and pastries. However, they cannot be used to broil or cook meat. So you might also consider a *broiler-rotisserie*, which toasts everything and comes with a grill for barbecuing and a motorized spit.

Slow cookers. Better known as *crockpots,* because the cooking surface is an inner ceramic pot, these are relatively new electrical appliances. They are being made by at least 20 different manufacturers and have run up phenomenal sales. And for good reason. For the woman in a rush they make it possible to prepare long-cooking dishes like stews and pot roasts in the fcw minutes it takes to ready the ingredients. Put the food in the pot in the morning, set the control at low (about 200°F or 100°C), and go about your business. No stirring, no peeking, no worrying about food burning. They cost only pennies a day to operate (as much as one burner, not one oven), and the slow-cooking method is particularly good for tenderizing cheaper cuts of meat.

One disadvantage is that the sealed-in heating element cannot be repaired if it breaks. The other disadvantage is that you might, like me, be performing like an eight-armed Indian goddess before breakfast in order to get the family on the road, and not be able to spare even those few minutes to prepare ingredients for the crockpot. In which case I suggest you prepare it the night before, when cooking the evening meal (not after eating it, when the Inner You tends to run down).

Margaret Drabble told me that the Victorian writer, Mrs. Gaskell, was once asked how a woman could be a successful writer. She pondered, then answered, "Get a slow casserole cooking first thing in the morning, then you can concentrate on your work." Were she living today, I'm sure she would have an electric crockpot.

VACUUM CLEANERS: Though vacuum cleaners have become lighter and more elegant since they were introduced in 1908—some models now have built-in headlights and a whistle to alert you when the dustbag is full—apart from such amazing innovations they have not changed mechanically very much.

Upright versus tanker and canister. There are 3 types of vacuums: canister, tank, and upright (or a combination). All work basically by suction, like an elephant's trunk, but the *upright* has a spinning beater-brush that beats dirt up and *out* of carpets. The upright comes with attachments for draperies and upholstery, but these tools generally are not as easy to use as those that come with the tank-canister type. *Tank* and *canister* machines, though not as good on carpets as the upright, are more versatile and work better on bare floors and above-floor cleaning. The combination model has a tank or canister plus a motorized rotary beater.

Which type you need depends, again, on your life-style

and your nerve ends. (Some people hate the entangling cord that trails behind them when they use tank or canister cleaning attachments.) There are also lightweight models, sometimes called electric brooms, which are relatively inexpensive and good for a quick pickup. But I think that if you're investing in a machine, you should *never* get one that does only light work; your circumstances might easily change, and there you may be next year up to the armpits in fitted wall-to-wall carpeting with this underpowered broom. . . .

Which make should you buy? I know of no Electrolux owner who has been dissatisfied and they last and last and last.

CLOTHES WASHERS: The washing machine is certainly the greatest invention since soap. The modern washer is an incredibly sophisticated machine that, when started, fills and empties itself, washes, rinses, spins fabrics damp-dry, regulates the temperature of the water, and even dispenses detergent and bleach, all without human guidance.

In homes with children, it is an absolute essential. Since a machine can do the laundry while you do something else, it's a good idea to have it near the kitchen; some people prefer to have it close to bedrooms and baths, which makes sense if they don't have a tribe of kids trooping through the house with dirty clothes.

Washers have a wide range of settings, so that you can toss even delicate fabrics into the machine. (Although I never would.) The different fabric settings are merely a basic thermostatic control that adjusts the water temperature from high (for white cottons) to low (for wool). There's nothing more magic to it than that.

Except for heavily soiled or greasy clothes, it is not necessary to use hot water. (But when using cold water, use a special cold-water detergent, such as All.) The machine should be fully loaded to save energy, but not overloaded. Most models have a variable water-fill capacity that can be regulated according to the size of the load.

Size. The average household needs a machine capable of holding from 9 to 16 lb. of dry clothes, but there are portable models for people who need less capacity. The manufacturers offer many different kinds of laundry equipment, so you can usually find a size and model that fits your space and needs. Amazingly, a good machine seldom goes wrong. Except for simple repairs, such as replacing a faulty water pump or clearing a clogged water hose, it's advisable to hire an expert technician if the machine does go on the blink.

DRYER: In sunny weather, sheets and towels that have dried outside smell marvelously fresh, like grandma's, but a clothes *dryer* is another essential if you don't live in the Sunbelt. Dryers run on either gas or electricity. The clothes are tumbled in a drum until they are dry. Dryers can be very sophisticated (unnecessarily so, I think) with several operating thermostats to provide a variety of temperatures and drying cycles to accommodate different kinds of fabrics. With a modern dryer, equipped with knit, permanent-press, and wrinkle-relaxing cycles, there's really no reason to do any ironing except for a few odd jobs such as the occasional man's shirt for the occasional man; permanent men should know better.

STEAM IRON: Still perhaps needed for a few cotton garments, for touch-ups, and for steaming woolen skirts and pants. If your man insists on cotton shirts, send them to a laundry or let him iron them himself. Fine linen table-cloths and napkins should also be entrusted to a good hand laundry (if you can find one). Permanent-press sheets should never be ironed or they lose their perm.

The best steam irons have stainless steel or aluminum bases (or soleplates), some with a nonstick coating. Stainless steel heats more slowly and is more expensive, but is less susceptible to scratching.

SEWING MACHINES: A sewing machine is a very good investment. I know women who are still using their 50-year-old foot-powered machines and getting satisfactory service.

A sewing machine is a wonderful slave for mending, making alterations, and plain sewing, such as seaming fabrics to make curtains. If you haven't learned to use one, it's a good idea to take a few lessons. Almost all stores that sell the machines, department stores with fabric departments, YWCA's, and high schools offer sewing courses. Whether or not you use the machine to sew clothing really depends on skill and a flair for putting together fabrics and patterns and learning to fit garments. The kind of machine to get depends on the kinds of sewing for which it will be used.

The "Model T" versus the "Porsche." The simpler the better to start with, a sort of Model T is what you need; a really complicated machine may awe you into inaction, as it did me. Sewing machines are powered by electric motors. They range in size from lightweight (18 lb.) portables to complicated automatics set in large cabinets. The criterion for choice of a sewing machine is whether or not you want to get into elaborate stitchery.

If you seriously plan to sew clothes with embroidery, shirring, and ruffling, then by all means get a complex zigzag machine. The simple straight stitching machine has a needle that goes up and down and sews in a straight line. The zigzag machine's needle can also move from side to side, and in a circle or semicircle. Disks or cams are used in the zigzag to enable the machine to make complicated stitches like hemstitching, featherstitching, embroidery, and buttonholing. (You turn a dial or lever on the head of the machine to the required setting.) It is also easier to sew on knit and stretch fabrics with a zigzag machine because there are more adjustments.

Portables. A portable machine comes in a carrying case or can be set in a specially constructed table. A nonportable machine is a piece of furniture. A portable in a carrying case requires storage space and, in addition, a sewing box. Before deciding on a portable (which is really only portable if you're an amateur weightlifter or want merely to put it in the car to transfer it, say, to and from a summer home) you should consider that the machine will have to be placed on something for sewing. Card tables aren't sturdy enough and dining tables can be a bit high. I wham away at my desk.

A good compromise is a simple console, which looks like a small occasional table, and a carrying case into which you can put the machine to lug it from one place to another when necessary. Sewing machine consoles can be quite large and come equipped with storage space for sewing equipment like thread, buttons, scissors. Some look like tables; some like cabinets, and they come in different styles and wood finishes; choice depends on taste and the amount of space you have for it.

A lightweight portable is not suitable for sewing heavy fabrics. If you are planning slipcovers with corded seams or winter woolen coats, you had better get a heavier machine (but not otherwise). The lightest weight machine is not the cheapest because it is made of aluminum rather than cast iron. There are heavier portables in the 25- to

30-lb. range, and there are zigzag portables. Elna puts out a good zigzag portable, but prices start at $350 and run to over $500. Singer's lightest machine costs about $220 and is excellent. A really good portable Singer can be bought for as little as $130, but this machine is heavy and does only straight stitching. Singer also puts out a slant-needle machine. The only advantage to a slant needle is that it is easier to see the stitches while sewing. But there are many makes and models available, so comparison shop.

Don't buy a sewing machine that has plastic parts. Your best buy may be a secondhand, reconditioned machine. These usually come with guarantees and can give excellent service. You should, of course, read the warranty and/or guarantee very carefully, and know just what you are getting. Before buying you should test the very machine you're purchasing.

SEWING MACHINE CHECKLIST

- Is the control—foot pedal or knee lever—comfortable?
- Is the light in a good position? Is it easy to change the bulb?
- Are the markings on the machine for tension and stitch adjustment clear? Are these adjustments easy to use?
- Is the machine quiet?
- Is it easy to insert the bobbin and to wind the thread on it?
- How is the machine oiled?
- Is the wiring protected?
- If the cabinet has a hinged lid, is it properly supported when open?
- Are the spare parts for the machine readily available? (For that reason alone it is inadvisable to buy an unknown or weird foreign brand; repairs may be difficult.)

Maintenance. A sewing machine should last more than 20 years (in fact more like 100 years if the parts are not plastic), but the machine needs some care. Lint should be removed as it accumulates. The tension disks, bobbin case, and levers should be wiped with a soft cloth. The moving parts should be oiled unless the machine is self-oiling. The machine should be cleaned periodically.

GARBAGE DISPOSERS: These omnivorous marvels attach to the kitchen sink and grind up food wastes, leaving only the nonsmelly residue of paper, glass, cans, rubber, and olive pits to be hauled away by the garbage collector. They are prohibited in many cities such as New York, but often come as standard equipment in new houses in suburbia where local sewage lines are big enough to handle the volume. (If you have a septic tank, check with local public health authorities to be sure that you have sufficient capacity to handle the extra load.) If you live in the country you may want a trashmasher (see page 64). If you have a garden and believe in ecology, you will want to transform the biodegradable food waste into rich compost for your plants.

I can happily live without an electric garbage disposal, mainly because I have a private horror of absentmindedly plunging in my right arm and pulling out a bloody stump. In my kitchen I prefer to leave a space under the working surface next to the sink and to stick a 24-inch-high plastic trash can with swing top there. I also use a disposable bag in the can. If you do get an electric garbage disposal, get the sort that resets itself at the press of the button and keep that H-shaped wrench, which unjams it, NEAR AT HAND. And buy 100 percent more teaspoons.

DISHWASHERS: In the average American household, some 40,000 glasses, dishes, cups, plates, and what-have-you have to be washed each year. The advantages of having a dishwasher are obvious: They consume less energy than you'd use cooking up a batch of waffles. Also, they thoroughly sterilize the dishes. However, they can be wasteful if there are only 2 of you and you don't eat at home or entertain much.

Don't expect a dishwasher to dispense with your dishwashing problems, but it will halve the job and provide a painless, built-in discipline for clearing up immediately after meals. People with dishwashers always seem to have tidy kitchens. Some hardy types claim that after scraping the dishes and pots, you might as well go the whole hog and wash 'em. However, if you have a good-sized family and/or like to entertain, a dishwasher is definitely liberating; it should save you at least 250 hours a year. A dishwasher requires only 10 minutes of *your* time to stack a load that would take 45 minutes to do by hand.

Most dishwashers have several cycles, and many of them wash pots too. The water should be between 150° to 160°F. The machine must be carefully loaded, the dishes should be scraped, a special dishwasher detergent must be used and, although these machines generally do a good job, they will ruin wood, bone, horn, hand-painted or delicate china, cut or etched glass and most plastic (although Melmac and Melamine are supposed to be dishwasherproof.

ELECTRIC BLENDERS: Superb for soups, purées, health food vitamin drinks, milk shakes, desserts, pancake batter. Escoffier would have swapped his sous-chef for one. The new models have a number of speeds to regulate the degree of fineness into which food is cut.

FOOD MIXERS: These range from portable hand mixer, which is an inexpensive, easy-to-store version of the old egg beater, to the super-sophisticated food processor such as the French Cuisinart or the Bosch Magic Mixer from Germany. These are supposed to be strictly for serious cooks who want to simplify and streamline their procedures. In my opinion the best, though unfortunately the most expensive, of the food processors is the French Cuisinart (the cheapest model costs about $180). It is as simple to clean as it is to use, and although I sternly tell myself I could live without it, I don't really want to try because it really does take the grind out of cooking. It looks good, is neat, simple, amazingly easy to dismantle and wash, and you can keep all the accessories in an elegant, wall-hung holder.

This food processor is a first-class investment because it kneads, chops, binds, slices, scrapes, grinds, mixes, folds, and beats. In fact, it deals with almost every food preparation chore in the kitchen. It liquidizes ingredients for soups, gravies, and sauces; it purees for fruit desserts, milk shakes, and vegetable drinks (if you buy a food processor, you don't need a mixer); and it enables you to turn meat trimmings into pet food, grind hamburgers, and produce sausages, baby food, soufflés, raw vegetable salads, terrines, pâtés, stuffings, to mention but a few possibilities.

Using the processor. Basically, the machine consists of a strong plastic bowl with 4 different rotating blades that fit into the base. One is for cutting, chopping, mincing and puréeing; 2 blades are for slicing and shredding (different finenesses); and the plastic blade is for mixing and blending. You feed food through a funnel onto the slicing disk in the bowl.

You can't overload the machine because it has an automatic cutoff. To stop the motor you just twist the lid to one side. It's safe with children because the machine won't work unless the bowl cover is securely fixed—and then they can't get at the blades. At times you might find the bowl a bit small; for example, if you were kneading bread, you might have to repeat the procedure a few times.

ELECTRIC COFFEEMAKERS: They can make good coffee, but not the best, particularly the relatively new vacuum type, which brews the coffee automatically and keeps it warm (you tend to get a warm, rather than a hot, cup of coffee) until the machine is turned off. (Norelco, Braun, and Mr. Coffee are popular brands.) They only make sense if you and your family are in permanent need of a cuppa.

WATER SOFTENERS: If you can't work up a lather in your house, you need some kind of water-treatment device. A water softener is necessary in areas in which the water is so "hard" (loaded with minerals) that it reacts with soap to leave rings of sludge around the tub, besides making the coffee taste terrible. Softeners cost between $380 and $800 installed, though your hard-luck story may be softened by the manufacturers' claims that the average family of 4 can save about $60 a year in longer-lasting clothes and water pipes.

FREEZERS: Whether or not to own a separate freezer (almost all refrigerators come with some type of freezing compartment) depends on your life-style.

Advantages. If you *grow* fruit and vegetables, or catch your own fish or shoot your own birds, or like to buy them in quantity at peak season for use year round, freezing is a good way to preserve them. A freezer can also be a good way of cutting down cooking time if you cook double quantities and freeze half: 2 entrées, 4 loaves of bread, 12 pizzas. Many people also find it comforting to have that large reservoir of goodies available when they feel exhausted, lazy, short of cash, or swamped by hungry tribes of relatives, friends, and kids' pals in various combinations. A freezer is a useful ally in any plan to shop only once a week and a boon in planning painless parties.

Disadvantages. The main disadvantage of having a freezer is its cost: not only the original price of the appliance, which is not cheap, but also its operation. A freezer is one of the most energy-hungry appliances in the house and, including the cost of paper for wrapping foods, USDA estimates that freezing food adds at least 10 to 25 percent to the cost of the food itself. A 12 cu. ft. freezer costs around 50 cents a week to run economically. However, very few people take the necessary care to run it at this minimum expense.

TO RUN A FREEZER ECONOMICALLY

* Check that the thermostat isn't set too low.
* Choose a cool site, if possible, and certainly insulate if placed near any hot appliance, such as a stove.
* Ensure adequate ventilation around the unit.
* Keep motor unit and condenser grill free of dust.
* Never overstock with warm food.
* Keep the freezer full (freezing air is expensive).
* Never leave the fast-freeze switch on for more than 24 hours.
* Open the door as little as possible.

If you need a freezer only as a supplement to the weekly supermarket safari, 2 cu. ft. per family member is sufficient. (Each cu. ft. holds approximately 35 lb. of food.) If most of the food used in the family comes from the freezer (if you buy meat in bulk twice yearly), as much as 10 cu. ft. per family member may be needed. But please remember that no food is as nourishing as fresh food.

Types of freezers. Freezers are either *chests* or *uprights.* They come as *self-contained units* or *in combination* with a refrigerator. There are side-by-side combinations (2 parallel doors, one for the refrigerator and the other for the freezer), a bottom freezer combination that rolls out like a drawer or with separate door, and a top freezer combination. All of these are *separate* freezers, having their own temperature controls, and not freezer sections within a refrigerator.

The frozen food compartment within a refrigerator (meaning one that does not have a separate door or control) is *not* an adequate food freezer. If the temperature is kept cold enough to maintain the frozen foods, it is too cold in the rest of the refrigerator, and you are likely to end up with iced milk and frozen eggs.

Chest freezers are lower in cost, cheaper to maintain, and it is easier to pack more into them than you can in an equivalent capacity upright. Also less cold air is lost when the chest lid is opened. On the other hand it is far easier to organize an upright freezer. In a chest you often have a hard time finding things because there are fewer partitions, and you have to rummage around in it. They invite frozen fingers and slipped disks. You may have to dive in and burrow like a dog after a rabbit for whatever frozen package you want, which may be at the bottom under everything else. You will then have to repack the thing.

Uprights occupy less floor space but in turn concentrate more weight on a small area of floor; they could be a problem on old wooden floors upstairs. Unless this is so, I advise you to buy an upright.

There are manual defrost freezers, automatic defrost, and frost-free units. Frost-frees are more expensive to operate than the others and, because fans continually circulate cold air through the freezer, some food might dry out if not placed in moisture-proof containers. I would get an automatic. You may think it is hardly worth the extra use of energy and the extra initial cost. Since a freezer usually needs to be defrosted only once or twice a year, (and it's a good idea to check on the older contents), you may do better with a manual defrost—one in which you have to turn a switch off to start defrosting, and then turn it on again when the process has been completed and the freezer washed. A collection of frost on freezer walls or shelves causes the temperature to rise. If the frost is scraped away with a wooden or plastic putty knife when it forms, it will need to be defrosted less frequently, but please be careful. My mother jabbed too hard with a steak knife and had to buy a new freezer. (She will be ashamed to read this, but why should I always be the fall guy?)

Defrost completely before the frost reaches a depth of $1/2$ in. over a large area of the surface. Also defrost if frost begins to accumulate on packages that have been stored in the freezer only a few hours. If possible, defrost when the amount of food in the freezer is low because all food will have to be removed from the freezer during defrosting. To get the food as cold as possible before defrosting, set the temperature at its lowest setting overnight. Then remove the food, defrost, clean the unit. The inside should be washed with a quart of cool water (never warm water) containing 1 tsp. baking powder. Be sure to wash the gasket. The outside of the freezer should be cleaned by washing with soap suds and rinsing off. Wipe with a dry cloth and start the freezer again. Set the freezer at its lowest temperature until it is down to 0°F, or lower the temperature at which the freezer must be kept. Be sure there is a theromometer in the freezer, and maintain 0°F in the warmest part. It is also a good idea to keep foods with the fastest turnover in the warmest location and to rotate the food packages so that the oldest packages are used first. You can do this by filling one shelf or basket at a time and always filling from *back* to front.

What happens if there is a power cut? If the freezer is fully loaded and the door is not opened, the food will remain frozen for about 48 hours. If the freezer is only half-full, it may not stay frozen for more than half a day. Dry ice can be packed in, but open the door or lid as little as possible. Cover the food with newspaper, place heavy cardboard over it, and the dry ice on top. It probably also helps to cover the freezer with blankets, placing newspaper between the freezer and the blanket.

LIFE EXPECTANCY OF APPLIANCES

	YEARS
• Washing machines	11
• Spin dryers	10
• Clothes dryers	14
• Refrigerators	16
• Freezers	15
• Ranges	
electric	16
gas	16
• Vacuum cleaners	
upright	18
tank	15
• Sewing machines	24
• Toasters	10
• Televisions	
black & white	11
color (figures vary, but approximately)	7–8

Source: Marilyn Doss Ruffin & Katherine S. Tippett. Estimate from the U.S. Department of Agriculture.

Energy- and Money-Saving Tips on Appliances

- They should be kept in good repair to save energy.
- A gas flame should have a distinct blue inner comb with soft tips and no trace of smoke. If not, call your gas company.
- Water temperature for dishwashing in a dishwasher should be between 140° and 160°F. Water loses 1 degree per foot between the heater and the faucet. The pipe should be insulated.
- You can save electricity on a dishwasher by canceling the remainder of the drying cycle just as it begins. Open the dishwasher door, and allow the dishes to air dry—it will be fast, because the dishes are still very hot.
- If you have a self-cleaning oven, clean immediately after use, because the temperature of the oven will still be high.

How to Buy Appliances

"CONSUMER REPORTS BUYING GUIDE": Look for it at your local library.

BUY FROM A LOCAL DEALER: He has a reputation to maintain. This is a good idea even if it costs a bit more.

SEEK YOUR FRIENDS' ADVICE: Ask them which brands they've *not* found reliable, instead of letting yourself be stampeded by glamorous advertisements.

BUY THE MIDDLE-OF-THE-LINE: An appliance in this category is not the cheapest, which may be flimsy and have fewer features than you need, nor the top-of-the-line, which comes with all sorts of expensive complicated doodads. The more complicated the machine, the more it is apt to break down.

UNDERWRITERS' LABORATORIES UL SEAL: Electric appliances should carry this seal, which means it meets safety requirements.

BLUE STAR OF THE AMERICAN GAS ASSOCIATION: Gas appliances should have this symbol, which certifies safety.

ASSOCIATION OF HOME APPLIANCE MANUFACTURERS SEAL: This seal certifies that the net refrigerated volume and shelf area of refrigerators and freezers are as stated.

READ THE WARRANTY OR GUARANTEE CAREFULLY: There is no difference between a warranty and a guarantee as they are now used by manufacturers. Some guarantee the appliance only against defective parts and for a limited time. Some include labor in the replacement of a defective part. But know what you are getting! They may be vague in this area: Insist on having *in writing* what you are getting and what you are not getting. (Your trump card here is that it's your money they're after.)

KNOW WHERE THE APPLIANCE CAN BE SERVICED: Quite often the dealer will not take care of it, and it is important to know if the manufacturer has a service station nearby.

IF AN APPLIANCE IS DEFECTIVE: You should be aware that if you cannot get it repaired or replaced by either the dealer or the manufacturer, you may appeal to the industry's ombudsman group, the Major Appliance Consumer Action Panel (MACAP), 20 North Wacker Drive, Chicago, Illinois 60606. [Call collect: (312) 236–3165.]

When it comes (as it will) to appliance repairs: Stand over the man who's repairing your tumbler dryer and see what he does and make a note of what was wrong with it, along with the date and what it cost. This might be useful ammunition with which to complain if the machine develops the same fault 3 times a year; or it might eventually teach you to empty the lint bag of your tumbler dryer.

PHONEMANSHIP

A telephone can be a shrill, insistent, selfish nuisance, if you let it dictate to you and if you obey its call slavishly whether it suits you or not. (I know a family who had their phones disconnected for neglecting to pay the bill and found phonelessness such a blessing that they didn't have service restored for a month.)

KIDS AND THE PHONE: There is probably no way you can stop children from tying up the phone with incessant calls, but there is a way to spare yourself the endless bother of acting as an answering service for them: Have a separate listing and number for the children's own phone. Just make sure the kids don't abuse this privilege. Encourage brevity by suggesting that they pay a preagreed portion of the bill (from 10 to 50 percent depending on their allowances).

ANSWERING MACHINES AND CORDLESS PHONES: An automatic answering and tape recording machine is a necessity for taking messages at home if you do much business or have a secretaryless office. A reliable machine costs around $160. A portable cordless extension costs about $325, but can cut down on the number of extension phones you have to rent from the phone company. It's also quite convenient at times to be able to conduct a very personal phone conversation in a bathroom or even a closet where neither little ears nor big ones can tune in.

TO STAY COOL IN SUMMER, WARM IN WINTER, SAVE 50 PERCENT ON YOUR FUEL BILLS, AND FEEL GOOD, TOO

You may expend too much energy on the tennis court or the golf course, in the house, on the job, or in bed. That's between you and your glands and your doctor and mates and bosses, but essentially it's your own affair because all that kind of energy belongs to *you*. What does *not* belong to you is the energy you burn and pay for as a consumer. This is the fuel—whether it's gasoline or natural gas or propane or kerosene or electricity or coal or wood—that you need for comfort, mobility, and survival. You can hardly be unaware that the world's existing fuel sources are running out. You *must* be aware from your monthly bills that all the energy that once came so cheap is now costing you a frightening amount of money—for a few people as much as, or even more than, their home mortgage payment each month.

Conserving Fuel

You *can* and *should* cut that outlay for at least 3 very good reasons: (1) Waste, of anything, is foolish and immoral. (2) There are so many more delicious and rewarding things to do with money than to lavish it on predatory, fat-cat oil, gasoline, and electric companies. (3) We are entering an increasingly energy-scarce era in which we will have to cut fuel consumption.

You may think that Big Industry devours most of the world's fuel and drives up prices, but that's not quite true. Considering that you are not, as a family, making anything salable, you and your home are the most prodigal energy gobblers of all time. According to the Stanford Research Institute homes account for 19 percent of all the energy consumed in the United States.

Homes use 50 percent more energy than all the autos in the United States. Of this, 57.5 percent is used in home space heating, 15.1 percent in heating water, 10.9 percent in lighting and operating miscellaneous appliances, 5.7 percent in cooking, 5.7 percent in refrigeration, 3.6 percent in air-conditioning, and 1.6 percent in drying clothes.

According to one official estimate, 18 percent of the average household budget goes into heating the home; keeping it cool in summer can account for even more.

HOW TO CUT YOUR FUEL OUTLAY (for Electricity, Oil, and Gas) by at Least 50 Percent

- *Cut the heat.* Try gradually turning down your thermostat to 68°F, in order to acclimatize your family to a lower temperature. You may find that you're more comfortable with less heat. At night do as the Europeans do: Use your own body to keep warm with good blankets or continental quilts, or even sleeping bags for the kids. (No bed-making rows.)
- *Maintain heating equipment.* If you have an *oil furnace*, have it thoroughly cleaned and adjusted (in summer, when the service man is available). You will save twice the cost of this service (about $25) each

year. If you have a *forced warm-air system*, like 30 million other Americans, once a year you should have it tuned, like a car, by an expert. You can help by cleaning the filters twice a year.

If you have a hot-water central heating system, you need to bleed the air out of it at least twice a year to maintain optimum efficiency. Put a bucket under the air vent on the radiator and open the vent, which will emit a hissing sound (the escaping air). Close the vent when the water comes. Do this room by room.

• *Insulate.* An *attic* or crawl space and an unheated *basement* need to be insulated against heat and cold. In an attic put the insulation under the roof or, preferably, between the joists of the floor space. Use *at least* 4-in.-thick fiberglass. In an unheated basement you need insulation on the ceiling. Attic and basement insulation may cost around $400—less if you do it yourself—and will save you that amount in fuel bills over a 4-year period. A 6-in. layer of insulation in the attic alone can cut fuel consumption 25 percent.

• *Seal.* Keep the cold air out in winter and the cool air in all summer by sealing the house. *Caulk and weather-strip* all doors and windows. (You can use cheap, puttylike, plastic weatherstripping to close all cavities for the winter.) Close all unnecessary exits during winter. Put on *storm windows and doors.* If you're building a house, make sure that all windows are double-glazed (i.e., with 2 layers of glass) which can be 3 times more effective as insulators than single-glazed windows. Better yet, install *triple-glazed windows,* which are 50 percent more effective insulators than double-glazed.

In your present house, if properly installed by a skilled mechanic, double-glazed windows will cost around $1,500, at time of writing, (this is an average figure). You will recapture that outlay in reduced fuel bills and the higher value that accrues thereby to your home. (A New Jersey firm, Marjo Systems Inc., is selling its Thermal-Gard triple-glazed windows for the same price as its double-glazed and promises to keep this bargain in effect as long as there is enough demand to maintain production.)

All of which is fine and dandy, but possibly you don't have that $1,500 for fancy thermopanes or custom-made storm windows. Do what a friend of mine has done. From a roll of *heavy-duty polyethylene,* cut a piece large enough to cover each window from the outside, including frames. Tack or staple this in place and use 1 x 2 ft. pine strip lumber to frame it, to keep it from blowing away.

Make sure that heating and central *air-conditioning ducts* are insulated if they run through unheated or uncooled areas.

- *The open- and closed-door (and window) policy.* On hot *summer days,* keep all windows and doors closed to exclude the heat. Draw the blinds and pull down the shades. Turn off all unneeded lights; these heat up the atmosphere. Keep a fan or two going to circulate the air. At night, throw open the windows and doors (provided, of course, that they are screened) to bring in the cool, nocturnal air. This routine alone can substantially cut your air-conditioning bill. An old lady I know who has a beautifully cool house on the edge of the Mojave Desert has never installed an air-conditioner, thanks to her open-and-closed doors and windows policy.

- *Air-conditioner maintenance.* The commonest ailment in these units is *clogged filters,* which block the flow of air. Clean or, better, replace these at the start of each cooling season, and then clean them once a month. Central air-conditioning systems are very complicated, so your best bet is to have a maintenance contract with the installer.

- *Auxiliary heat.* A fire on the hearth is a joy forever. A *well-ducted modern fireplace* that returns the heat to the room can be a pretty efficient auxiliary heating system as well. Low-polluting firewood (which is a nonexhaustible resource and therefore ecologically okay) is even today fairly inexpensive, and the cost doesn't begin to cover the esthetic delight it affords. For long-lasting fires, try to get oak, ash, beech, birch, or maple wood. Mix these with the woods of fruit trees, such as apple and cherry, and nut trees, such as hickory and pecan, which give heat plus fragrance. If you don't have a fireplace, you can put in a Franklin stove, or one of the super new variants. Coal is still relatively cheap, so that if you have a cold area such as a utility room, you might, as a long-term investment, put in a potbelly stove (order from the big catalog mail-order stores). You can also do some cooking on it. However, coal is a dirty business.

If you have a fireplace, *always* close the damper in winter when the fire is out. A chimney is the most efficient method ever devised for draining heat *from* a house when the fire is not putting heat *into* it. It's a large hole that goes straight out to the open air.

• *Humidifying.* All types of heating systems leave the air very dry. This makes you feel uncomfortable, dries your throat, and warps your antique furniture. The answer is to put moisture back into the air. You can attach a humidifying device to the central heating system, but the simplest solution is to buy one or two portable electric humidifiers. You will feel more comfortable in the cooler temperatures, your complexion will not dry out, and you will save on fuel.

Calculated Cool

In most of the United States air conditioning has revolutionized living. Where average summer temperatures are in the 80s or above—and particularly in regions in which humidity turns swelter into swoon—air conditioning and cool dry air may be a necessity rather than a luxury.

If you are lucky enough to have a new home, you may have central air conditioning built in along with the heating system. However, a central system is extremely expensive to install and run in an older home, particularly if you live in an area in which the summer blahs set in for only a couple of months. So, like 30 million other homeowners, you may decide to install one or more room air-conditioners, for example, in the master bedroom and living room.

The benefits of air conditioning. An air-conditioner is basically a heat pump, removing hot air from the room, dumping it outside, and replacing it with refrigerated air. Besides *cooling* the air, it *removes moisture, filters out dust,* and *circulates* the air inside the room, like a fan. The second function alone, filtering, makes air conditioning a must for many people who are allergic to the dust and pollen that float in through open windows.

Cooling with care. As I said earlier, air conditioning

consumes expensive energy with the speed at which Henry VIII went through wives, so use it carefully and intelligently. Never leave a unit on when you're out of the house or room. Use the air-conditioner as you would use an electric heater. Turn it on *only* when you go into a room, and turn it *off* when you leave. MAKE SURE THE UNIT IS THE RIGHT SIZE FOR THE ROOM IT'S SUPPOSED TO COOL. Of course, more than you need would give more than enough profit to whoever is selling it, not to mention the cost to you in unnecessarily high electric bills all summer. Don't *refrigerate* your house. Don't be like those people we all know who wear sweaters and jackets to brave summer in their air-conditioned "Alaska."

How to buy an air-conditioner. Until fairly recently, when we all became energy-conscious, air-conditioning performance was rated solely in British Thermal Units (BTUs). Now American pragmatism has taken over, and air-conditioners are rated as well by their energy efficiency ratio (EER). The *higher* the EER, the more efficient the air-conditioner.

Try not to install an air conditioner in a window, where it will cut out light and look tatty: fix it flush in the wall.

Select a machine with units that come close to your estimate—within 1,000 BTU/hr for smaller conditioners or 2,000 or 3,000 BTU/hr for larger ones. A conditioner with too little cooling will leave you soggy on hot days; one with too much will keep the space cool but will not dry out the air sufficiently, leaving you clammy and cross.

Space to be cooled	Cooling needed
Medium-size bedroom	5,000 to 6,000 BTU/hr
Medium-size living-room	8,000 to 12,000 BTU/hr
Several connected rooms	15,000 to 20,000 BTU/hr
Medium-size house	24,000 or more BTU/hr

THE ATTIC: This is your front line in the battle to keep cool in summer and warm in winter and save energy all year round. It *must* be insulated, either under the roof, or preferably, on the floor. This will greatly lighten the air-conditioner's load. I can vouch for this because I spend the summer in an old farmhouse which is half-insulated. The insulated part is always noticeably warmer in the chilly mornings, and far cooler during the day than the uninsulated part.

25 FUEL-SAVING TIPS

- Dine by candlelight. It's not only romantic and flattering, it saves electricity. (Phyllis Diller adds that the dust won't show.)
- In areas such as the kitchen, utility room, basement, workshop, and garage, consider using fluorescent lighting. It's much cheaper to operate. A 25-watt fluorescent tube gives as much light as a 100-watt conventional incandescent bulb. (Personally, I hate fluorescents in the kitchen, I like flattering, soothing light from spotlights bounced off walls or ceiling, or else directed onto the stove or sink.)
- In the summer serve at least one entirely cold meal a day. This makes for a two-way saving: You don't use fuel to heat the meal, and you don't heat up the house by using the stove.
- Cut clothes-drying time in your machine 10 to 15 percent by hanging clothes and sheets outside to dry in warm weather.
- Have your gas appliances serviced regularly so they operate at peak efficiency.
- Get *dripping hot water faucets* repaired. They waste a surprising amount of water as well as energy.
- Fix a *hand shower* to a showerless tub. It will soon pay for itself by halving your bath-water bills. The average bath uses 25 gal. of hot water but an average shower uses only about 10 gal. And it's useful for cleaning the tub.
- *Don't do the dishes* unless you have a sinkful or a machine load. Leave small items for a big wash because an average sink wash and rinse uses 6 gal. A complete dishwasher cycle uses 15 gal. of water for a full load.
- Never wash dishes under a running *hot water faucet*; it can run away with 2 to 3 gal. a minute.
- Don't heat more *water* than you need. If you need 2 pt., it is throwing money away to boil 3 pt.
- Defrost your *refrigerator* regularly and avoid thick ice buildup.
- Plan menus to make full use of oven space—you can cook a whole meal using the oven only.
- Use your *toaster oven* to full capacity. It's cheaper to toast 3 slices at once, instead of 2.

- Use the correct *saucepan* for a particular job, not an overlarge one.
- Cover *pans* to keep the heat in, utilizing the hot steam for cooking.
- Adjust the flame on a *gas burner* to remain under pans and not come up the sides.
- After a pan has reached boiling point, turn the heat as low as possible. Cooking will continue.
- Use a *pressure cooker*. It uses less energy and you can cook a variety of foods in one cooker on one burner.
- Consider replacing old, inefficient, or irreparably broken *appliances* with efficient new ones, which use less fuel to give the same amount of heat.
- If you are going away for the weekend or longer, turn off the *water heater* and lower the *thermostat* to 60°F.
- Set the *clock thermostat* to give heat only when it is needed. Systems vary but I suggest you try half an hour before getting up and half an hour *before* going to bed (because the system will take half an hour to cool down).
- Switch off *radiator valves* and close *warm-air registers* in rooms that are not being used. Close the doors that lead to them, of course.

CAUTION! Leave valves and registers slightly open in very cold weather.

- Turn an *electric heater* off when you leave the room.
- Don't open a *window* if a room gets too warm; turn down the heat.
- Don't draw *curtains* over the radiator or heat will simply be wasted through the windows. If you have full-length curtains either shorten them or fit a matching blind to the window so you don't have to pull them at night.

CAUTION: Don't cut the heat where there are invalids, young babies, or elderly people.

My family mostly lives in Canada and they used to laugh when I visited because I was always turning things *down* or off; but I was trained by the frugal French and I notice now that the family no longer laughs, they copy.

HOW TO COPE WITH ELECTRICITY

Do you really save money if you turn off the light bulb on the landing, as Dad says? Or do you save only 2 cents a month, as kid brother insists?

If kid brother leaves both upstairs and downstairs hall lights burning when he goes to bed, 200 watts × 5 hours works out to 4 cents a night at an average utility company's rates. If I leave the electric oven on all night (and this has been known to happen), the cost would be about 90 cents.

Make sure you won't need electro-cardiac treatment the next time the bills come in: switch off the appliances that are a lot more likely than electric light bulbs to cause heart flutters . . . these are your HEATERS. All electrical appliances with heating elements (like clothes dryers) cost more to run than those that just have motors (like clothes washers) because they burn up a lot more energy. These include toasters, irons, hair dryers, and electric baseboard heaters.

A *kilowatt hour* (kwh.) of electricity is the amount needed to produce 1,000 watts of electric power for one hour. Thus, a 1,000-watt baseboard heater will use 1 kwh. per hour. Running from 8 A.M. to 9 P.M daily, it will cost about $15 a month.

A 100-watt light bulb uses 1 kwh. in 10 hours.

HERE'S HOW
GADGETS BURN UP ENERGY

	AVERAGE ANNUAL CONSUMPTION IN KILOWATT-HOUR
Air-conditioner (average size)	2,000
Can opener	0.3
Clock	17
Clothes dryer	1,200
Coffeemaker	100
Dishwasher (with heater)	350
Electric blanket	150
Fan (attic)	270
Fan (furnace)	480
Fluorescent light (3 fixtures)	260
Food mixer	10
Freezer (16 cu. ft.)	1,200
Frying pan	240
Garbage disposal	30
Hair dryer	15
Iron (hand)	150
Light bulbs (for average house)	1,870
Radio (solid state)	20
Radio phonograph (solid state)	40
Range	1,550
Refrigerator (frost-free, 12 cu. ft.)	750
Sewing machine	10
Shaver	0.6
Television (black and white)	400
Television (color)	540
Toaster	40
Vacuum cleaner	45
Washing machine (automatic)	100

Citizen Action Guide.

The Electricity Bill

Electric bills commonly represent a flat fee for the first 20–25 kwh. with additional kwh. being toted up at decreasing rates; so that the next 75 to 100 cost, say, 3.6 cents, the next 200, 3.2 cents, any additional kwh. costing 3 cents. However, in some localities, you are charged a flat service fee for electrical service, and every kilowatt hour you use is charged on top of that, at the same standard rate. In addition, there is often an energy or a fuel adjustment charge that varies from month to month according to how much the utility company must pay for its fuel. This is worked out as some fraction of a percentage, and the amount you actually pay is based, again, on the number of kwh. you consume.

To know how much electricity you use in a week, learn how to read *your* meter. This is much easier than it sounds,* although they used to look to me alarmingly like the control panel of a 747. In fact, modern meters read a bit like the mileage recorder of a car dashboard. Older meters have 5 circular dials equipped with pointers recording the numbers of kilowatt hours in 10,000s, 1,000s, 100s, 10s and 1s. Read the meter from left to right, taking the lower number if the pointer is in between 2 digits.

Electric Meters

CYCLOMETER-TYPE ELECTRIC METERS: The easiest electric meter to read is the cyclometer type (see diagram), which displays a kwh. count on number wheels like those of an automobile odometer. The numbers are read directly across the face, giving a cumulative consumption figure, which is converted into a monthly consumption as shown here. This meter is a relatively modern design, more expensive than the pointer type, and less widely used.

---

* And much easier than reading an electric bill.

Cyclometer-Type
Electric Meter

KILOWATT HOURS

POINTER-TYPE ELECTRIC METERS: The common pointer-type electric meter (see diagrams) looks a bit like a set of one-handed clocks (some have 4 dials and others have 5) with crazy hands. (The method for reading this meter has just been described.)

Here's a code to crack the cryptic figures below the dials.

CL200—the meter will measure current up to 200 amperes.

240V—the meter is designed for a 240-volt power supply.

3W—3 wires are used to conduct electricity to the meter.

FM25—the manufacturer's code for the meter's internal wiring scheme.

TA30—the meter's accuracy was checked under a 30-ampere current.

Pointer-Type
Electric Meters

KILOWATT HOURS   KILOWATT HOURS

Some new homes and apartment buildings now use off-peak meters, which have 2 rows of dials (see diagram): The black set operates during on-peak hours of 7 A.M. to

11 P.M.; the red dials record electric use from 11 P.M. to 7 A. M. These are read the same way as the conventional pointer-type meters, and added together in order to bill you.

Know Your Electricity Supply

Circuit breakers and *fuses* safeguard your electrical system against overloads that are put on the wiring if you try to draw more electricity through the wiring than it can safely carry. They also protect against fire hazard from flaws within appliances or frayed wires in the house wiring system that could cause short circuits.

You can save lots of blood, sweat, toil, and tears by getting your house fitted with circuit breakers in place of fuses. Circuit breakers are switches which trip to "off" if the circuit is overloaded. After you have repaired or remedied the cause of the overload (i.e., unplugged that extra heater), you reset by simply flipping the switch back to "on."

Electricity enters your house through the heavy supply wires of the utility company, and once inside the house it passes through your fuse box or circuit breaker panel and is distributed through separate runs of wiring called circuits. Each circuit is rated for the strength of electrical load it can carry:

- 15 amperes, 120 volts for rooms (bedrooms, living room), which need only lighting fixtures and *small appliances* such as stereo, TV set, sewing machine, dehumidifier, and the like.
- 20 amperes, 120 volts for rooms in which you are apt to use appliances requiring *heavier use of power* (kitchen, basement workshop, garage, or utility room).
- 30 or 50 amperes, 220 volts for *major appliances* (electric stove, water heater, or electric clothes dryer), which should each be wired to a separate circuit.

Air-conditioners are high consumers of electrical power, and some of the big ones need to be wired into a heavy-duty 220-volt circuit, like the electric range and the water heater. Except for the small units, it is better to have a separate circuit into which to plug your air-conditioner, or you will be constantly blowing fuses when you switch lights on while the air-conditioner is running. Make sure you check the adequacy of your wiring when buying a new air-conditioning unit; you may have to call the electrician to come and put in another circuit before you can plug it in.

HOW TO HANDLE GAS

DON'T STRIKE A MATCH IF YOU SMELL GAS: *Do* open all windows immediately. Extinguish fires, naked flames, and cigarettes. Make sure that a gas valve has not been left on accidentally or a pilot light blown out. Turn off main supply valve and, even if you are in doubt, telephone your gas company immediately.

NEVER LOOK FOR A GAS LEAK WITH A NAKED FLAME: Remember the gas or utility specialists are the experts when it comes to gas. If there is a leak in the service pipe supplying the meter or in the meter itself, generally no charge is made for repairs. Don't turn the gas on again until the gasman tells you it's safe to do so. If you feel you *must* check a possible gas leak, coat the suspect area of piping with liquid detergent. If there is a leak, you'll get a lot of soap bubbles where the leak is.

CAUTION IS THE WATCHWORD WHEN DEALING WITH GAS: *Don't* have your appliances connected by anyone who is not a qualified serviceman from a reputable, specialist firm. Check on anyone who claims to be. If you have *any* worries concerning the safety of your gas supply or appliances, telephone the gas company immediately. *Don't* buy a gas appliance that does not carry the American Gas Association seal.

PIPE SAFETY

PRECAUTIONS: If you are leaving a house empty for more than a day during cold weather: (1) turn off the taps at the water mains; (2) make sure no plugs are in the sink or bathtub; (3) *drain* all pipes; (4) turn off all taps firmly so that they don't drip; and (5) have all exterior pipes carefully lagged (covered with a protective casing in case of rust).

LEAKING RADIATOR PIPES (OR VALVES): An emergency treatment is to wrap a bandage or a towel around the pipe below the leak and wind string or thin wire around the towel, then lead the end of the string into a pail or bowl. If possible, shelter the string by making a shield of kitchen foil and place this under the string from leak to pail.

BURST PIPE: Turn off the supply of water to the pipe that is burst. If the burst is in a pipe supplying the water cistern, the tap may be outside the house. If the burst is in a pipe from the cistern to the tap and there is no tap on the cistern, block the exit from the cistern by pushing a cork with a cloth wrapped round it into the pipe opening inside the cistern. You'll probably get pretty wet groping around inside the cistern. If a hot-water pipe bursts, turn the hot-water tap full on and *put out the fire that heats the water at once* (i.e. switch off the immersion heater or turn the boiler off). Otherwise you may have a fire as well as a flood.

Burst hot-water pipes are usually caused by pipes furring, so boilers should be cleaned out regularly in accordance with the supplier's instructions to avoid a burst *boiler*.

FROZEN PIPES: If a tap is not running because the pipes are frozen, pour hot water over the tap itself. If this doesn't work, very gradually pour hot water back along the pipe. Where this is not possible, apply hot cloths: no great heat should be used or a burst pipe will result. If a waste pipe freezes, try thawing it first by pouring salt down it, and, if that fails, with hot water. If it still doesn't run the block may be outside the house: wrap up well and try hot cloths on the outside pipe.

MS. FIXIT
A Home Maintenance Guide

If you're lucky enough to have access to a man who can not only fix things around the house but is actually willing to do so, treat him gently and feed him well. If your man is unwilling, do not force him by any method, whether this be a reproachful glance as you hammer your thumb or a list of what your friends' husbands do for *them* (they're probably lying anyway). Men are extremely good at being helpless; the cleverer they are the more helpless they are, and the cleverest ones offer proof of this by making things *worse*. Anyway, you don't want to find yourself patching up a marriage. (See Your Man's Attitude, p. 299).

Often (they tell me) men don't want to do a maintenance job because they don't know *how* to do it, and its unmanly to say so. Just as women supposedly spring from the womb with an inborn knowledge of housework, so men are supposedly born knowing how to be the Compleat Home Handyman. If your maintenance problem is really a blockage in your man's brain, set up the job yourself and ask him to come and read the instructions from this book. Then he'll tell you when you're doing it wrong ... Then you hand over ...

It is also still possible, in some neighborhoods, to find a handyman by pressing an able teenager into service, but they tend to be elusive, as is their concept of punctuality. They need endless admiration and encouragement, not to mention ruinous quantities of Cokes and cookies. As for the plumber and electrician, indulgently encouraged my efforts to "do-it-myself" perhaps because they are embarrassed by the amount they had to charge just to come over and replace a washer or rewire a lamp.

In my experience, it's quicker, cheaper, and less harassing to keep a list of all the jobs that need doing, and keep a day completely free to do a lot of them. Whoever gave wives and mothers the idea that the whole weekend was time off anyway?

If your house is falling apart, your local newsstand can

supply you with a copy of *The Family Handyman*, which is published 9 times yearly, or you can subscribe to it by writing to the Webb Company, 1999 Shepard Road, St. Paul, Minnesota 55116. It not only tells you how to do what but also inspires you with enthusiasm and convinces you it's FUN (which, for me, it damn well isn't). *The Family Handyman* covers anything that the do-it-yourself amateur can handle, from changing that faucet washer to building an addition onto a house or installing your own central heating system. You might graduate to the alluring *Popular Mechanics* magazine (which already has a *million women readers*).

According to them, women are getting more and more adventurous all the time, and some think nothing of wiring up a new circuit while the washing is drying, or building in a few bookcases over the weekend. Nothing impresses or depresses me more than a woman who does BIG JOBS. I like to think they're lying but I was once on television with a woman who had installed her own central heating, double glazing and insulated her loft *while carrying twins*. I didn't attempt a thing for weeks afterwards.

The man to give you confidence is your hardware-store owner. Cultivate him. He can give you all sorts of free advice and tips on the best materials to use for the job you are undertaking, and very often suggestions of a better method of going about it. Do not hesitate to give a full description of your "problem." Quite often the store owner will go off and fumble in the back room and then produce a miracle piece of equipment that will provide you with an easy solution, saving you time, money, and frustration. Shop around until you find the right hardware store and owner. This can be a very worthwhile relationship, so devote some time to cultivating it.

Your first purchases should be a transistor radio (for company) and a strong, solid ladder (wooden ladders are sturdier than aluminum), and if possible don't do anything on a ladder unless there is someone else in the house to hear you holler for help. You will also want to find a place to keep your tools and supplies in a well-organized fashion so that you don't spend your first hour on the job digging out the tools you need.

THE WORKING WOMAN'S TOOLBOX

*Our motto: A plumber's help
is cheaper than a plumber*

You don't need a man (well, not for home maintenance) if you have a proper toolbox fitted with a reasonable set of tools. I can never fit the instruments back into their neat little places. Instead, buy a cheap plastic toolbox (or a fishing-tackle box) with a handle and several self-raising, subdivided trays, or you can settle for a plastic cutlery tray in a drawer, or even a cardboard box. And make sure to get a strong padlock or lock it away from your friends and children. Alternatively, keep an assortment of your most needed odd-job tools—screwdrivers, hammer, scissors, pliers, adjustable wrench—in a plastic bucket. Take the whole bucket with you when you go to fix something and you'll save that constant running back to get just one more tool. The disadvantage is that you can't lock a bucket.

An investment in a toolbox is going to show returns faster than anything else you can buy for your home. I tried to pare down the following list of suggested items, as it's meant to be a toolbox for the inexperienced. "All the more reason for getting the right tool for the job," sourly commented a high-powered male handyman; however, he did agree that none of the tools listed are difficult to use. Anyway, I've starred the basic essential items for a beginner's tool kit.

Not all items in the following list are traditionally kept in the toolbox, but I can't think where else I would keep them.

★ • A pair of rubber gloves (never do any electrical work without wearing them). A pair of heavy work gloves to protect your hands.

★ • *Adhesive bandages, ointment* for burns, Band-Aids.

★ • *A set of adhesives:* (1) *white glue* for porous and semiporous materials, such as paper, wood, cloth, pottery; (2) *rubber glue* for paper, photographs, leather, plastic; (3) *contact or instant-bonding cement* of which some can be used on just about any material while others are made especially for plastic laminates like Formica; (4) *epoxy glue* for bonding almost anything including china, glass, metals, wood; (5) *latex-base glue* for fabrics and carpeting. (See How to Stick Almost Anything, p. 187).

★ • Assorted *balls of string, rubber bands, clear plastic tape, picture wire.*

★ • *Box of matches, flashlight* and *spare batteries, transistor radio, extra batteries, candles,* and *Sterno* for cooking in case of a power failure.

• *A carpenter's level* (18 in. long) [45 cm]. It is vital if you want to hang shelves straight.

• *Folding carpenter's ruler.* This is easier to use when taking vertical measurements since it does not buckle like a measuring tape.

• *A center punch.* A short rod used to start holes for screws and nails. Also used to drive a pail down flush with the wood without leaving hammer marks.

• *Chisels.* You will need a ½-in. cold chisel for cutting through bolts and nails; 1 or 2 wood chisels (½ in. and 1 in.) for chipping out bits of wood.

• Several *C-clamps* in different sizes and a couple of *spring clamps.* They hold things you are sawing, or clamp things you are sticking.

• *A combination square.* Use for marking and measuring 90-degree and 45-degree angles, for measuring, or as a level.

• A battery-powered *continuity tester.* Enables you to test appliance cords or lamp wiring to make sure the wiring connections are unbroken. Clip the tester to one end of the wire and touch the probe to the other. If the wiring is unbroken the tester lights. If it does not, there is a break somewhere, and you should replace the cord or rewire the lamp.

★ • Spare *curtain hooks.*

• *A ⅜-in. electric drill,* with an assortment of bits for drilling wood, masonry, and metal. You *can* get a hand-operated drill, and this should be your first power tool. (If you ask for one as a gift, you'll probably get some Chanel No. 5 as well, out of sheer pity, if nothing else.)

• *An electrical voltage tester.* This is used to check whether or not there is current in the outlet or appliance you are working on. (You touch the 2 probes to the terminals of a light fixture, or put them in the slots of the outlet, and if there *is* a current, the light glows.)

★ • *Faucet washers;* to fit *your* faucets, extra *O-rings* as required, or a roll of *self-molding packing.*

• *A funnel.*

★ • *Fuses.* Have an assortment of extras in the proper amperages to match those in your fuse box.

★ • *Hammer.* Buy a good 16-oz. one with curved-claw back for yanking nails out. The front is, of course, for crushing rose stems.

• *Insulating electrical tape* and *insulated staples* for attaching electrical wire to the top of baseboards.

• *A roll of 2-wire lamp cord.*

• *Masking tape.*

• *A flat metal file* and a *round file* for shaping wood.

• *A miter box.*

★ • Assorted *nails:* brads, finishing nails, common nails in different lengths, tacks, thumbtacks, upholstery tacks, pins, molly bolts, toggle bolts.

★ • *Penetrating oil* for dissolving rust. *Lubricating oil,* for squeaking doors, window hinges, locks, etc., and for lubricating the blender and sewing machine.

• *A paint scraper* and *putty knife.*

★ • *A penknife.* I'm not quite sure why, but I feel safer with one around.

• *A small* and a *large (14-in.) pipe wrench* for plumbing jobs.

• *Plastic wood-filler,* or wood putty, or spackle (water cement that looks like flour) for filling screw holes and cracks.

★ • *Pliers.* You will need *slip-joint* pliers for bending and twisting wire and gripping things; *long-nosed* pliers for twisting ends of electrical wiring into loops, for gripping small screws and other tiny objects; and *vise-type* pliers, which have a locking-grip feature that holds them in place when you clamp them onto an object: they also incorporate a wire cutter.

• *Portable work light.* Make sure yours has a heavy-duty cord, a wire cage to protect the bulb, and a hook to hang it up.

• *A pry bar.* Among other things, this is useful for digging out nails and prying up loose boards. (You can use your claw hammer, but a pry bar is best for stubborn immovable objects.)

★ • *A rubber plunger* (C cup size) or an *auger* that snakes through and unblocks drains if the plunger doesn't work.

• *Sandpaper* in assorted grades.

• *Saws.* A 24-in. crosscut is a good general purpose saw but too large for me to handle. I prefer a *10-in.* saw: It has a stiff back, smaller teeth, and you don't have to be as strong to use it, although it doesn't get the job done as fast. Perhaps you prefer to compromise and have one *18-in.* saw. A small *keyhole* saw is handy for cutting holes in things; you can get one with interchangeable blades—one for cutting wood and a hacksaw blade for cutting through metal.

• *Scissors.* Keep a small, large, and serrated one handy. Serrated scissors grip what you are cutting.

★ • *Screws.* Have an assortment in different lengths and sizes, some with flat heads and some with round heads.

★ • *Screwdrivers.* You will need at least one; but even better, get a set of at least 4 regular-tipped screwdrivers with shanks and tips of varied lengths and sizes and 2 Phillips screwdrivers for different sizes of cross-topped screws. Get good-quality hardened steel screwdrivers: The tips of inexpensive ones tend to chip off.

• *Soft lead pencil and eraser* so that when hanging pictures you can mark up your walls in the wrong places and then rub the marks off.

• A heavy *staple gun* and *staples* (a great shortcut for fastening jobs and swift upholstering).

★ • Flexible *steel measuring tape.* It should be at least 12 ft. long (20 ft. would be better), marked in inches, feet, and with 16-in. markings for helping to locate studs in walls.

★ • *A utility knife* with interchangeable blades for cutting linoleum and many other materials.

• *A vise.*

• *A whetstone* for sharpening your chisels, penknife, and any other blades.

• An adjustable *wrench.*

WHAT EVERY WOMAN SHOULD KNOW

You will find that the hardest part of the simple jobs described in this chapter is to overcome your early conditioning. You were probably brought up to switch your mind off at the unladylike suggestion that you should use a screwdriver. But there isn't always a man around when your sink gets blocked, and even if there is, it's probably quicker to unblock it yourself than nag him into doing it for you.

Skip this section and turn to it only in time of crisis. It probably won't make sense until you are forced to do something.

Electricity—Handle with Care

- *Word of warning:* Most of us know as much about electricity as Thurber's aunt, who feared that her light bulb leaked it. Electricity is potentially dangerous, so treat it with respect, keep it away from water and always wear rubber gloves when dealing with repair jobs.
- *Always* cut off the power at circuit breaker panel or fuse box before starting a repair job.
- *Never* poke *anything*—a finger or scissors—into a light bulb socket or wall socket.
- *Never* touch an electric gadget if you are also touching water or you will risk electrocution. Remember that James Bond once killed a villain by throwing a plugged-in electric heater into the bath in which his enemy lay soaking. So *don't* hold a plugged-in appliance with wet hands or if you have wet feet or when you are standing in the bathtub or with your feet in a bowl of water.
- *Don't* switch a light switch with wet hands.
- *Don't* use water to put out an electrical fire in an appliance that is plugged in. Unplug it, then use a chemical fire extinguisher. If the fire is still smoldering (as it easily can in a sofa or mattress), smother flames with a coat or blanket and call the fire depart-

ment! Never use water on a kitchen grease fire—it will make it worse. For more on fire extinguishers see Fire Prevention and Protection, p. 269.

How to Change a Fuse

WHAT TO DO WHEN THE LIGHTS "BLOW" OUT: When a bunch of lights goes out, you have probably blown a fuse. The cable of a light that plugs into the wall, or any light that doesn't have a plug, goes back to the fuse box; so if that light blows, then every other light on the circuit will also have gone.

How do you discover which, of a number of lights now not operating, is the villain? (1) You turn them all off. (2) You replace the fuse or reset the circuit breaker. (3) You turn them on again, one by one. When the fuse blows yet again you have found the culprit. Switch off lamp, replace the fuse, then get an expert to deal with the faulty fitting. At this point in your maintenance education, this is an electrician's job. Don't call an expensive electrician until you have checked (1), (2), and (3) above.

EVERYTHING YOU NEVER WANTED TO KNOW ABOUT FUSES: If you can change a light bulb you can change a fuse. A fuse is a deliberately weak link inserted into an electrical system to stop it from being overloaded. A fuse blows quite easily because the metal strip through which the current passes won't carry a strong load and melts. When the little glass window of a screw-in fuse is clear; but the metal strip has melted in the middle, it usually means you have overloaded the circuit by plugging too many appliances or lamps into it. If the glass window of a blown screw-in fuse is clouded, it is usually a sign that there is a short circuit somewhere in the wiring or the circuit or in one of the appliances plugged into it.

Fuses are marked with the number of amps they can carry without blowing. *You should never replace a blown fuse with one rated for a higher amperage or you will be creating a fire hazard.* (Never, NEVER replace a burned-out fuse with a copper penny, even if it means letting everything wait until you run down to the hardware store for a supply of fuses.)

You can get an *S-type nontamper fuse*, a special kind of fuse that once installed will put you beyond all temptation to replace a fuse with one of a different amperage. These fuses, which are color coded, come with special screw-in adapter bases. Once the adapter has been screwed into the socket in the fuse box, it is virtually impossible to get it out. Most importantly, when a fuse does blow, the adapter base will only accept a fuse of the correct amperage. These S-type fuses will also incorporate a "slow-blow" or time-delay feature found in certain other screw-in fuses, which enables them to permit a brief upsurge of current before blowing. They are particularly handy for circuits used by appliances that have an initial heavy surge of power consumption while starting up. If you find that a fuse is blowing every time your washing machine or air-conditioner starts up, you might try one of the time-delay fuses.

When *changing a fuse*, switch off all the lights and appliances on the circuit, and make sure you are not standing on a wet floor. Do not touch anything but the rim of the fuse you are unscrewing. In fact, it is probably a good idea to keep your other hand in your pocket, so you won't be tempted to grab hold of a nearby water pipe for moral support (thereby grounding yourself), while taking out the old fuse or putting in the new one.

If you have *cartridge-type fuses* that do not show any visible signs of being blown, what can you do? Keep a supply of spares and check each fuse in the box by replacing it with a new one. These fuses are usually housed in a little metal box that pulls out from your main fuse box; you simply pull the old cartridge free from the spring clips that hold it in place, and snap in a new cartridge. Cartridge fuses are commonly used on circuits controlling major appliances. If your dishwasher stops, it is worth this trial-and-error checking to see if the fuse is blown before you call the costly serviceman.

Identify your fuses before they blow. A fine rainy-day activity for you and a child. Turn on everything in the house. Then go to the fuse box and unscrew or unplug one fuse after another while your helper makes the rounds with pad and pencil, noting which lights are out in which rooms. Then put stick-on labels next to the fuses, indicating which room lights and outlets they control.

How to Change a Plug

It takes a lot of time and effort to fit a conventional plug on a 2-wire 1-amp cord. Use a convenient snap-on plug instead. All you do is pull up the lever at the top of the plug, push the cleanly cut end of the 2-wire lamp cord into the hole at the side of the plug as far as it will go, and push the lever down into place. Metal prongs inside the plug press through the insulation of the cord, making connection with the copper wires.

How to Make Your Own Electric Extension Cord

LIGHTWEIGHT CORDS: You can make a light-duty extension cord by buying a matching socket and wiring it to the other end of the cord to which you've attached a plug. Snap-on sockets work in the same manner as snap-on plugs. These lightweight cords should be used only for lamps and very small appliances that do not draw a lot of electricity.

HEAVYWEIGHT CORDS: For use with heavier appliances, you may want to make a long heavy-duty extension cord so you can vacuum the car and use an electric lawn mower or power saw.

Buy heavy-duty 3-wire electrical cord in the length you need. This cord comes in different gauges of wiring, so check with your hardware or electrical supply store to make sure the cord you buy fits the power needs of the use you plan for it (tell them the amperage of the appliance you want to attach to the cord). Also buy a heavy-duty 3-prong plug and matching socket. The 3 wires inside the cord are color coded: green, black, and white. The 3 terminal screws inside the plug and socket are colored green, gold, and silver. Follow the color coding. Attach: green wire to green terminal screw, black wire to gold-colored screw, white wire to silver screw.

Here's a memory aid:

> Green to green is easily seen
> Black to gold is coal when it's sold
> Silver to white is a moonlit night.

How to Stop a Dripping Faucet

If a faucet is dripping it probably needs a new washer. Your hardware or plumbing supply store will sell you one, but take along the old washer to make sure of getting the proper size: There are an incredible number of different sizes and shapes. You may feel like a deranged Swiss watchmaker in mid-job, but if you lay out the parts on the sink drainboard in order of removal (left to right), it makes the reassembly job more orderly.

REPLACING THE WASHER: First turn off the water under the sink if possible. (If there is no shutoff under the sink, you'll have to turn off your house's main water supply, and better wait until no one is home to do your repair!) Open the faucet to let the water drain out of it, then plug the sink so screws cannot fall down the drain. Unscrew and remove the handle of the faucet. This may take a bit of ingenuity as the screws are sometimes hidden under those chrome covers that say H and c. But persevere. There has to be a way to get it off.

Once you get the handle off, unscrew the nut that holds the faucet stem in place. Use an adjustable wrench. (When you use a wrench on any chrome plumbing fixture, cover the chrome with masking tape to keep from marring its finish.) After you've lifted the nut off, pull out the faucet-stem assembly. At its base, usually held on by a screw, is the washer. (There are *some* washers that are just pushed into place over the stem end.) Remove the screw, replace the washer with a new one, replace the screw, and reverse the above procedure to put the faucet back together.

REPLACING THE FAUCET SEAT: If the faucet still drips, the "seat" of the faucet, where washer meets inlet pipe, may be worn. Replacing this requires a special tool, and it's probably best to call a plumber. The necessary tool is called a seat wrench. Insert it into the hole left when you remove the faucet stem until one of the hexagonal gradings on its shank meshes with the diameter of your faucet seat. Unscrew the faucet seat, take it to the plumbing supply house to match it with a new one. Screw the new seat tightly into place using the seat wrench. (It's easier to do than to read.)

REPLACEMENT PART KITS: Many of the modern single-stemmed mixing faucets can be repaired with kits of replacement parts put together by the manufacturer. Mercifully, these come with complete instructions and diagrams, as some of the parts are quite complex. If you have one of these modern wonders note down the name of the manufacturer and the model number (usually engraved on the chrome somewhere), so that you can pick up a replacement kit at the plumbing supply house.

How to Stop a Leaking Faucet

If water seeps around the top of the faucet, you may need to tighten the packing nut, replace the packing, or change the O-ring, depending on the kind of faucet you have.

PACKING NUT: If your faucet has this fitting, cover the nut with masking tape and tighten it with an adjustable wrench. If it still leaks, remove the packing nut (no need to turn the water off to do this). Under the nut you should find a domed washer. If it appears worn, take it to the hardware or plumbing supply store and get a replacement. If you cannot find an exact replacement, you can repack the faucet with self-molding packing, a soft putty-like material that's sold in small strips. Just wind it round and round the top of the faucet stem, and screw the packing nut back on top of it.

O-RING: If you have a faucet with this attachment, shut the water off, remove the faucet stem, take off the O-ring, and get a replacement.

Helpful hint: Virtually everything screws in clockwise and unscrews counterclockwise. Bear this in mind if you find yourself working upside down in cramped quarters under a sink, with your back against the wall.

How to Stop Water Pipes Banging

If water pipes bang and shudder when you turn faucets off, you have a condition called "water hammer" and will probably need to call a plumber to drain your plumbing system. There are usually special lengths of piping hidden in the walls above the supply pipes to your fixtures which contain air that cushions the shock of water in the pipes when it is suddenly cut off by your shutting a faucet.

When most of this air has become absorbed by the water in the plumbing system, which it will do in time, you get water hammer. The plumber will drain all the water out of the system and let some cushioning air back in through an empty faucet. Watch him. You can do-it-yourself the next time.

How to Unblock a Sink Drain

CHEMICAL DRAIN CLEANERS: Products such as Drāno and Liquid Plumber can help to open a partially clogged drain (they are not so good for old plumbing), but remember that these substances are highly caustic and dangerous, so use rubber gloves because chemical drain cleaners can burn you. In any case, they won't work on a drain that's really and truly stopped, but it's always worth a try to avoid the plumber.

A RUBBER PLUNGER: Next, try this plumber's helper, which can be bought at any hardware store. You can buy plungers with cone-shaped adapters on them that can be used both for sinks and for toilets. Just shove the cone of rubber back inside the rubber suction cup of the plunger for use on a drain.

Block up the sink overflow with a damp cloth in order to create a vacuum, grease the edge of the plunger, fit it over the sink outlet, and pump several times. Very satisfying.

UNCLOGGING DOWN UNDER: If the plunger fails, put a bucket under the U bend, or trap, in the outlet pipe under the sink. Use an adjustable wrench to remove the cleanout plug in the trap. (If the trap hasn't a cleanout plug, remove the whole trap by unscrewing the slip-nuts that hold it in place.) Be very careful and WEAR RUBBER GLOVES when doing this if you have used a chemical drain cleaner.

Try to scrape out the blockage with a bent coat hanger, or better still, a plumber's snake or auger. Insert wire or snake in the cleanout plug, and work it up toward the sink drain until you can catch hold of and remove the blockage. Don't remove bucket until you've replaced everything.

This is also the way to recover anything valuable that has slipped down the sink outlet, such as the diamond out of your engagement ring.

How to Solve Toilet Problems

(This deals with tank-type toilets only. Most bathrooms with pressure flush valve toilets are in big apartment houses, and the super should cope.)

IF WATER WON'T STOP RUNNING INTO THE TOILET:

Check the tank ball. It should be cutting off the flow into the bowl from the tank, but may be failing to do its job. Shut off the supply of water to the toilet; you don't have to bail it out with your bathroom glass. After turning off the water supply (wherever it is), just flush the toilet until there's no water left to flush away. Then lift off the tank top, flush the toilet, and observe the tank ball to see that it is dropping smack on top of the outlet hole into the bowl. If the guide wires that attach the tank ball to the lift arm of the flushing handle appear to be misaligned, straighten them out or, if they are badly bent, replace them with a new set from the hardware store. If the tank ball itself seems badly worn, it may be letting water seep down into the bowl. Unscrew it from the guide wires and replace it with a new one. Clean off any scum around the opening into the toilet bowl.

Check the float and intake valve. If the tank ball seems to be working properly, the problem may be that the float attached to the filler valve of the toilet is floating too high in the water and failing to shut off the water coming through the intake pipe. With the tank full, try lifting the float slightly. If this fails to stop the running water, the trouble is probably a worn part inside the intake valve—in which case you'd better call a plumber to replace it, though you can *try* to take it apart and replace the washer. (You're going to have to call the plumber anyway.) If you do call a plumber, you may want to have him install a more up-to-date ball cock (float valve). The parts cost less than the labor!

If lifting the float does stop the running water, bend the rod connected to the float *down* slightly so the float shuts off the water when it reaches a level an inch or two below the top of the intake valve. It may also be that the float has sprung a leak and become waterlogged. Unscrew it from the rod and shake it. If there is water inside, replace it with a new one from the hardware store.

IF THE TOILET FAILS TO FLUSH THOROUGHLY: This indicates there is not enough water flowing through it. Try bending the rod attached to the float *upward* slightly so the water level in the tank can be higher.

IF WATER LEAKS OUTSIDE THE TOILET: This may be condensation, in hot weather. If not, it is a faulty gasket in the intake valve or under the toilet bowl. Call a plumber.

IF THE TOILET BOWL IS CRACKED AND LEAKS: Before investing in a plumber, try draining toilet and using a sealer, such as G.E. Seal, applied to the inside. This saves replacing the toilet.

How to Hang Pictures

PICTURES: There are various kinds of picture-hanging hooks available at hardware and five-and-dime stores. For fairly lightweight pictures and small mirrors you can use hooks attached to self-adhesive backing, but these will not stick to wallpaper or unfinished wood surfaces. However, I hate using these because someone else always hangs something too heavy on them, then WHAM! Another broken picture frame.

Metal picture hooks. Use picture hangers made of a bent piece of metal that consists of a hook and a triangular brace through which you drive a nail into the wall to secure the hook. These are available in different sizes and can hold up to 100 lb. The triangular brace guides the nail down into the wall at an angle; and when the nail has been been driven in properly and the hook lies flat against the wall, you have a very secure mounting. With large pictures, it is a good idea to use 2 hooks, spaced about 1 foot apart, so the picture will not slip and require constant straightening.

To mark the spot correctly for your hook, pencil a little "X" on the wall where you need to drive the nail. (If you have a crumbly plaster wall, stick a piece of Scotch tape over the X before nailing, and the plaster will not flake off so easily.) Put the nail through the two guide holes on the picture hanger, holding the hanger and nail against the wall so the point of the nail is on your X-mark. Give a gentle first tap with your hammer, then drive the nail in, tapping harder as the nail becomes more firmly seated in the wall.

Picture wire. Be sure to buy picture wire that is the correct strength to support whatever you're hanging. Don't use natural fiber string or cord, which can rot and drop your picture with a bang. This happened to me once in the middle of the night. Bump, bump, bump down the stairs it went, like a drunken burglar. In bed and terrified I telephoned the police who, having nothing better to do that night, arrived in 3 squad cars, with 2 mounted searchlights and an eager Alsatian dog. Now I always use wire or nylon cord for picture hanging.

SHELVES AND HEAVY PICTURES: If you are hanging up something very heavy, or putting up shelves that will have to support a great weight, you usually have to use some sort of screw or bolt. The kind you select depends on the type of wall you have: plaster, wood, wallboard, concrete, etc. To determine what your wall is made of, you might have to drill a hole in it and analyze the debris that comes out. Don't use an electric drill unless you have practiced a bit under the supervision of someone who knows how; otherwise you might break the drill or even your wrist. When drilling walls be careful that you drill only into *wall.* If you drill into water pipes or electrical conduit you could be in trouble or even dead.

If your drilling produces a white powder and the drill goes right through the wall quite easily, you have some sort of *wallboard,* usually nailed up over wooden studs. *Plaster* is usually applied over concrete, cinderblocks, bricks, or wooden lathing. If it is over a solid concrete or other masonry wall, your drill will not break through, and if you gather up into an envelope the dust that comes out from behind the white plaster dust, you can get your hardware man to help you determine the kind of fastener to use to attach the shelves to the wall. Plaster and *woodenlathing walls* require the same sorts of fasteners as hollow wallboard walls.

There are special masonry nails that can be used in cement, brick, and other such walls to hang relatively light loads. For hanging heavy objects on *masonry walls* you will need long bolts or a combination of a bolt and screw with some sort of expansion plug, which you insert into a hole you've drilled in the wall. The expansion plug gets compressed into the hole by the screw, and helps grip the wall more securely. For *hollow walls*, there are several different kinds of fasteners, such as molly bolts and toggle bolts.

Molly bolts. To use a molly bolt, first drill into the wall a hole that's the diameter of the sleeve that encases the bolt. Push the sleeve into this hole and screw the bolt into the sleeve, holding the sleeve in place with a special little gripper tool, which the hardware man will give you free when you buy the mollies. Screwing the bolt into the sleeve causes the sleeve to crimp up on the far side of the wall, gripping itself in place. To hang up an object with a molly bolt, you must then unscrew the bolt, run it through the object you wish to attach to the wall, then screw it back into the sleeve.

Toggle bolts. These bolts have a pair of collapsible wings screwed onto them. To use these fasteners, first drill a hole into the wall, the diameter of the folded-up toggle "wings." Then remove the toggle, put the bolt through the object you are hanging, and thread the toggle back onto the bolt. Push the folded-up toggle through the hole in the wall and tighten the bolt. The "wings" of the toggle will open on the far side of the wall and hold the bolt firmly in place. Toggle bolts can support heavier weights than mollies, but you cannot unfasten and reuse them; once you undo the bolt the toggle will drop off behind the wall.

If, in a fit of insane ambition, you are trying to hang heavy shelves on a hollow wallboard or plaster and lath wall, you should get your fasteners into the studs behind the wall covering. Studs are 2 × 4 upright wooden beams to which the wallboard or lathing is attached. They are generally set 16 inches apart (although sometimes in older houses this is not the case), measuring from the center of one stud to the center of the next. Assuming that there is a stud at the corner of your room, you can measure down 17 inches from the corner and, with any luck, be at the center of the next stud. To be sure, drill a hole, using a small bit on your electric drill. You can patch up misplaced holes with a bit of spackle (it's water-cement that looks like flour) and paint. Fasten things to studs with the proper size nails or screws, depending on the weight of the object your are mounting.

HOW TO STICK ALMOST ANYTHING

In my experience, there is no such thing as an all-purpose adhesive, any more than there is an all-purpose book or all-purpose food or an all-purpose shoe. A home needs more than one adhesive to hold it together, because the secret of sticking is to select the most suitable goop for the job. And there does seem to be an adhesive for just about any kind of material you may ever have to work with. Before using . . . CHECK THE SOLVENT.

CELLULOSE CEMENTS (MODEL AIRPLANE GLUE): Thick, clear glue that comes in a tube. Very good *general-purpose* stuff that will stick together both porous and nonporous materials. Spread a thin coating on both surfaces. For porous materials, let glue dry, then press surfaces together and clamp. For nonporous materials, press surfaces together immediately after applying glue, and clamp. Remove excess with nail polish remover.

CONTACT CEMENTS: Thin, syrupy substances, used to apply plastic laminate, such as Formica, to countertops. Spread evenly on both surfaces, let dry, and press surfaces together. Bonds *instantly*, so you have to be very careful and dexterous to use these adhesives—you cannot pull the glued surfaces apart if you have misaligned them. Remove any excess with nail polish remover.

New instant-bond cements are also available that can be used to bond *any* two surfaces together on contact. They are very potent and must be handled with care (some "handymen" have found themselves in hospital emergency wards to get their fingers unstuck). These glues are packaged in thumb-size tubes.

EPOXY ADHESIVES: These come in 2 parts—a resin and a hardener—sold in separate tubes. Mix equal amounts together (on a piece of foil), spread a thin coating on the broken surfaces, press together. Remove excess with hot water and soap while still wet. One of the strongest of all adhesives, epoxy can be used to bond together almost anything—glass, metal, wood, stone, etc. It is expensive and more difficult to work with than ready-to-use adhesives but not as scary as the instant-bonding glues. Great for repairing ceramic ovenware.

LATEX-BASE ADHESIVES: For gluing together *fabrics, carpeting, paper, cardboard.* Sold in tubes or cans. Heat and water resistant. You can use this stuff to hem drapes; the bond will hold throughout laundering, but fabrics so glued must not be dry cleaned. (Dry-cleaning fluid dissolves latex and rubber.) Apply a thin coat to one surface, smooth the other surface on top of it: Clean up excess glue with a damp cloth while glue is still wet.

PVA (POLYVINYL RESIN) ADHESIVES: Carpenter's "white glue," often sold in plastic squeeze bottles. These come closest to being all-purpose household adhesives. Used to stick *wood, paper, cloth, leather, most porous materials.* Spread the glue on one surface of the object you're sticking together, clamp the pieces together if necessary, and wipe off any excess glue with a damp cloth. This kind of adhesive dries clear. It will come unstuck if exposed to high heat or moisture.

SILICONE ADHESIVES: Clear thick glue, sold in squeeze tubes, smells like vinegar. Use for *china, glass, ceramics, tiles.* Spread lightly on both surfaces to be glued, let dry until tacky; clamp together until hardened. Water and heat proof. (You *can* put the mended teacup in the dishwasher.) As a solvent use paint thinner while adhesive is still wet. Once dry, you have to scrape off the excess with a sharp knife or razor blade.

RUBBER CEMENTS: Thick rubbery glue, often sold in jars with brushes in the lids. For gluing *paper, photographs, rubber, leather, plastic.* Use whenever flexibility is needed. Apply to both surfaces, let dry until tacky, press together. Nail polish remover will remove excess.

How to go about it: Start sticking by making sure, if possible, that whatever you're fixing is on something that can be thrown away, such as old newspapers. Wear an old smock or shirt and have at hand the proper solvent so you can get the stuff off your hands and immediately clean up any mess you make. Find a quiet, uninterrupted time in which to do your sticking. Take the phone off the hook. At the moment of truth, when you're about to apply a new countertop using contact cement, it helps to take a few steadying breaths.

KEEPING THE COLD AND DAMP OUTSIDE

Fall Check List

Maintenance of the outside of the house is, for the most part, best left to professionals. However, if you are a house owner, keeping a solid roof over your head and maintaining sound walls and foundations, it is probably the most important part of home upkeep. You should check the outside of your house periodically to determine what needs repairing. Do this well before bad weather sets in, so you allow time for the roofer, painter or mason to fit you into his schedule and get the work done so your home is snug for the winter before he leaves on his annual vacation.

Annual inspection of the exterior of the house and regular maintenance will enable you to plan ahead and spare you the nasty shock of discovering that suddenly that roof you'd never given a thought to has got to be completely replaced—perhaps with the very money you'd been looking forward to spending on a much-needed re-decoration of the interior of the house.

LOOK AT:

THE ROOF (use binoculars, do NOT try to climb up there): Check for broken or missing shingles, and for gaps, crumbling areas or signs of corrosion.

THE CHIMNEY: Are there any cracks?

THE BRICKWORK: Check for cracks or gaps in the mortar joints.

GUTTERS: Check gutter outlets so that fall leaves and birds' nests don't block them. Get screens installed, or at least put balloon-type strainers over the openings of the downspouts (they look a bit like a nineteenth-century lady motorist's hat and will prevent debris from getting into and clogging downspouts).

Check gutters for leaks at the joints. Evidence that water may be running down the outside of a wall may mean that the gutters are broken or blocked at the joints, so that water pours over instead of being carried away. This can result in damage to the walls which can result in dry rot. You will probably want to call a roofer to make any necessary repairs, but if you do have a very low house then you can patch up leaking gutters with a tube of sealing compound. Leaky old gutters should be replaced with stainless steel ones that won't corrode. Get the roofer to fit them with screens and strainers while he's at it.

EXTERIOR WALLS: Check wooden siding to see if there are any loose or rotting boards that will need repair or replacement. Check the paint for any blistering or peeling areas that should be repainted. Check shingled walls for broken, missing, or warped shingles. Check stucco walls for cracks. Check for any cracks in the foundation, and check the foundation and adjacent woodwork for any traces of termites. You will probably not see the termites (the ones that do the damage do not come out into the light) but you may notice the little tunnels of mud they build up over the stone foundation of your home to get from their underground nests to your woodwork. Call a reliable exterminating service (check with a neighbor if you don't know whom to call). If you should happen to find little piles of sawdust munchings in the course of your inspection, you may have carpenter ants, and should again call an exterminator.

BASEMENT FLOOR AND WALLS: Check for any sign of moisture. There are damp-proofing solutions that can be painted on to interior basement walls. However, if the trouble is due to substantial cracking of the walls, you'd better call a builder to have a look at it. And if there is a lot of water in the basement, it could be a major undertaking to correct the condition, involving digging up all around the outside of the foundation. Be very wary of outfits that claim they can come over and waterproof your basement from the inside. If you have a serious water problem, their treatments are unlikely to work—at least not for long. Get professional advice from an architect.

SKYLIGHTS: If they are ill-fitting, get a builder.

WINDOWS: Broken windows can be replaced with panes of glass pre-cut to size by a glass dealer (often your hardware man), which are held in place with little metal triangles . . . called glazer's points, and then sealed with putty. Get glass 1/16 in. (1.5 mm) smaller all around the frame. Remove the old glass (wear cotton, non-slip gloves!), put a little putty around the frame and place the new glass against that. Press the glazier's points into the wood, sliding them in flat over the glass, and pushing them into the wood with the edge of a screwdriver. Put a 1/2-in. (12-mm) rope of putty (roll it out between your hands) all around the frame. Smooth and trim the putty with a putty knife. Let dry, and paint.

Get a carpenter to plane *jammed windows*, then prime and repaint bare wood as soon as possible.

Defective sash cords are, again, a professional's job but if you are a do-it-yourself debutante, cotton sash cords should be replaced with nylon cord, which won't rot, or with chain, which won't stretch.

Once you have fathomed the mystery of the double-hung window, (an ingenious bit of Rube Goldbergman-ship to the uninitiated) it is not too difficult *to replace sash cords*. Each half of the window, top and bottom, is hung on two cords, with one end of each cord tied in a knot that fits into a slot at the edge of the window sash. The other end of the cord goes over a pulley and disappears into the window frame where it is knotted to a heavy weight. The trick is to get at the weights. Pry off the moulding that runs vertically on either side of the window. Use a flat-bladed chisel and brace it against the wood-work with a towel, to protect the paint. Once the moulding is off, you will see a rectangular "pocket" of wood held into place in the window frame by two screws. Undo the screws, remove the block of wood, and you will unveil the weight. There are, of course, four "pockets" and four weights per window, one on either side at the top to sup-port the upper window sash, and two below to support the lower sash. To get at the top weights, you will also have to pry off the vertical strip of wood that separates upper and lower sashes. Once you know how, this is *almost* fun to do, but it helps to watch someone else do it the first time.

Persistently rattling window frames should be replaced by a carpenter.

PLUMBING: No home can be warm or comfortable if pipes are frozen or burst. Wrap insulation around internal pipes, especially those in an uninsulated attic.

Cracks and Gaps

REALLY LARGE CRACKS IN A WALL (more like splits, that open again when you fill them) are usually a sign of foundation problems. Consult a qualified builder, or the local building inspector.

SMALL CRACKS IN WALLS OR CEILINGS can be patched up with spackling compound, which mixes like a cake mix without the added egg. Be sure to brush out all loose and flaking material before starting to fill the crack, otherwise your patch might wobble loose. Wetting the edges of a crack slightly will help the spackle adhere. Mix up the spackling compound in an old can or bowl and apply with fingers or putty knife, smoothing flat with the latter.

CRACKS IN WOOD can be filled with special wood fillers or wood putties which you squeeze into the crack, let dry and sandpaper smooth.

CRACKS IN BRICKWORK OR CEMENT can be sealed with a ready-mix mortar which you buy at the hardware store. All you do is add water, like a cake mix.

GAPS WHERE THE WOOD IS MISSING (gnawed by gnomes or rats or cats): It's a carpenter's job because the damaged wood will probably have to be cut away and a new piece glued and nailed into place and repainted.

GAPS BETWEEN FLOORBOARDS AND BASEBOARDS (where the draft whistles through): Bridge that gap with a length of quarter-round moulding which, seen end-on, looks like a quarter of a broom handle. Use small finishing nails or brads to keep it in place because they're fine and won't split the wood.

GAPS BETWEEN WALL AND CEILING: Structurally it's rarely serious, but it looks a bit impoverished. Filling the actual gaps is usually a waste of time because they may reappear (they are often due to seasonal expansion and contraction of the walls). Put up wooden or polystyrene moulding along the top of the wall and paint it to match the rest of the woodwork. Nail the moulding to the wall or the ceiling—but not both or it will get pulled away at the next expansion or contraction.

DOOR AND WINDOW GAPS (which can often be the cause of drafts and rattling): Weatherstrip (see chapter on heating and cooling).

BATHROOM GAPS BETWEEN WALL AND TUB OR BASIN: Can be sealed with bathtub caulking, a putty-like substance you squeeze out of a tube and smooth out with thumb or a wooden popsicle stick. (A marvellous miracle material for which you will devise many uses.)

Remember: Drafts are responsible for most heat loss in the average home. Try making a "gap check" in yours with a wet finger on a windy day.

Squeak and Rattle Check

Oil anything which squeaks, from chair castors to curtain runners. Alternatively, rub vaseline on it.

CASTORS: If a castor isn't moving smoothly check that dust or cotton thread hasn't become wrapped around the wheel or axle. If it has (and you can get at it) cut it away with a sharp knife. Oil the castor while working it around, then wipe surplus oil away.

If chair castors are loose, tighten the screws. If one of the screws turns maddeningly around insert used matchsticks to jam it. Alternatively, remove screw, insert plastic wood into the hole, and wait overnight while it hardens, then re-insert the screw. If the shank of the castor is loose, remove castor from socket, wrap shank with masking tape or electrical tape and then try to reinsert it into the socket, where it should grip better. Then buy a new castor because it won't last more than a fortnight.

DOORKNOBS: If a doorknob is loose and rattles, there's a good chance that all you have to do is tighten the tiny screw behind the handle. It's called a set screw and is also the screw you have to undo to remove an antique brass doorknob in order to give it a real polish for the first time in a hundred years.

Before unscrewing it is vitally important to open the door wide and wedge it (with a wad of newspaper). Otherwise, what invariably happens is that you drop the screw, the door swings shut, and you find yourself grovelling for a set screw in a locked room which no one can open.

If you tighten the set screw and the doorknob still rattles uselessly, unscrew the screw again, remove the knob, pull the spindle that goes through the hole in the door out by drawing out the knob on the other side of the door, and replace the spindle (and knobs, if you want) with a new one from the hardware store.

HINGES: If door hinges squeak or seem to stick, put a little

oil on the hinge pins and move the door back and forth
to work the oil into the hinge. If it still squeaks, remove
the hinge pins, clean them (steel wool) and oil again.
Remove the lower pins first: hold a screwdriver against
the knob of the pin and tap on the screwdriver with a
hammer. Do one hinge at a time so you don't have to
wrestle the door back into place.

FLOORBOARDS: Squeaking floorboards should be nailed
down. Drive the nails in at an angle, and use a nailset to
bury their heads, filling the holes with plastic wood filler.
If this doesn't work, call a carpenter as the floor may need
to be reinforced from below.

WHEN YOU NEED TO CALL IN THE EXPERTS

DEAL ONLY WITH REPUTABLE FIRMS AND CRAFTSMEN: It is a
good rule to find out those who are best known and well
thought of in your neighborhood. This seems obvious,
but the lure of a bargain will lead one to forget now and
again. Do not, for example, get taken in by someone driving up to the door and offering to blacktop your driveway
for substantially less than a local firm might do it. By the
time the driveway has started to crack and disintegrate,
the people who did the work will have moved on to the
next state.

FIND OUT WHAT KIND OF GUARANTEE OR WARRANTY THE AP-
PLIANCE CARRIES: Check this out *before* you buy, and also
make sure you are not going to have trouble getting a
repairman to come over when the machine needs servicing.
Again, you may be better off buying from a smaller local
firm than from one of the big chain discount houses,
unless you can be sure (guarantee in writing) of getting
proper servicing.

TRY TO KNOW AS MUCH AS POSSIBLE ABOUT YOUR "PROBLEM":
When you do call in the plumber, electrician, furnace
repairman, or appliance serviceman say as little as possible. Just state the facts. Don't *you* say what you think
it is. This may cloud the issue and the diagnosis is *his*
problem and *his* responsibility.

I keep a repair list, jotting down the date and reason for the furnace's frontal lobotomy, as well as a quick, *intelligible to me*, explanation of what was done and what it cost. This is useful after one machine had apparently given up the ghost 3 times for the same, supposedly repaired, cause: When I looked up the bills they might have been written in Chinese for all they meant to me.

PESTS

Ants (insect)	Mosquitoes (insect)
Bedbugs (insect)	Moths (insect)
Carpet Beetles (insect)	Powder-Post Beetles
Centipedes (arthropod)	(woodworm) (insect)
Cockroaches (insect)	Rats (rodent)
Firebrats (insect)	Silverfish (insect)
Fleas (insect)	Spiders (arachnid)
Flies (insect)	Termites (insect)
Mice (rodent)	Wasps (insect)

Often, as with New York cockroaches, the pest problem infests the cleanest and elitist in the land. There is no shame involved, even in having bedbugs: They travel in cabs, like the rest of us.

I learned the hard way about the horrors of pests in the home when we bought a charming old stone French farmhouse, hung with vines and surrounded with lime trees. Our kitchen equipment was rudimentary (we were camping in): a tin tub for the water, 2 bookshelves for the food and crockery, and a sort of pale blue, jazzed-up bucket that called itself a field toilet. On the first day the ants appeared, followed by the flies, then the spiders and the mosquitoes, then the bats, and finally (on the fifth day) a sweet little field mouse. The mouse multiplied over the weekend and on the seventh day we rested not, because the rats had arrived. Our dream house was like being in the middle of an army training area with everything zeroing in on us. It is difficult to sleep with rats running all over the place; if you throw books and boots at them you quickly run out of books and boots, and they always miss the target.

On the eighth day, aided by the farmer next door, we ruthlessly invested in rubber gloves, assorted pesticides, and tins and heavy-duty garbage pails with lids in which to keep the food. There is *nothing* like a plague of rats to make you pest-conscious forever more. Pests (even the cute little field mouse) carry disease, often bite, and can take over the place incredibly fast if you allow it to happen.

In treating pests, prevention is better than cure. The weapon for fighting is *cleanliness*. Keep the house clean, avoid damp, and keep food away from them.

- *Clean up food spills promptly.*
- *Don't leave food in the open.* Keep it in the refrigerator or in airtight cans, jars, tins, or sealed containers (not plastic—rats and mice gnaw plastic.)
- Don't keep food or grain in the open, at floor level, in the kitchen or the larder. Keep the floor crumbless. Regularly clean out food cabinets.
- *Sweep thoroughly.* Don't leave fluff around for nests.
- Keep garbage in clean sacks and clean out garbage as fast as possible. (Or else keep in galvanized iron garbage pails.)
- Avoid having mounds of rotting animal and/or vegetable matter in home or garden.
- If you find you have a pest, empty and clean all shelves; throw away tainted food, such as rice, flour, or noodles; spray shelves with insecticide and leave for half a day before replacing contents.
- *Seal up the pest entrances* with a caulking compound. Pests like to breed in dark, quiet places, particularly in or behind wall cracks, baseboard cracks, electrical outlets, and cracks where water and radiator pipes go through the wall.
- *Use a pesticide if you already have pests.* There is no single "kill 'em off," so choose the right pesticide for your problem.
- There are many kinds of pests and pesticides. But you don't need 2 dozen. You probably need about 4 basics—flying, nonflying, mites, and rodents. You need "insecticides" to control insects, "miticides" to kill mites, and "rodenticides" to control rats and mice.
- Whatever the brand name, an *insecticide* should

contain lindane, malathion, or diazinon. Whatever the brand name, a *miticide* should contain malathion or lindane. *Rodenticides* have many different ingredients. Check with your local building inspector which to use. These should be handled with *great care* because some are lethal to pets and people.

• *There are 2 kinds of spray.* One is sprayed in the air (space sprays), for mosquitoes, houseflies, and gnats. The other is for surfaces, applied directly to areas where insects are likely to crawl. Either kind is available in a pressurized container. (Get U.S. Department of Agriculture Home and Garden Bulletin 96, "Controlling Household Pests," for further information. Send 50 cents to Superintendent of Documents, U.S. Government Printing Office, Washington, D.C. 20402.)

Remember That Pesticides Are Dangerous Products

Read the directions carefully each time you use them, wear rubber gloves when you go into action, and wash them immediately afterwards. If you get any pesticide on your skin, eyes, or mouth, wash quickly and thoroughly. Immediately wash any contaminated garment with soap and water. Wash hands and face thoroughly TWICE after using pesticide. Don't store pesticide near food or where children or animals can reach it. Make sure that any pesticide is labeled "nontoxic to humans and pets."

When you're using a spray insecticide don't spray it on food, drink, animals, or children. Don't breathe it in yourself. Don't spray near an open fire or throw a used can into a fire, unless you think that an explosion might enliven your afternoon.

Incidentally, as a result of the controversy over possible damage to the ozone layer from aerosol cans, many manufacturers have switched to a pump-type can that not only eliminates freon, the noxious chemical involved, but also gives you more insecticide, since most of the space in the conventional aerosol can is occupied by the gas (which also mixes with the product and can cause skin irritation). Inspect the can to see whether you're buying aerosol or a pump type, and always try to buy the pump type.

Pesticides will be in a clearly labeled container. *Don't*

transfer it to another container. *Don't* reuse the empty container. Keep it locked if possible (not necessarily in the kitchen), wherever you have a lockable drawer or compartment. Keep it in a wall safe, if you like, but not in that gloomy little hell hole under the sink, or at the bottom of a food cupboard, or near cooking utensils.

Keep children out of the way while you are using rat or mice poison, and also get any pets out of the way. (If it kills rats, it might kill cats, dogs, and birds.)

Eliminating Specific Pests

ANTS: Be especially careful in the summer months, when they are likely to invade a ground floor kitchen from the garden. Find their nest (watch where they carry the cookie crumbs). If you can't get to the nest to clean it out, spray it with a household insecticide. Spray the ant exit, then seal the opening, and spray the route from the ant exit to the food source.

Where you have a real ant problem, to prevent ants getting at food, stand the table legs in little tins of water at meal time and put the fruit in a bowl sitting in a bowl containing some water. Ants can't swim.

ANT

BEDBUG

BEDBUGS: If you wake up itching in the morning you may have unwelcome strangers in the bed. Bedbugs can enter your home via secondhand books and furniture, as well as beds. They are 1/4 to 3/8 in. long, roundish, brownish, and flattish. Their irritating bites leave large red patches and possible swelling. They suck human blood at night and lay eggs in cracks in the woodwork and behind wallpaper.

You will need to damp spray the mattress thoroughly with insecticide (top, bottom, *and* sides). Also spray the frame, springs, and slats of the bed.

Spray surrounding floor, baseboard of room, and any cracks in walls or floor (then seal them). Repeat this performance, two days running. (Don't sleep on the mattress until it's dry.) If none of this works, call an expert, who will fumigate the room by blocking all windows, ventilations, cracks, and keyholes. The room is then left sealed for some time before being aired and cleaned.

CENTIPEDES: Spray. Lever the corpses onto a bit of paper and remove to trash can.

CENTIPEDES

COCKROACH

SILVERFISH

FIREBRAT

COCKROACHES, SILVERFISH, FIREBRATS, AND OTHER FLYING OR CRAWLING INSECTS: Cockroaches are tough creatures. They have been on earth millions of years longer than man, and you're unlikely to master them without the help of science. They happen to prefer human habitations to any other kind and feed on garbage as well as food.

Cockroaches love moist, warm, dark places. Silverfish love cool, damp places. So watch water pipes underneath the kitchen sink and draining board. They can eat books, envelopes, wallpaper, and just about anything with great glee. Spray walls, floor, ceiling, and woodwork with insectide, liberally applied where you suspect their "run" is. If necessary holler for the public health inspector to trace the source of the trouble.

FLEAS: They are transmitted by any furry animal, not just cats and dogs. Each type of flea likes a different sort of host—horses, cats, rats, dogs, hamsters, or humans. Ani-

mal fleas will bite humans; some seem to attract them far
more than others. Their bites leave itching red spots on
the skin, which you should not scratch. They like darkness
and warmth, tend to lay eggs in floor cracks, and appear
in the warm, wet weather common to early summer and
early autumn.

If your pet has fleas, thoroughly vacuum floor, carpets,
rugs. If they are infesting something obvious and not very
valuable, such as the cat's bed, burn it. Otherwise, with
soap and warm water, thoroughly wash your pet's sleeping area. Wash any blanket or cushion. Spray the floor
and all surrounding baseboards and cracks in walls and
floor as well as any other places where a lot of dust collects. Spray anything that is infected, such as your bed.
If, 2 days later, you still have fleas, repeat the process. If,
in 4 days, you still have fleas, either fumigate the house,
room by room, or call the public health department for
advice.

FLIES AND WASPS: If this is a perennial problem, you should,
of course, fix outward-opening screens on all windows
and doors. You'll need 16-mesh-per-inch screens because
you might as well keep out everything equally irritating,
not just the flies.

Flies are the filthiest of all insects and possibly the most
persistent. Grab that can of Black Flag or else use flypaper
strip, which is peculiarly satisfying and cheap. Hang it
from the ceiling. You will subsequently find large numbers
of flies and any other flying insects stuck to the paper—
dead. If you run across a persistent flypaper-resistant
strain, ask the public health department for advice.

Flies love decaying food. Check that your garbage
receptacles have tight-fitting lids; spray the interiors. Use
the spray insecticide to squirt around generally, morning
and evening (making sure no food or cooking utensils are
in the open). Check that there is no pet excrement in the
house, and that the compost heap (a fly's equivalent of
Coney Island) is not too near the house.

FLEA

FLY

WASP

FURNITURE BEETLE (WOODWORM): Lays its eggs (which take 3 years to hatch) in cracks or crevices of *unpolished wood,* such as the undersides of chairs, backs of chests of drawers, flooring, and wooden panels. The baby beetle bites its way through to the open air leaving a 1/6-inch exit hole. Wood dust beneath a piece of furniture is a sure sign of "woodworm." Don't allow into the house any secondhand or antique furniture that has groups of tiny holes in it, unless you are sure that it has been professionally treated: You risk infecting your other furniture very quickly, as well as the woodwork of the house.

You can treat furniture with a woodworm insecticide from the hardware store. The best time is spring, because then you can get the babies (fiendish chuckle) but DON'T WAIT for spring to come around. Brush the insecticide well into the peppery-holed surface. (Treatment may discolor light woods.)

To eradicate woodworm, the specialists will heave up floorboards, inject every tiny hole in the house with a hypodermic syringe, and generally do a thorough job. Don't try to tackle it yourself, the risk is too great. Get a guarantee for at least 5 years.

POWDER-
POST BEETLE
    ADULT CLOTHES MOTH
    BLACK CARPET
BEETLE LARVA

MOTHS: It's the grubs, which like dark, warm places, that do the damage. Their favorite food is wool, fur, skin, and feathers. They attack clothes, carpets, rugs, drapes, upholstery, and mattresses leaving tiny but visible holes. They particularly fancy the area around the zippers of men's trousers. They do not eat cotton, linen, or synthetic fibers.

To prevent moths, never store dirty clothes: Dry clean first. During summer months, keep furs in commercial storage, with a furrier or at a big store that has a fur department that will not only store and renovate your furs but also ensure them against damage. All stored articles should be cleaned, frequently inspected, and protected by a moth deterrent such as naphthalene flakes or balls (mothballs to you), or a lindane or malathion spray.

What Kills Moths. Hang the naphthalene mothballs, or crystals, as high as you can in your closets, so that the vapor descends from above; it cannot rise, it's heavier than air. Useless to hang it low, therefore. Keep the closet clean and, if possible, airtight. Of course, cedarwood linings are best.

You can also mothproof your clothes, as well as your carpets, rugs, and drapes, by spraying them (follow directions on label). Your carpeting and drapes should be treated by a professional.

Where grubs have attacked an item, such as a stuffed bird, you should burn or otherwise dispose of it. If possible send other items to the dry cleaner. Otherwise, if you have moths in your clothes, empty your closets and hang clothes on a line to air in the open. Spray clothes closets and chests with insecticide, also baseboards, walls, floor cracks, shelves, and clothes rods of closet.

MICE: In spite of precautions you may be afflicted by mice. They shred and chew things such as newspaper and clothes, gnaw wire, and leave droppings that are like tiny brown seeds. Cheese in a trap only works for one mouse at a time, and they seem to breed as fast as the trap snaps.

And, if you trap them, you then have to deal with the bodies, which can be unnerving. I was once telephoned by a girl friend who lives alone; she was in tears because she had caught her first mouse in a trap and didn't know what to do next. She had run the bath and thrown it in, but the trap was wooden and it floated, and the poor mouse was squeaking piteously. She had let the water out, tried to put the mouse out of its misery with a hammer, but missed (because she shut her eyes) and cracked the porcelain bath. Well, what would *you* do? I'm afraid that what she finally did, in desperation, was to throw it out of the window, from the fifteenth floor. For her, the story ends there; for a passerby that's where it may have started. Anyway, what she *should* have used to kill mice and rats is a slow-acting dehydrating rat poison, so that they creep off and die wherever they live, rather than under your nose; then they're *supposed* to crumble quickly to dust, so you don't have to deal with the appalling problem of "dead rat odor." However, I have never found it as easy as that.

HOUSE MOUSE

If you really can't cope and are prepared for someone else to do your killing for you, hire your own hit man. Look in the Yellow Pages under "commercial exterminator" or "pest control operator."

MOSQUITOES: Their nasty buzzing can herald a sleepless night for all the wrong reasons. They breed near still, stagnant water, such as slimy ponds, water barrels, birdbaths, empty ornamental urns, or any upended pails kept in the garden. Any little saucerful of stagnant water is, to them, as inviting as a satin-sheeted king-size bed. They also breed in damp leaves, so watch the gutters.

Kill them with a spray insecticide for flying insects (which also includes moths) and use direct action. Aim and fire! At night, don't leave the windows open and the lights on (which also attracts moths).

MOSQUITO

RAT

RATS: The best way to keep rats out of the house is to seal all holes in exterior walls. Cats deal with mice but seldom with rats. Any sensible cat is scared by a rat. The first time I saw one in an empty house, I jumped on a chair, held my skirt around my legs, and gave a quavery little scream. You don't need me to tell you what a rat looks like—your instincts will inform you.

Rats carry very nasty diseases, so if you see a rat call the public health department and ask their advice. Because they're nasty beasts (the rats), try to avoid dealing with them yourself. If you have no alternative, ask the public health department which poison to use to pattern trap (like pattern bombing) the regular rat run. Ugh!

BLACK WIDOW SPIDER

TERMITE

SPIDERS: Most varieties are harmless, but 2—the black widow and the brown recluse—can inflict painful, and perhaps deadly, bites. Knock down webs and spiders with a stick or broom and crush them with your shoes. Spray with insecticide containing lindane. *Never* spray from directly underneath it, so that a spider can fall on you and bite you.

TERMITES: They crawl or they fly. Don't fool around. Call the pest control operator for heavy fumigation, hole digging around the house, and ripping off and burning any damaged and destroyed wood. These greedy creatures can cost thousands of dollars' damage to your home by lunching on all the wood, from furniture to structural beams.

TICKS: Take your animal to the vet to be doused in a tick-killing malathion solution. Or do it yourself, dunking him in it if your pet is small enough, pouring it over him if he isn't. Swab his ears with a sponge. If ticks are breeding in the house, treat with household insecticide.

You can make *your own flea shampoo* by mixing 5 cups of kerosene with ½ cup of oleic acid, and then adding ¼ cup of triethanolamine. Use it on your pet, preferably in the bathtub, just as you would use shampoo on your hair. Then give him a flea collar.

Other Household Nuisances

COMBATING MILDEW, MOLD, AND MUSTINESS: As *they flourish in damp, poorly ventilated, ill-lit areas,* clean, dry, air, and light those areas.

Never dry a damp room or closet with an electric heater. Ventilate with fresh air as thoroughly as possible by opening all doors and windows and perhaps simultaneously using an electric fan (but not a heater). Put a vent in the door or use louvered doors; install a low voltage ceiling light, high where nothing (such as clothes) can touch it and make a fire hazard. Use a chemical dehumidifier.

To discourage mildew, mold, and mustiness never store clothes when damp, *never* put damp or wet clothes in the clothes hamper (first hang them up to dry). Keep drawers and closet walls, floors, ceilings, and shelves clean. If you wash them, dry quickly and thoroughly. Spray with a fungicidal spray. Rugs, draperies, upholstery, or mattresses that smell musty or show signs of mildew should be vacuumed with a disposable bag vacuum cleaner, so that the bag can be thrown away (if you haven't one, borrow or hire one). Otherwise you risk leaving mildew spores in your cleaner.

To get rid of a musty smell on textiles, wipe them down with a Handi Wipe that has been dipped in equal parts of alcohol and water and then wrung out. Dry with clean cloth. When dry, treat with fabric fungicide. If you have a severe mildew problem get a copy of the U.S. Department of Agriculture Home and Garden Bulletin 68, "How to Prevent and Remove Mildew." Send 50 cents to Superintendent of Documents, U.S. Government Printing Office, Washington, D.C. 20402.

DRY ROT: It is *not* dry. A sinister, science-fictionish fungus, dry rot grows and feeds on wood and finally reduces it to a crumbling state that sounds "dead" when hit with a hammer; it has a nasty moldy smell. It starts in damp, unventilated places such as under floorboards and behind wood paneling. It spreads by thin rootlike strands that creep over nonnourishing brickwork to reach more appetizing wood. It produces flat growths rather like a cross between a pancake and a mushroom. If you suspect that you have dry rot, immediately call a building inspector. You need someone who's professionally qualified to discover the causes and then to deal with this very costly drama.

THE CAUSES OF DRY ROT

- A damp course rendered ineffective because someone has piled up coal, earth, sand, gravel, or something against an outside wall. (So don't do any of this.)

- A broken dampproof course. (As homeowners know, a dampproof course is a strip of nonporous material, such as lead, slate, or heavy-duty plastic, inserted into brick walls from 6 in. to 25 in. above ground level in order to stop moisture from rising up the wall.
- No dampproof course in your home.
- Not drying out wet boards before laying a floor covering such as cork or linoleum.
- Faulty plumbing that keeps floorboards damp, particularly hot water pipe joints behind a bath panel.
- Faulty, leaking drain pipes; possibly combined with worn mortar at the joints. (The wall should be repointed.) This was my Achilles' heel.

Once the cause has been analyzed, all rotten wood for up to 3 ft. beyond the infected area must be cut away and immediately burned. All nearby brickwork must be sterilized with a blowtorch, then, when cool, treated with a preservative. The wood can then be repaired with new wood, which should also be treated with a preservative.

WET ROT: Not as serious as dry rot, because it is easier to arrest. It is a timber fungus that grows in a *really* damp, wet place where you get leaking water, such as a cellar, shed, or medieval bathroom. The fungus, which rarely shows itself on the surface, makes the damp wood darken.

Treatment consists of checking the source of moisture and thoroughly drying the wood, which might have to be treated with preservative. Badly decayed wood should be cut out and replaced.

EXPERT TREATMENT: If your house has woodworm, or wet or dry rot, get expert treatment from a specialist. It's extremely expensive, but not as expensive as having the old homestead crumble around you.

On no account go only to one firm. Get several estimates, but don't necessarily accept the cheapest. Take the advice of the building inspector (I have found one firm to be as much as *10 times* more expensive than another). If the job promises to be expensive, you may find it economical to employ a surveyor to advise you and possibly supervise the work. I did.

ANIMAL CRACKERS: THE CARE AND CHOOSING OF PETS

Dogs, cats and some birds can be comforting, loyal and entertaining companions, especially to the young, the old, and the lonely. But think six times before you buy a pet. Think of:

- 1. The cost of food and vet bills.
- 2. The necessity for limiting reproduction by spaying or neutering them (which can cost more than a vasectomy).
- 3. The amount of time you'll have to spend on caring for and perhaps exercising your animals.
- 4. What will happen if you go away?
- 5. Space. It's cruel to keep any but the smallest dog untended all day in a city apartment—even if you have someone to walk it.
- 6. Are you prepared to have carpets, drapes, upholstery and furniture scratched, clawed and possibly ruined? I once had to start patching a wall-to-wall carpet four weeks after it had been laid, and before it had been paid for, thanks to an adorable kitten of similar age. Another time I had a sweet, lovable Weimeraner who felt trapped and caged and constricted inside a brownstone townhouse.

IF YOU WANT A DOG, BE PATIENT. Adopting a dog is, in many ways, like adopting a child. First visit an animal shelter in your area. The Humane Societies and other non-profit organizations are loaded to the point of despair with abandoned or unwanted dogs. Don't necessarily pick a dog you may recognize to be a pure-bred and therefore valuable (maybe its previous owner couldn't stand its nasty temper).

Suburban newspapers, office and campus bulletin boards, and friends and neighbors can often tell you of unwanted puppies or cats up for adoption. If you decide to *buy* a dog, in most cases it means that you want a pedigree puppy. Any community has reputable pet shops, as well as disreputable pet shops whose pitiful offerings have been bred like broiler chickens in some loathsome puppy factory. Check the pet shop with the Better Business Bureau.

Even better, ask anyone who owns the sort of dog you want where he or she bought it. Some of the nicest dogs I know came from registered local breeders who not only care about their dogs but are apt to be quite choosy about the people they sell them to.

If you buy or adopt a puppy, it should be no less than six weeks old or more than twelve weeks. Don't buy a puppy that doesn't *look* in good condition, fit and bouncy. Don't accept any explanations for a listless puppy. Don't pick the runt of the litter because it's so tiny and sweet and pathetic. You may be heading for vet's bills, and heartbreak.

A pedigree pup should have had rabies and distemper shots before it's sold and the breeder should provide proof of this, as well as its papers. Get a mongrel vaccinated. Consult the vet about worming. And get the pup licensed, or you may have to pay a fine. In some areas you may have to show proof that it has been vaccinated against rabies to get your licence.

Some communities charge lower fees if a female has been spayed.

Treat your puppy as kindly and gently as you would a baby. Keep him in a blanket-lined box with a ball and a few toys until he's three months old, when he can be promoted to a real live dog basket.

Only really big, hardy dogs should be kept out of doors in a kennel.

Housetrain your puppy by saying "NO" in a stern, authoritarian voice, when he seems ready to make a mess, and immediately take him outside. Exercise him straight away after meals, which is when he's most likely to mess.

Dogs need a regular, balanced diet, not just meat. Feed a puppy four times a day until he's six months old, twice a day until he's nine months old, then once a day in morning or evening. Keep to regular times. See that he always has fresh water. Bones are good for his teeth, but a plastic milk bottle will give him endless pleasure. Avoid chicken, rabbit or fish bones, which can splinter. Give your puppy chow or finely chopped meat mixed with puppy meal twice a day, and perhaps a lightly boiled egg twice a week. A dry dog cereal such as Purina chow gives it a totally balanced diet, though most canines—and cats—like to have a meaty or fishy canned food like Ken-L-Ration as variety. Remember: *cereal chow is cheap, meat treats are expensive.*

CATS: If you've set your heart on a cat, acquiring a kitten seems to be no problem. You just tell everyone you meet tomorrow that you want a kitten and strange kitten owners everywhere will be rushing around in no time. Or you can telephone the animal shelter, buy one from a pet store, or get a pedigree cat from a breeder. Again, don't get one less than seven weeks old.

Get your kitten checked by the vet and injected as necessary. Spaying or neutering is done four to five months after birth.

Don't pick up a kitten (or puppy) by the scruff of its neck or by its paws. Put one hand under its chest and nestle its hindquarters in your other hand.

Housetrain your kitten by putting near his basket a plastic cat tray or ordinary tin tray covered with newspaper, litter or earth. Clean the tray daily, Ugh! Swab it out with hot water and a little disinfectant. You can get a cat panel fixed to an outside door, if you have a yard or garden, or you can have a tiny glass pane that flaps up and down fitted to a suitable window.

Feed a kitten four times a day until it's four months old, three times a day until it's six months old, twice a day until it's nine months old and then once a day. Start it off on baby cereal mixed with milk and a little chopped liver, fish or good cat food. By the time it's two months old it'll be ready for dry cat chow. No cat *needs* expensive canned food. It does need a constant bowl of clean water.

SIMPLE FIRST AID FOR ANIMALS: A dog or cat that has been run over or seriously injured in any way can be dangerous. The most affectionate pet may not realize that you are trying to help it, and may turn on you. Approach an injured animal very gingerly. Muzzle a dog with a belt or a man's necktie or even a scarf.

If the pet is bleeding heavily, apply pressure on a sterile gauze pad or a clean handkerchief and tie it down with another handkerchief or strip of cloth. Wrap the pet in an old coat or blanket to keep it warm and prevent it from thrashing around while you rush it to the vet. (Gone, alas, are the days when vets paid house calls, even in emergencies.)

Dogs and cats often suffer *eye injuries*. Keep the eye moist by dropping cooking oil into the eye and, if it looks serious, take it to the vet.

Pets can eat *poison* by accident or someone's nasty intent. If it has the shakes, vomits a great deal or gets highly excited, wrap it in a blanket, scoop up (Ugh!) a sample of the vomit (which will indicate what foul substance it has swallowed) and rush pet and sample on a saucer to the vet.

If the dog or cat comes in stinking of *carrion* or *skunk*, wash it immediately with tomato juice, give it a regular shampoo and then rinse with a gallon (4 liters) of water with a teaspoonful of ammonia in it.

Dogs can be plagued with *ticks* and *burrs*, particularly if you live in the country or suburbs, though ticks can breed in an apartment. Rub your hands periodically over the dog's body to see if it has ticks. The lumps are easily detected, often under its legpits or ears. Remove these infectious nauseating bloodsuckers by dabbing them with kerosene and then twisting them off with tweezers—counterclockwise—so making sure that you don't leave the tick's head behind.

Disinfect the bite area with alcohol, burn the ticks and *wash your hands* (also see "Pests," p. 000). Newly acquired *burrs* can also be removed with tweezers, but if the burrs are embedded in the fur the best thing to do is to very delicately cut them out with nail scissors.

When a pet *limps* badly or seems unduly bothered by a leg (it may persist in licking a paw), it has probably been impaled by a thorn or splinter. Moving very gently, minutely examine the paw. If the thorn or splinter is still sticking in there, remove it carefully with sterilized tweezers. Then dab the pad with hydrogen peroxide. If the pad has been cut, dab with hydrogen peroxide, to prevent infection.

With any other ailment, consult the vet at the very first signs of illness.

The dog that constantly roams far from home disturbing other people's lives and garbage pails, is not exactly a first-aid problem, but may quickly become one unless you curb it. If it won't stay home, and you have a yard or garden, the only solution is to run a 100-ft (30-m) wire between trees or poles and attach a running chain to it, to which you firmly attach your dog's collar. However, if you give him good long walks, he may feel less inclined to be the neighborhood scourge.

Actually, most pets, if well exercised, properly fed and sensibly treated, seem less likely to get sick than the average human. Come to think of it, they have pretty soft lives.

HOW TO KEEP A HAPPY CAR

Most women feel that a car should appreciate in value and give as little trouble as emeralds; but a car depreciates, like a fur coat, so you must treat it with tender loving care. All you need to know is how and why.

"You can always find a woman who doesn't know how to care for a car," I was told by an officer of an automobile club, "but for every woman you will also find a man." Sweet of him. The main reason for joining an automobile club is for its emergency road service. If you do a lot of driving away from home, particularly if you are apt to be driving at night and have an older car, it is comforting to know that in the event of a breakdown you can call your automobile club, or one of the affiliated service stations listed in your handbook, and have the assurance that help will arrive. The services and benefits provided by clubs vary greatly, however, and you would do well to make sure your anticipated needs will be covered before taking out membership in such an organization. (Some clubs will only reimburse you for services provided by an affiliated garage, for example.)

If you do a lot of driving alone, it might also be a good idea to get a CB radio in case of trouble or breakdown.

Following a Maintenance Routine

Regularly check, or have a gas station attendant check, the battery fluid, the oil level, and the tire pressure of your car. It is vital to do this before a long trip as any breakdown in alien territory can be particularly exasperating and costly.

BATTERY: Once a month, more often in hot weather, unscrew the filler caps and check the level of the fluid in each of the battery cells. It should completely cover the lead plates inside the battery. If it does not, add clean tap water or distilled water. Do not overfill. Battery fluid is a mixture of water and acid. If it seeps out at the top, it can corrode the battery and its terminals.

Make sure that the terminals—the knobs where the thick wires join the battery—are free from dirt and corrosion. Clean them with an old toothbrush and a weak solution of water and baking soda, and grease lightly with petroleum jelly.

SPARK PLUGS: Check that the spark plug cables leading from the distributor are in good condition (insulation uncracked) and securely attached. Otherwise your engine won't work properly. Replace spark plugs at least every 10,000 miles. Spark plugs in good condition keep the engine running smoothly. Aging spark plugs can result in a considerable, and progressive, inefficiency in the performance of your engine.

RADIATOR: Check the level of the water and antifreeze mixture in your radiator every month or two (not necessary with sealed radiator). Do this when the engine is cold, and you won't run the risk of burning your hand on a hot radiator cap or, worse, having scalding, pressurized fluid spurt up in your face. If the fluid is low (check your owner's manual to see what the level should be), refill the radiator with a half-and-half mixture of water and antifreeze. (You can use plain water in a pinch, but it is better to maintain the proper mix of antifreeze to keep the engine cool in summer and unfrozen in winter.)

OIL: Check the level of the engine oil every time you go in for gas. Pull out the dipstick, *wipe it clean*, then reinsert it all the way, pull it out again, and check the oil level. Add oil only if the level is at or below the "add" marking.

REPLACEMENTS: Just as some things, like men, shoes, or scrubbing brushes, need renewing from time to time, a car needs occasional replacements. Replace *tires* whenever you can see bands of smoothly worn rubber across two or more adjacent grooves on your tires. This means that the tread has worn down to 1/16 in. across these bands, and that's not much rubber between you and the road!

Treat yourself to a new pair of *windshield wiper blades* before each winter. Not only do you risk developing crow's feet as you peer ahead, but it is dangerous to drive with a dirty windshield.

CLEANING: You're supposed to keep your car exterior in good condition by cleaning it or getting it cleaned once a week. One way is to drive through a car wash. The bliss of yielding the car up to be soaped, washed, and brushed by those trembly machines is equaled only by the luxury of having a maid to iron your scanties.

If doing it yourself, first spray all over with a strong jet from the garden hose, to wash away the worst grime trapped around chrome and hubcaps. Working from the roof down, wash one section at a time with a solution of mild liquid soap and water using a soft cloth or sponge. Rinse each section with the hose before going on to the next. Clean windows with a household window cleaner. Dry the car with a chamois or a soft cloth.

When the car is really clean and dry, you can make it even cleaner and shinier by applying a liquid polish. Pour some on a clean cloth and cover one section of the car at a time with the polish. Let it dry completely, then rub off with another clean, dry, soft cloth.

To protect the finish of the car you can put on a coating of wax. Usually 3 to 4 times a year. When raindrops roll off your car as though it were a duck's back, the wax is still good. When they flatten out and just lie there, it is time for another waxing. Rub the wax on with the usual clean soft cloth (dry, if you're using a liquid wax, damp if you're using a paste wax—*read the instructions*). Let the wax dry and polish up the car with a chamois or yet another clean cloth.

You can get special cleaners for the chrome on the car, but once chrome is deeply rusted, nothing simple can be done to eliminate it. You have to have it rechromed or buy a new part.

CORROSION: You are unlikely to get salt under your car in summer unless you race it along the beach, as in a cigarette ad. You are far more likely to get plastered with municipal salt sprinkled on winter roads, so get a garage to hose underneath the car in winter if you have been doing a lot of driving. If you think this is unnecessary, try soaking an ordinary pair of steel scissors in salt water for a couple of hours, whereupon they will start to rust, whereupon they won't work so well, and thereupon you will see what I mean.

What and What Not to Keep in the Car

ITEMS TO STORE IN THE GLOVE COMPARTMENT: Owner's manual, maps, flashlight, hard candies (chocolate melts), sunglasses (a genuine safety precaution), tissues, pencil and paper, small first-aid kit, your automobile club membership card and handbook, your insurance identification card, and if you want to be *really* boy-scout prepared, an insurance accident form. Heaven knows where you will keep your gloves. The car should also have some kind of litter bag and a snow scraper.

ITEMS BEST KEPT ELSEWHERE: Leave the insurance policy and the certificate of ownership in a safe place at home. Carry your driver's license and the automobile registration in your wallet. Keep a spare car key in your jewelry box and another (in case you lock yourself out 200 miles from home) taped inside a headlight, or some similar hiding place.

TOOL KIT: Check to make sure you are carrying a jack, an adjustable wrench, a screwdriver, a spare tire, an extra fan belt, pliers, a tire-pressure gauge, and flares in case you have a breakdown. Also, an aerosol can of tire inflator in case you have a flat.

If you do have a flat, take the tire inflator can and simply screw the plastic can nozzle to the tire valve stem, and the tire will reseal and reinflate within minutes. Then drive slowly to the nearest service station and have the tire checked.

Dramas

IF YOUR CAR WON'T START: Have you switched the *ignition* on? Is the car in *Neutral* (if it is a manual-shift), or in *Park or Neutral* (if it is automatic-shift)? Do you have *gas*? Does the *battery* need recharging (check by switching on the headlights)? Now you can go for help without feeling like a real idiot.

Before you skip merrily to the next page, pause. . . . Now imagine a lonely road, night is falling, it is raining. Your tire has just blown out. There is no service station or telephone in sight. Somebody will have to do something and *there is only you.* Now read on.

CHANGING A TIRE: Tires always seem to flatten or blow out in calamitous conditions, so practice changing a wheel somewhere near your local garage. How that friendly mechanic will chuckle if he has to hop out and rescue you!

HOW TO CHANGE A FLAT TIRE

- Ease the car off the road. Never change a tire near a drain or the nuts may jump down it. Put out distress signals: flares, a flasher, a handkerchief tied to the door, emergency light on.
- Put the brake on and leave the car in gear (or in Park if it's automatic), so it won't slip and run over your hand Put a block against at least one wheel—a stone or a brick or *something* to stop it moving. (If changing a front tire, block the rear tire diagonally opposite it; block both front tires when changing a rear wheel.)
- Remove the hubcap with the handle (the pointed end) of the jack.
- Loosen nuts with the wrench-end of the jack, but DON'T take them off yet.
  Jack up car (the owner's manual tells you correct position for jack) until the wheel has cleared the ground by a couple of inches.
- Remove nuts and put them inside the hubcap.
- Heave wheel off.
- Put on spare.
- Replace nuts, then tighten.
- Lower car, until wheel just touches ground.
- Tighten nuts again.
- Check you've done them all.
- Remove jack.
- Replace hubcap.
- Remove blocks against wheels.
- Drive off and double check fit plus tire pressure at the nearest garage.
- Have punctured tire repaired as soon as possible.

Alternative Transportation

One way of cutting down on energy and combining transportation with exercise (when transportation for only one is needed) is to imitate the French women: Young and old they all zip around on MoPeds or motorized bicycles, which can be mastered in 5 minutes and cost very little to run.

A MoPed is a bicycle with a motor; if it doesn't have pedals, it's not a MoPed. One by one, state motor vehicle bureaus are allowing the MoPed, as a motor-assisted bicycle, on the public roads, unfettered by some of the regulations that affect motorcycles.

You can pedal a MoPed for exercise like an ordinary bicycle, then, when your thighs are thin enough or you come to a hill, you can just flip a switch to engage the motor and nip in and out of traffic effortlessly at 30 mph and 200 miles to the gallon.

I found that having a MoPed amazingly simplified my life—you can always find a parking spot, and traffic jams and rush hours no longer have the power to irritate you. I felt quite wicked once when I whizzed through a traffic snarl-up jammed with Lincoln Continentals. Charming men talk to you at the lights, kids wave hello, and suddenly life seems less harassing. I found the bike easy to ride when pedaled and light to push, although it weighs a sturdy 62 lb.

At present, over a dozen makes are available in the United States, all imported, including Puch (one of the best), Peugeot, Vespa, and Velosolex. All machines have automatic transmission and an engine size of about 49 cc. Because regulations differ according to state, there are 20, 25, and 30 mph versions of most MoPeds. In some states you can operate this machine without carrying excessive insurance or paying registration or license fees. Recently though, other states have enacted stricter legislation. To get current information on MoPed operation in your area contact the Motorized Bicycle Association, 1001 Connecticut Avenue N.W., Washington, D.C. 20036.

Expect everything to go wrong, then you won't feel quite so bad when it does. As part of your moving budget, plan some selfish treat for yourself after the first week in your new home. Think of this promised indulgence when things get bad. Be prepared for friends who delight in breaking bad news. Remember that tears will get you nowhere.

WHO TO USE AND HOW TO USE THEM

Choosing a Suitable Mover

For reasons beyond my control (briefly, money) I once moved 5 times in 18 months. The first time I hired a boy and a truck, and the agony took 3 days and the breakages were appalling. My slipped disc alone cost a small fortune to repair. The second, third, and fourth times, I hired a specialized moving company. A team of 5 men, used to working together, moved steadily over the house like locusts, leaving a trail of newspaper in their wake. They packed and moved me out in 2 hours and were into the new place and unpacked 2 hours after that; they were charming, and the whole adventure was most enjoyable.

The fifth time I couldn't be present, but I engaged moving men from one of the world's most famous stores. A bunch of surly, gnarled, near-old-age pensioners turned up; they looked too weak to carry a chair upstairs; I was afraid we'd have a group coronary. They took 5 days instead of 5 hours, and the mess took weeks to clear up. The moral of this story is: However well known your movers might be, check and double-check on them and the insurance they carry. Book well in advance, preferably 6 weeks before (I got the gnarled dwarfs because I didn't do this).

The major moving companies (consult your Yellow Pages) provide useful, if not totally candid leaflets covering the difficulties of interstate and other nonstraightforward moves. Large moving companies can be cheaper than small companies on long-distance moves because additional unloading staff can be made available from branch offices at the other end.

If you can't afford specialists, haven't got anything difficult to move, and aren't moving far, the cheapest way is to hire a truck (you can drive a truck up to 4½-ton capacity using an ordinary driver's license). You can rent a truck with a power-operated back platform that raises and lowers itself to take your sofa and lift it up to van height and down to the ground again at journey's end. Hire of truck plus man costs more. Try not to carry anything yourself. You're supposed to be the field marshal, not the infantryman.

The "Best" Time to Move

Not too surprisingly, moving firms have peak demand periods: the period before the day the rent is due, at the end of the month, on end-of-quarter days, and during the spring and summer—especially in the school vacation period. So these are the most hectic and sometimes, if you are moving within your state, most expensive times to move. The cheapest time of the year for an intrastate move is probably on a Monday in mid-February.

If your move takes you across state lines, the moving company is regulated by the Interstate Commerce Commission (ICC). They have fairly tough rules, one of which is that the moving company must give you an ICC booklet covering your rights at least 24 hours before you sign a contract for your move. The ICC also requires that the moving company must give you a "report card" on its own past performance, which includes such items as its track record on pickup and delivery and frequency of loss or damage claims. Thus you can evaluate the different firms. In any case, try to choose one that belongs to the National Furniture and Warehousemen's Association.

Estimates and Contracts

Get quotes from at least 3 firms. You may be surprised how much they vary (up to 50 percent in my experience). It can be, literally, a shattering experience to discover on the day of the move why the price from the firm you accepted is so low, namely, because of their inefficiency.

AN ESTIMATE IS NOT A FIXED PRICE: If you are moving locally, you may get a *cost-per-hour* estimate, which an unscrupulous salesman may underestimate in order to get the job. If you are moving interstate, the cost of your move is determined, by law, *according to the weight of your goods and the distance* they're going. When getting an estimate for either kind of move, be sure to show the mover's representative every last tool in the garage and box in the attic so he can give you an accurate estimate. (Also draw the estimator's notice to any antiques that will require especially careful handling.) This is for your benefit, since in order to obtain your goods at the other end of the move you must hand your driver—in cash or a certified check—(1) the full cost of the move, if the same as the estimate, or (2) if more, 110 percent of the estimate, the balance to be paid within 15 working days.

One young couple of my acquaintance, overestimating their own strength, told their mover's representative that they planned to bring this box and that table and that chair by themselves, but when the time came to move they abandoned their self-help plans. The mover, however, had made arrangements for only a small van and had to make the trip twice in order to transport all the household goods. As he was charging by the hour, the costs of the move were doubled. So try to be realistic about your own abilities.

If there's not enough furniture to fill a van, you will get a cheaper quotation. Some items can be moved as a "part lot," which means the firm will fit it in when they have a van in that area, but you must be prepared to wait for delivery.

Find out *how many men and trucks* there will be on the job and ask for separate *estimated times* of arrival, loading, journey, and unloading. Ask if there will be any *extra costs*. In interstate moves the *actual arrival time* of your possessions is something that few companies will ever predict with any accuracy. This is particularly true if your belongings are not a "part lot" but unfortunately still leave enough room in the truck for the company to pick up another load en route; this can delay your stuff for days. *Be very tough on this point when getting estimates from different outfits*. If your family has to wait in a motel and eat in restaurants while your belongings zigzag across the country, it can be a very expensive proposition.

FIND OUT WHAT THE CONDITIONS OF THE CONTRACT ARE: In other words, find out what you're getting for your money and *check that it covers insurance* while packing and unpacking, loading and unloading in transit, and whether it covers damage to clocks and electrical equipment. Get proof of insurance in writing and also check with your own insurer by telephone, to sort out any problems.

On an interstate move you are entitled to insurance of 60 cents per pound per article at no extra cost. *For an intrastate move* insurance depends on the individual carrier —check the different costs on the different estimates. You may want to insure your goods, either as a full lot or for certain specific pieces, for more, either with your own insurance company or your carrier. The amounts must be noted on the bill of lading.

Extra insurance is well worth a few extra dollars, and it is essential if you have valuable pictures, china, crystal, or antiques. The movers won't be responsible for the safety of jewelry, money, or documents, so you should pop these in your bank or sew them into your stays or whatever means of safekeeping you decide on before you move. A moneybelt belted around your waist is a good idea for cash and keys.

Read your contract carefully; there are limitations to the contractors' liability. Get confirmation of the following points *in writing*, together with a written estimate. When you confirm the estimate ask for a receipt and make sure that you get it or you risk being liable for any unspecified discrepancies.

POINTS A CONTRACT SHOULD COVER

- Acceptance of estimates.
- Accessibility of premises.
- Delays caused by events beyond company's control.
- Responsibilities of the client.
- What an estimate does not include.
- What cannot be removed or stored.
- When charges are to be paid.
- The company's rights when charges are not paid.
- Extent of company's liability.
- The submission of claims.
- Arbitration procedure.
- Use of subcontractors.

CLAIMING DAMAGES: There's generally a time limit in which to claim or complain. I have tried to avoid boring legal jargon in this book, sticking it in only when vital. It's so easy for the eyes to glaze over and the brain to blank out at the sight of a paragraph like the one in bold print below. Only when your Ming is in bits, your pots have lost their handles, the crate of your best china is missing, and one piano leg has disappeared may you see the point of it.

IMPORTANT LEGAL POINT: Normally, if Party "A" [that's you] accuses Party "B" [that's the moving company] of negligence, the burden of proof lies with the Accuser (Party "A"). When Party "A" is the Client (called the Bailor) and Party "B" is the Mover (called the Bailee for reward), the burden of going forward with the evidence is transferred to Party "B" who must show that any loss or damage to belongings did not arise through his fault. It is sufficient for Party "A" merely to claim that the damage was done by Party "B" and not to establish how, why, or where it was done. It is also necessary for Party "B," if he is to be successful in rebutting the charges of "A," to prove that he has not been negligent.

Quite simply, what this means is that instead of scream-ing at the mover, "You broke my piano leg. You did so," and having the mover retort, "No, I didn't and you can't prove I did," if the piano leg has been broken, the mover has to prove that he *didn't* do it; you don't have to prove that he did.

If you're moving, that interesting little point is worth the cost of this whole book. It can mean that instead of your having to prove that the movers broke your Ming, they are responsible unless they can prove that they didn't.

Even if you have signed a release saying that your effects are in good order, most reliable movers will assume responsibility for damage if you report it in a day or two. If you have any trouble, write a letter of complaint to the ICC, Washington, D.C. 20423, sending copies of the letter to the company, the Better Business Bureau, and the At-torney General in your old and new states. If you have any trouble the ICC has a "hotline" for complaints. Call (202) 343–4761 or (202) 343–4141.

COMPARISON OF LEADING MOVING COMPANIES

Listed by groups in order of overall service, based on each company's 1974 performance report for C.O.D. ship-ments. Within groups, listed alphabetically.

	Shipments Underesti-mated	Shipments Picked Up Late	Shipments Delivered Late	Shipments with Damage Claim of $50 or More	Average Time to Settle Claim
ABOVE AVERAGE	%	%	%	%	*Days*
Bekins Van Lines	23	6	12	16	18
Engel Van Lines	8	5	12	16	52
King Van Lines	25	+	20	12	26
Republic Van and Storage Co.	23	+	16	11	32
AVERAGE Aero Mayflower Transit Co.	24	5	19	23	42

American Red Ball Transit Co	24	5	23	17	40
Atlas Van Lines	26	4	24	13	46
Fernstrom Storage and Van Co.	21	2	16	19	37
Global Van Lines	20	8	14	13	46
Greyhound Van Lines	16	18	21	15	45
John F. Ivory Storage Co.	16	11	26	12	20
NATION	25	1	27	20	44
Neptune World Wide Moving	21	+	14	26	28
North American Van Lines	27	13	15	16	50
Pan American Van Lines	30	2	12	17	67
Trans-American Van Service	19	10	18	11	43
United Van Lines	25	16	15	13	31
Wheaton Van Lines	17	3	23	13	46
BELOW AVERAGE Allied Van Lines	25	16	21	24	54
Burnham Van Service	21	21	30	17	24
Lyon Moving and Storage Co.	11	7	30	16	63
AVERAGE FOR ALL 21 CARRIERS	21	7	19	16	41

* Includes only shipments where actual cost of move was under-estimated by 10% or more.
+ Less than 1%

Source: Consumer's Research Magazine.

WHAT TO ARRANGE IN ADVANCE

TRAFFIC RESTRICTIONS: If any apply to the area to which you are moving, tell the mover well in advance so that he can ask for police cooperation.

FIXTURES AND FITTINGS: Make sure you have ascertained in advance what fixtures, fittings, appliances will be left at your new home. Get it in writing from the old owner of the property.

Rose bushes, hydrangeas, and doorknobs naturally come into this category, as well as curtain rods, light fixtures, TV aerials, shelves, and closet fixtures. I have suffered from finding all the above items surprisingly missing upon my entry and very tedious it was at the time. No use hollering for a lawyer when dusk is falling and you are roaming in the gloaming on a Friday night with no doorknobs and nothing to hang your clothes on. Also, check the type of electric sockets in your new home to ensure that ranges, refrigerators, and lamps will work on The Day.

SERVICES: *The telephone company* should be notified of your move a week beforehand. *The gas and electric companies and water authority* can usually be notified 48 hours in advance, but check with them on this.

Ask for services to be turned on the day before you arrive at your new home (or on the actual day if entry is impossible before you arrive), and turned off and the meters read in your old home on the morning of the day you leave. Be there to see that they are, or complain if they're not. Keep carbon copies (dated) of your letters and send all letters certified mail because you cannot assume that the service companies are more efficient in your new, unknown area than they were in the old one.

It is wise to get, and file, a letter from all these utilities confirming that you will not be responsible for bill payments after the move from your old home. I speak as one who was billed for 6 months by one utility for hundreds of dollars currently due on houses that I had left respectively 2 and 3 years earlier.

Locate the local *doctor, hospital, bank, police station,* and *fire department* in your new area, noting telephone numbers and addresses. Don't forget to contact the milkman if you need home delivery. Ask your neighbor which one she uses—a good way to meet your neighbor.

ELECTRIC AND GAS FITTINGS: If you take your *major appliances*, have them disconnected by qualified workmen. Moving men won't disconnect any electrical or gas apparatus or take down electrical or gas fittings if wired up to the main switches. Nor will they take down or reinstall *TV aerials*, so arrange separately for this. Your mover may subcontract these jobs for you.

Refrigerators should be defrosted before loading. And you should start to deplete any freezer supplies (that is, eat the stuff) as soon as you know you're going to move, because a freezer is a heavy, delicate item and should be empty when moved.

CHANGE OF ADDRESS: Visit your local post office to tell them of your intended departure. They will give you free of charge a stack of change-of-address postcards. They will also give you forms to fill out to ensure that they forward your mail. Send change-of-address postcards to your friends, the magazines you subscribe to, the income tax people, your insurance company, credit card companies, and all firms where you have charge accounts.

UNWANTED ITEMS: Make an inventory of what you want to (1) move, (2) sell, (3) throw away. Call the Salvation Army or some rich charity (poor charities don't pick up) to collect unsalable items, or just leave a small heap on the doorstep with a notice saying "Please help yourself." You'll be amazed how fast your junk disappears.

If you're moving into a smaller house and have more furniture than you will be able to accommodate, if you are planning to redecorate, or if you just don't want to pay for hauling heavy objects like kitchen tables and lawn mowers, have a garage sale. If this is too much bother and if the surplus objects have any value, *give* them to a non-profit thrift shop and get a receipt for their estimated worth—which is then tax deductible as a charitable contribution. (Volunteers of America will let *you* value the property and give you a receipt.)

Remember that no charity or hospital is thirsting for your broken television set, empty bottles, or beat-up old armchair with the broken arm.

PACKING: Find out whether cartons, wardrobes, and other packing materials are provided by the moving firm, and at what cost. If you have bulky, heavy, breakable furniture, it's best to let the movers do the packing. If you're contemplating frequent transfers, you can save moving bills by buying lightweight, indestructible, disposable, or easy to assemble and disassemble furniture.

Otherwise, if you decide to do your own packing—or at least part of it—plan to use sturdy objects as containers, such as waste baskets or laundry baskets. And since you probably won't want to bring your crummy old garbage pail to your new home, you might as well buy new plastic ones and use them as packing containers. Stick a numbered label on each case listing its contents, and keep a list of contents clipped to a notebook as well (never be without a notebook, especially in a move), because then you'll know what's in the packing case that mysteriously disappears.

If you have a lot of books, it saves a mint to pack your own. If you have a reference library, you can pack it so that it arrives in the right order, not with painless-childbirth manuals mixed in with the philosophical works. (Moving is also a godsent opportunity to weed out ancient and forgotten best sellers and torn and disintegrating not-so-best sellers.) Used supermarket cartons are perfect for packing books. Your appliance dealer generally has a surplus of the super-large cartons that his ranges and refrigerators were shipped in. Use them whole or divided into sections for cooking utensils and other items that are fairly nonbreakable and/or of small value.

I find that it's best to leave wall-to-wall carpeting and drapes behind. It will help sell your house if you declare your intention to leave them to the prospective buyer. Besides, they probably won't fit your new pad, unless the rooms are smaller. Same goes for major appliances, unless you're in love with one or some.

ON-THE-SPOT MOVING INSTRUCTIONS: Write 2 copies, 1 for you and 1 for the foreman.

Make a neat plan of the dear old home. In red, number each piece of furniture. Get large-size sticky labels, number them, and stick a *number* on each piece of furniture as per your old-home plan.

Make a neat plan of the new home. Use a blue pencil, and indicate a *letter* for each room. Then add the appropriate letter to the numbered label on each piece of furniture. Each item should end up labeled something like "Item 29. To Basement Utility Room. Room G."

Then Write 2 Transfer Lists. The *first* is a room-by-room list from the old home, giving each number an item. A particular armchair would be entered as "From Room A. Armchair 29 to Room G." The *second* is for each room in the new house, giving each item and number. For instance "Room G. Armchair 29, table 17, television 22 . . ." *This is your Master Plan* and both you and the foreman must hang on to your copies at all costs. (Best to Xerox a few extras.) This may seem a tedious procedure, but it is indisputable and it *works*.

SLEEPING AND EATING ARRANGEMENTS: If possible, move ahead of the family and try to straighten things out (sort of) before they arrive. If the company for which you work is paying for the move, then you probably don't have to worry, and they can check into a motel until the new dust settles. Otherwise, arrange for them to sleep somewhere near the old home, perhaps with relatives or friends (big present afterward to the hostess). You might not like the idea of imposing on your friends, but plenty of people don't mind putting a sofa or spare room at your disposal for a night or two. I have often offered mine to friends about to move; they've never taken advantage of the offer (I refuse to list possible reasons), but it's reassuring to know that you have an emergency plan.

Plan on noncooked meals, whether it's a box of sandwiches, a picnic basket, or a drive-in restaurant.

CHILDREN AND PETS: Do your best to *get rid of the children* while you're packing. Send them to relatives, neighbors, parks, movie theaters, and baby-sitters. It's also a good idea to locate baby-sitters in your new area in advance. Keep a predetermined temporary entertainment area for placebos: soft drinks, toys, games, books, TV.

One moving expert stresses that parents must be extra kind and considerate during the whole of the moving period. Let calm and patience be the key words, advises this obviously childless fellow. Keep babies, young children, and pets out of the way. Moving men don't like stepping or tripping over them.

A *good place for pets is the bathroom*, since your movers won't be going in and out of there, except for the usual. Don't offer pets food for at least a few hours before the move—to avoid stomach upsets because of nervousness and/or traveling—but do provide fresh water. Move your animals last of all (it's a good idea to put them in your new bathrooms until the movers are no longer underfoot and the front door is closed).

Understandably, domestic animals can become unusually aggressive when bewildered and upset by a change in routine and environment. You can get cheap cardboard carrying cartons for transporting cats, small dogs, and turtles. Birds should be taken in a covered cage or a cardboard box with airholes punched in, then they won't flap around and risk injury. Carry fish in water in any waterproof container for a short journey, or sealed plastic bags with plenty of air in relation to water. For larger animals consult your vet because, like children before a long flight, they can be tranquilized for the journey.

If you're driving a long distance to your new home, say, taking the kids on a scenic, 3-day, leisurely trip, it's probably better not to take your pets along. You might arrange for them to stay with your old vet, or friends, until you reach your destination, then have them flown to you. Some moving companies will put your pets on a plane and arrange for pickup and kennel service at the other end. It's not a cheap service, of course, but cats especially will tolerate a short plane hop better than a long car trip. Airlines now have pressurized luggage compartments. I know of plenty of people who have shifted pets in this way with no problems, and of course the airlines will tell you it is safe. Indeed, if they could guarantee that the airplane would take off immediately, it *would* be safe. But if the great flying bird stays motionless on a really hot or really cold runway for a couple of hours, your pet could suffer. However, you are allowed to take pets in the cabin with you provided they are in proper carriers; this is the best way for them to fly, if possible.

On "The Day"

PACK AN EMERGENCY SURVIVAL SUITCASE: It should contain essential items, other than food and drink, such as toothpaste and toothbrushes, toilet paper, soap, towels, can opener, corkscrew, rubber glove, sleeping pills if you take them, aspirin, Band-Aids, coat hangers, flashlight, and a couple of spare light bulbs.

Give instructions only to the foreman. When the moving men arrive, go around the house with the foreman. Check the inventory he takes to ensure that every object described, and any existing damage, is listed accurately. Point out to him anything extraordinary that might need special attention. Don't forget outside items, such as garden tools, statues, and planters. What you must remember about moving men is to keep your Master Plan simple, keep out of their way, and communicate only with their chief wizard. I may be cynical, but I budget for half of a generous tip in advance, give it to the supervisor and hint that the other half may be forthcoming upon his final departure. Allow $5–$10 per moving person per day at least. I don't believe a *few* beers may improve their disposition. Think of the Ming.

WHAT YOU CAN LEAVE FOR THE MOVERS TO DO: A good moving company will pack *everything,* if you wish: books, china, pots and pans, toys—the whole lot. Needless to say, this is an additional expense. (In larger homes the delicate stuff, such as china, glass, and small items, may be packed the day before the move.) Bedding should be folded and left for the men to pack. Their tasks include taking apart and reassembling large pieces of furniture such as bedsteads, wardrobes, desks, and kitchen cabinets. They sometimes take down curtains and take up carpeting at your request and expense. However, they do not rehang or relay it at the new home, except by previous arrangement. Nor do they rehang wall decorations such as mirrors and pictures.

Very small valuable items, such as miniature carvings, should be packed in cotton in a box by the owner. Tie or tape all furniture keys to the piece to which they belong, if they haven't already been filed in your organization drawer (see The Drawer with the Answer to Everything). Stereo equipment, say experts, should be specially packed in the original cartons if possible. As you threw these away when you originally unpacked it, the stereo should be carefully packed in cartons after screwing down the turntable and playing arm according to the manufacturers' instructions. On my last move I wrecked a good stereo by not doing this.

Don't pack anything dangerous or inflammable such as matches, chemicals, kerosene.

LEAVING THE OLD HOME: Lock the door after you finally leave and make sure that your moving impresario has a key to your new home as well as the address.

If the old house is likely to be empty for a few winter days, it is advisable to drain pipes and tanks, which you do *after* the water supply has been turned off, by you or the water company, by taking all the plugs out and turning all the faucets on until the water gives out. Leave a note on the kitchen faucet to say what you've done.

Check that you have left your home as neat and clean as possible, as you would hope to find your new one, in fact.

ON ARRIVING: Stick large letters on the doors of every room in your new house, according to your plan. Check that every piece of furniture that is carried in bears a number and a letter.

YOUR JOB AS SUPERMOVER

- It is your duty on The Day to *keep especially silent.* Don't moan; it doesn't help. Don't carry anything; save your strength for cleaning up. The most exasperating clients, say moving men, are those who tell them their jobs. Keep calm and within range, but out of the way.
- Keep track of 2 sets of *keys.* Keys to the old home and the new should be kept in your handbag and, if possible, the foreman should also have a set.
- *Make notes.* List anything that's been forgotten, lost, or broken.
- *Make drinks.* The last things stored in the van (and therefore first out) should be the kettle—or a plug-in heating element—milk, instant coffee, bouillon cubes, tea bags, plastic or disposable cups (china always gets broken and anyway never holds enough).
- Keep hold of the emergency survival suitcase.
- Keep your head when *checking your list of possessions* upon arrival, and get the foreman to sign it at the out and in stage. *Don't you be rushed into signing anything.* His next job is not your problem.

This avoids later arguments as to whether the Colonial loving cup wasn't in 3 pieces when they packed it. Of course, most movers do not hang around while you unpack, but do your best to assess the condition of your belongings.

- It's all those *packing cartons* or orange crates that make the muddle, so if you're moving without professional help, move them into the new home first and keep them in one room near the front door. Move *heavy pieces*, such as gas stove and washing machine, before the lighter stuff. Do not unpack cartons of china, glass, ornaments, books, until the furniture is in place.

- At the new house, *check utilities and other necessary apparatus*. Are the sink, stove, toilet, bath and basins working correctly? Is all drapery-hanging apparatus ready and working? Check light bulbs, light shades, and electric plugs. Move drapes and carpets, ready for the furniture.

- If all services have not been turned on, telephone (if the phone is working) and complain. *Keep cool and reasonable when complaining,* do not sound harassed, or you will be written off as a hysterical woman (which, of course, by now you are). Always sweetly but firmly ask for the names of the people you talk to. You may want to complain about THEM later—which is, of course, why they may be reluctant to divulge their names.

- *Get to know the neighbors fast,* so that you can tap them for water, extra milk, some instant coffee. Just take a deep breath and knock on the door; then smile hopefully.

  The friendliest way for *you* to greet a new, harassed neighbor is to offer your telephone and tea bags or a needed kettle or saucepan. If your budget can stand it, offer them a bowl of fruit or a bottle of wine on the evening of the first (always the worst) day.

- *On the day after,* if services still have not been turned on, complain again. Catch up on everything you thought you would be able to finish faster than was in fact possible. Continue to congratulate yourself on keeping calm.

LONG-TERM STORAGE

If all or some goods are being moved into storage, ask in advance what the cost of storage and insurance will be and how stored goods will be covered for loss or damage through fire (for any reason) or flood.

Container-loading

By far the safest, cleanest, most trouble-free, and expensive form of long-term storage is the relatively new concept of container loading. This involves prepacking the goods into standard-size plywood containers that are sealed with metal clamps, stacked in a warehouse, and unsealed only when you want them.

Paste "keep out front" labels on to the few stored items that you might need earlier than the rest, such as a desk, bed, or baby carriage. Once the goods are stored away it can be expensive to locate separate items.

If you pack any woolen garments, blankets, or fabrics in trunks and chests, liberally scatter mothballs. Storage contractors are not responsible for moths. It's best if carpets and rugs are cleaned before storage and also treated with a moth deterrent.

Don't store anything liquid or inflammable.

SETTLING IN

Probably a solicitous Welcome Wagon lady will drop by soon after your arrival. Her job, of course, is to introduce you to local merchants who want your business, and they may have some worthwhile discount offers and free gifts for the newcomer. *Very occasionally*, this lady may be genuinely interested in helping you settle down and make friends, but don't count on it. A conscientious real estate 'agent will sometimes go out of her/his way to help you find good stores and make friends. I know of one elegant real estate lady who even gives wine and cheese parties (several each summer) on her patio to introduce her clients to the community and will go to almost any lengths to settle their gripes with the utility or phone company or with the former owner of their house. Again, don't count on it; you will generally have to depend on your own initiative.

Join Everything

Participate in as many activities as possible: Join churches or synagogues where appropriate, the PTA, the pool (car or swimming), the library, the League of Women Voters, the nursery-school cooperative. Use your children to make friends; send them on errands to the neighbors, offer to baby-sit for other families in return for the same service. Car-pool to school, on outings, to the train station. Innumerable families have become friends through the Great American Car Pool.

Get the Kids Involved

If you're moving in the summer, as many families do, find out beforehand what summer facilities are available—summer reading clubs, puppetry classes at the local playground, various arts and crafts courses and theater groups at the local schools, Bible classes—and sign your children up so that they will be immediately caught up in new activities and not so likely to miss their old home and friends. On hot days you might set them up to sell lemonade. On cooler days stick them outside with a table and a chair, some old comic books and a sign that says "Comic Trading Post." It's difficult to make the effort at the beginning when you have so many other things to do, but if you have children, they should be your first priority, and that also applies to getting them out from underfoot.

Having accomplished all this, you are now ready to enjoy your new home!

SPENDING MONEY

Mr. Micawber's crisp advice on budgeting hasn't been improved on in the past 100 years: "Annual Income twenty pounds, annual expenditure nineteen, nineteen six, result happiness. Annual Income twenty pounds, annual expenditure twenty pounds ought and six, result misery." What's sound advice for pounds and pence is also sound advice for dollars and cents.

If there's trouble in a home, it isn't necessarily in the bedroom—it's quite often in the budget. I wouldn't be surprised to learn that more families fight over money than over sex and mothers-in-law combined, usually because they've built the battleground into their lives by planning their expenditures badly or by not planning them at all. My hunch is backed up by Frederick Humphrey, associate professor of Family Relations at the University of Connecticut and president of the American Association of Marriage and Family Counselors, who says, "Sometimes I think families are more reluctant to discuss money matters than sexual matters."

Finding a Single System

The first financial fact that a couple should discover is *what system works for both of them.* One couple might institute a simple solution based on a piggybank and a two-sided purse. Another couple might positively enjoy having 6 bank accounts plus an accountant. But woe betide the togetherness when *she* controls the piggybank and *he* divides the laundry bill into his, hers, and theirs with the aid of a pocket calculator.

According to some marriage experts, a good test of a relationship is supposed to be whether a man and woman can successfully operate a joint banking account. You might find it safer to try going over Niagara Falls in a barrel. All I can tell you is that no system will be any good unless you *both* understand it and agree to use it.

Your Housekeeping Budget

AN ANNUAL BUDGET: Basically consists of 2 simple lists. *List 1* notes money coming in from all sources during the year. *List 2* notes money spent on various items over that time. If you get paid each week, it's sensible to work out a weekly budget; if you are paid twice a month, as more and more people are, a biweekly budget will be the answer; if you're paid monthly, work out a monthly one.

You can estimate the totals for these weekly or monthly lists based on the previous year's income and expenditures. Experts advise that you be precise in your accounting—no rounding out sums to the nearest dollar. State the actual amount coming in or going out down to the last cent.

THE PURPOSES OF A BUDGET: The point of a home budget is threefold. (1) knowing what you want to do with your money; (2) keeping track of where the money actually goes (theoretically these 2 figures should be the same, but

Your Housekeeping Budget

Item	Cost		Cost per week		Cost per year	
	$	¢	$	¢	$	¢

life isn't always that accommodating; (3) and making sure that you don't overspend and get into debt, without realizing it.

CATEGORIZING BUDGET ITEMS: In working out the budget all those concerned should be absolutely clear where even the smallest expenses fit in and that every expense does fit in somewhere. Your budget items should be grouped under 3 headings: "Essentials," "Necessities," and "Luxuries." I call an "essential" something that you can't get along without—like bread. A "necessity" is butter or margarine. A "luxury" is jelly. I can't tell you which items fit under which heading because one woman's necessity is another man's extravagance. Whether your car is a luxury or a lifeline may depend on how far you live from work or the shopping center. Are cigarettes a necessity to be bought regularly and paid for on the weekly supermarket bill or are they luxuries to come out of individual personal allowances? What I can tell you is everyone concerned should decide in advance which item comes under which heading, in order to ease short-term economizing if it becomes necessary.

Put a *Mistakes and Contingencies* allowance into your budget. This is the disaster fund (unpredictable "act of God" stuff) for which you should allot a really pessimistic amount. After all, if you don't use the money for emergencies, you can divert it into savings or a buying spree at the end of the year. But, believe me, you will use it. **So the budget for savings should NOT be lumped with the disaster fund; keep them separate or your savings will just melt away.**

Some people operate a *painless savings account*, into which key post items in the annual budget that can be marked "P$" (*Painless Saving*). The idea is to make regular installments into an interest-bearing savings account against the day when these expenses will have to be paid. Household insurance, for example, is frequently paid annually; you can be collecting interest on your money as you save for that payment. The same is true of tuition costs, Christmas expenses, and vacation spending. Consider putting P$ money in a separate account (or a second housekeeping account, see further on) to avoid raiding your regular savings and disaster accounts.

LISTING ITEMS IN YOUR BUDGET

- **Home** Mortgage payments or rent (including local property taxes) (P$)
gas and electric (P$)
telephone (P$)
repairs and maintenance (P$)

- **Food** groceries
eating out (including lunch at work)

- **Clothes** new clothes and shoes

- **Insurance** property (P$)
life (P$)
health (P$) (may be covered in part by employer's insurance plan)

- **Health** doctor (P$)
dentist (P$)
drugs and medicines

- **Education** tuition for children or self (P$)
books and school supplies (P$)
newspapers and magazines

- **Transportation** car payments (P$)
car upkeep
commuting transportation (bus, subway, etc.)

- **Personal** hairdresser and barber
other

- **Entertainment** movies and theater
hobbies
vacation (P$)

- **Domestic** cleaning help
baby-sitter
gardener

- **Dues** union (P$)
clubs (P$)

- **Charities** church
community chest
other

- **Savings** You may prefer to include regular savings in your P$ account until you have accumulated enough to invest.
bonds (P$)
annuity (P$)
other

- Gifts   family *(P$)*
                       friends *(P$)*
- Christmas   food, drink, presents, parties *(P$)*
- Mistakes and
  Contingencies   regular contributions *(P$)*
- Debts   installment payments *(P$)*
                       charge and credit card accounts *(P$)*
                       other

SAVING MONEY

Save what you can in a *savings account* in a commercial bank or a savings and loan association; by purchasing *stocks and/or bonds;* by creaming part of the savings off into *mortgage repayments* (since bricks and mortar are also an investment); or by purchasing *antique silver,* furniture, jewelry, or potential old masters (but never on your own judgment, unless you happen to be an expert).

How much should you save? It depends on what for and for how long and how much is coming in. If you can manage to save 10 percent of your total income a year, good for you. If you can't seem to save money, but really want to, you can force yourself to save by taking on savings commitments and having your employer enforce them, such as *paycheck deductions* to buy *U.S. Savings Bonds* or to go directly into a savings account in your name. You may wish to buy a retirement *annuity,* join a monthly *investment plan,* or buy into a *mutual fund;* consult your broker on the available plans and their performance history and prospects. Also available are *Keogh* and *Individual Retirement Plans* that permit you to invest up to a certain stated percentage of your income each year, tax free till you retire, if you are self-employed or your employer does not offer a pension plan. In any case, the object is to choose a savings system that will keep abreast of inflation.

The installment plan can be a great way to save up for things but only if you are buying something that is likely to appreciate in value such as real estate, and only if you don't allow more than 10 percent of your annual income after taxes for the purchase. I know a girl who bought a diamond tiara this way. It's the smallest tiara in existence and she's never even worn the thing because it always seems to be in hock for more urgent financial needs. But it certainly was a glamorous way to save, and the value of the piece has increased 6 times in 10 years.

If you are self-employed allow for taxes when budgeting. Work out what your tax should be and deposit this money regularly in a savings account where it will earn interest until the tax man claims it, as he eventually will.

SORTING OUT INCOME

Two Breadwinners

If there is more than one contributor, either (1) sort out responsibilities or (2) pool the family income (salaries, allowances, dividends, earnings, legacies, or whatever) and add it up. Try redistributing it under the previous headings.

When a young husband and wife both work they sometimes feel it is better not to rely on the wife's pay in case she stops working to raise the children or for any other reason; this way there is not so likely to be a painful adjustment to a lower standard of living. Provided there is some compensatory form of security for the wife, such as having a hunk of the family assets in her name, it seems reasonable that the money she earns be earmarked for major but slashable items such as central air conditioning (if you own your own house), a new dishwasher, or quadrophonic sound equipment.

If you both work, you may not want to have a joint mortgage for tax reasons; the interest is a substantial deduction.

SEPARATE BANK ACCOUNTS: You cannot afford to be sentimental about money. If you and your husband are madly in love, well that's wonderful, but statistically you have a good chance of falling out of love and divorcing. So without being offensively self-protective, avoid entwining your money or goods with those of your husband (or with any other member of the household). Not to be mean, just to keep things straight. I consider that having only one joint account for 2 people puts the budget, as well as the relationship, at risk; the judge who lives next door to me agrees. His nonworking wife has a personal account and a housekeeping account.

Some people feel that it is important for the chief earner not to think that because he (or she) brings in the money he (or she) has a greater right than the rest of the family to determine how it should be spent. A husband might work and get paid and a wife may work full-time in the home and not get paid. He is the breadwinner for the family but she is not just a bread-consumer. Some wives feel that he gets paid (to a greater or lesser degree) for both their work. That's certainly the main reason that was given by men for unequal pay. But the days are gone when you could get a woman to work for a week merely for full board and a roof over her head.

SEPARATE TAX RETURNS: If you have a separate income, your tax return (separate or joint) should also depend on which way saves you the most money. Keeping a joint housekeeping account (unless you maintain careful records of the contribution of each of you and how the money is spent), can mess up your tax deductions at the end of the year.

For example, interest on installment buying and all loans, including mortgages, is deductible. If you pay for a large purchase, such as a refrigerator or car, out of a joint housekeeping account, the tax man may have a few questions as to how that deduction is allocated. You may find that for tax reasons one of you should pay the installment bills (and collect all the deductions) and the other pay the current bills, each out of your separate accounts. It would be wise to consult an accountant or tax expert at the beginning of your budget year or before making a major installment purchase. With his advice you can work out the fairest and most economical approach.

There are other living arrangements that also require careful consideration of your tax circumstances. If more than 2 earners are sharing a home (husband, wife, and wife's mother; mother and sons; two or three friends), each might pay an agreed sum regularly (every week, month, or quarter) into the joint household account for the purpose of running the home. When a mother and son live together, if the son is the wage earner, it means a tax benefit for the "head of household." And if the mother, under such conditions, is handling the household account, beware that this account cannot be construed as "income." A tax consultant can advise you on these special situations. (Although consulting an accountant or tax expert is an initial extra expense, such advice may save you money and sanity.)

KEEPING PERSONAL PRIVATE MONEY APART FROM THE HOUSE-KEEPING MONEY: You can manage this by having 2 purses, or a purse with 2 pockets, or 2 separate bank accounts and checking accounts. For me, in fact, the secret of keeping track of home budgeting is to reduce as many outgoings as possible to a regular basis, and for this I opened a *second housekeeping account for regular payments*. (It's a variation on the painless saving system, but for house-keeping only, not for health insurance, car payments or vacations, etc.)

To do this, first add up all your regular payments for *everything*, from the milkman to the dog license. Estimate what fuel and telephone bills will be by looking up last year's costs. Take a deep breath and don't panic—the total amount is bound to be truly staggering. Divide it by 12, prune, then arrange to have the resultant sum paid monthly into this number 2 account. All regular bills are paid from this account, so I don't feel faint at the very thought of opening the electric bill every month. If I am a little overdrawn one month, it should theoretically balance out in the following months. Food and unexpected or un-budgeted expenses are paid from my number 1 house-keeping account. It might cost a little more to have sev-eral bank accounts, but I prefer to pay for clarity rather than to constantly have to add and subtract to find out whether I can afford to buy a new umbrella or have my teeth capped.

If you decide to carry more than one account, you may want to look into the checking facilities of savings and loan associations so as to reduce the cost of sheer bank-ing. Some of these institutions will permit free checking if you carry a stated minimum amount in a savings account (which is not a drawback since you should want some kind of savings account anyway).

HOUSEHOLD BOOKKEEPING: I do as little as I can get away with and so should you. If you refuse to even consider organizing your money, stop reading. Come back to this page again if you start raising poodles or get into a money muddle.

The easiest form of house bookkeeping (or business bookkeeping) is a *cash book* (bought at a stationery store) —it has lines and columns conveniently ruled for you. Fill in the date, money that comes in (noting where from, perhaps), and money that goes out (noting where to, *definitely*) in 4 separate columns. I don't mean the cost of every head of lettuce . . . I just fill in "food" as such. This book calms you when you wonder where on earth the money went, or when someone sends you a second bill for something you've already paid for, or when you want to check how many times the vacuum cleaner has been repaired since you bought it. It is also a good indicator of where you can economize.

It is a good idea to make a point of entering checks in the book *before* filling them in, otherwise you tend to forget to enter them at all. To pay bills, sort them out alphabetically, enter them in your cash book, fill in the check stubs, then steel yourself to make out the checks.

Cash statements. If you want to know exactly where you are financially, you can do a satisfying bit of arithmetic that grandly calls itself a cash statement. It is ideal even for an advanced muddler because an average 13-year-old who is weak in math could do one.

The easiest time to do this is when your bank statements come in (or calculate up to that date). Your statement will contain your canceled checks and notes of your deposits. Bank statements used to arrive on the first of the month, but then they were computerized and now they seem to arrive any old time. However, they will arrive at the same time each month, depending on where you are in the computer cycle. If you don't like adapting to their schedule and prefer doing monthly accounts ending on the last day of the month, simply chop your statements up, rearrange them into monthly periods, and Scotchtape the pieces together.

The canceled statement will record your balance as of the date the statement was sent out. Simple subtraction of remaining outstanding checks noted in your checkbook will tell you *Where You Are Now*. And then, by subtracting the bills still to be paid, you can find out *Where You Will Be*. If this appears to be disaster, note any money due to come in that will perhaps alleviate the trauma. You don't really have to understand the system; just write it down accurately under the right headings and it will work out to *Your True Financial State*. Use a different column for each bank account.

A SIMPLE STATEMENT

Date	Personal	House-keeping	Second Account
State of accounts	+ $ 2	+ $20	+ $200
Deduct bills to pay	0	− 17	− 120
Deduct checks not yet withdrawn	− 1	0	− 32
SUBTOTAL	+ 1	+ 3	+ 48
Add checks not yet deposited	+ 13	+ 10	0
FACTUAL TOTAL	+ 14	+ 13	+ 48
Add, tentatively, money due in	+ 25	0	0
THEORETICAL TOTAL	$39	$13	$ 48

Your True Financial State is therefore $39 + 13 + 48 = $100.

FAMILY FUNDS

Getting Everyone into the Act

Some families have regular conferences about money, once every 3 months, say. Get the children in on these as early as possible, even though they may be bored, and treat their contributions with respect. (You are encouraging them to learn how to handle money.) After discussing the budget, analyze disasters to find out how to prevent them, suggest amendments to the budget (more pocket money may mean a less expensive vacation), and take account of future changes, such as rising costs. After this you should all go out to dinner—even if it's only hamburgers or pizza—to cheer yourselves up.

Major expenditures should, ideally, be discussed and approved by all the family. If he wants a scarlet sports car, you want a dishwasher, or your eldest daughter wants to spend a year traveling, it's a matter that all the family should know about if footing the bill will affect the finances of the whole household. This is what the quarterly conference is for. If one adult member of the family tries to explain a major expense that the rest can't see the sense in (for example, how the aforementioned sports car will actually *save* money), the best way would be to get him/her to explain it in front of the family accountant who can then act as an impartial adviser. But you may not have a family accountant who has time for this sort of arbitration, in which case common sense can be a pretty good guide.

All this may sound horrendous, but my pretty cousin Corinne, a comparatively new bride, says she's eternally grateful to her father for doing this. Not only did she, as a little girl, see the point of switching heaters off (more money for holidays) but she sailed into marriage able to run a budget, without ever realizing she had been taught to do so.

WHAT TO DO IF YOU'RE A CASHAHOLIC

A cashaholic is someone who's hopeless with money. Psychologists say that such extravagance is inculcated in children by parents who, instead of giving their children a proper allowance and teaching them to spend it responsibly, give only pocket money for treats and presents. The result is that the child, when grown up, thinks of money in terms of treats and personal pleasure as opposed to dreary things like taxes and insurance premiums.

CONTROLLING YOUR HABITS: I've never really found a cure for this condition, but you can survive solvently as a cashaholic by treating yourself as an alcoholic and locking up the "bottle"—don't own a checkbook, certainly don't own a credit card, deal only in cash, and when your wallet is empty stop spending. Form a Cashaholics Anonymous with a similarly afflicted friend and telephone her when you get the urge to spend; she can reel off a litany of bills and responsibilities and, in theory, deter you. Make up a shopping list of *essential* and *necessary* items; stick to it; don't add one extra item. As a last resort shop by telephone; it's more expensive, but you will avoid all sorts of extravagant temptations.

There is another method, if you can afford it. That is, turn your income over to a professional money manager. He doles out your spending money, pays your bills, and organizes your financial life. He draws up a cash flow on your financial position and helps you to produce a sensible, workable budget. He also collects a small percentage fee, from you, for taking your money problems off your hands. Your bank, credit union, or the local Better Business Bureau will give you the names of reputable finance counseling firms.

Finally, commit your money in advance to some sort of savings, such as buying a home.

BRINGING UP FINANCIALLY SENSIBLE CHILDREN: You won't raise a generation of cashaholics if you teach your children how to handle money as soon as they can buy their own ice cream.

Involve them in the family's affairs as soon as possible, as I have suggested, and give each child an *allowance*—yearly, every third month, monthly, or weekly—to cover all that he or she spends; older children can have clothes on their budgets, plus hobbies, sports, travel, school expenses, movies, and sweets. Expect some drama during the first 6 months, when they learn that overpurchasing of ice cream can mean no money to get into the local pool or skating rink. *Stand firm.* Kindness will not equip your offspring to stand on their own feet in later life. It's your responsibility to teach them that money is an important and permanent background to life and freedom.

You may be shelling out the allowance on a periodic basis, but the children should be encouraged to put some of it in their own *savings accounts.* My children had bank accounts since they were 8. I paid their allowances regularly, and they sorted out everything for themselves, including mistakes and contingencies. Although I advised them, I never bailed them out.

They both started their own businesses at 18 and my eldest son sold out when he was 21.

This system can save an enormous amount of money on children's clothes and shoes because they take better care of them. An added refinement before switching to contact lenses was the *eyeglass bonus*, paid at the end of each school term if they weren't broken. (The figure dropped immediately and dramatically from 3 pairs a term to 0). For their part, they had to promise to have proper school clothes. When they were younger, I kept, in my own closet, a spare pair of jeans, socks, and a sweater for each child, for occasions on which I wanted them to look decent.

Two extra points: I have always paid in full for their overcoats (the child who is willing to save for his own overcoat does not exist), and to encourage them to save for items that seem impossibly beyond their small allowance, by prearrangement I pay for half of anything that can be termed "equipment"—this can vary from a bicycle to a professional drawing board (of course, the trick for them is to get everything classified as equipment).

BUSINESS FINANCES

Bookkeeping

If you have your own little cottage industry steaming along nicely (embroidering blouses, making ceramics, canapés, or jewelry, freelance writing), you should keep account of income and expenses. On the left-hand page of a cash book (separate from your housekeeping book), keep a dated list of the invoices you send out (how else will the accountants of other firms know they owe you money?). On the right-hand page enter the date when payment is made. Anything undated on the right-hand page is unpaid.

An *invoice* or bill should be an exact account of what they owe you—how much and for what. It should be sent at the same time as the goods, unless you have made other arrangements. A short summary, or *statement*, giving the overall sum owed should be sent at the end of each month.

Business theory says that bills are paid at the end of the month after the first statement has been sent. By invoicing on the 29th, rather than the 1st of the next month, you should theoretically get paid a month earlier. You may have sensibly made arrangements that the goods be paid for *before* delivery, in which case you just bill in advance and don't hand the goods over before payment is made. (It's called a pro-forma invoice.)

It is inadvisable to sell goods on a sale or return basis —"on spec." Your goods are gone, and the shop hasn't invested in them, so it might be less keen on selling them than some other product in which the shop's money is tied up; responsibility for possible dirt or damage can also be tricky. I mention these points because, though they are simple, I have seen many housewives who have never been in business mess up a good start by not understanding sound business procedures.

Keeping Tabs on Business Expenses

I find that a simple notebook system works best. It is especially indispensable on out-of-town or foreign trips. What you want in this instance is a quick record of expenses while you're rushing around on business in some strange city or country. You also want to be able to understand your record so you can analyze it all when you get home. Remember always to ask for *all* bills and *all* receipts. Shove them in your bag, and then into a folder in your hotel room. When you return home carefully file them. Also, when using a foreign currency *write your expenses in that currency*. If you try to translate it as you go along, you'll be inviting headaches and inaccuracy.

Get a small lined notebook with columns (or draw 6 columns in yourself, see chart below. Write what you spend your money on in the ITEM column. When you receive cash, note it in the IN column, along with the sum you listed when you began your trip. (Record monies spent and received in the same currency in which the transaction was made.) Note personal purchases in the PERSONAL column and business purchases in the BUSINESS column. At the end of the day or week (it is unwise to leave it longer), add up each "money *out*" column. Add the total, subtract it from the sum you started out with (plus any monies received) in the IN column and, given a bit of luck, the answer should be about what you still have in your purse. Of course, the calculations are easier for domestic business trips, but just as essential if you want to keep track of your hard-earned cash.

Expenses on Domestic Trips

Date	In $	Item	Personal	Business
5/1	$400	Air Fare to S.F. (economy round trip)		$180.00
		Cab to app't		13.00
		Lunch (Chinatown)		15.50
9/1	$250	Chinese kimono	$16.20	
		Bus! to airport		3.50
		TOTALS: (Remaining Cash $371.80)	$16.20	$212.00

Expenses on Foreign Trips

Date	In $	Equivalent Foreign Exchange	Item	Personal	Business
9/10	$150	£100 sterling	Cashmere sweater	£18.75	
			Cab to Ritz		£2.25
			Drinks with contact		£4.40
			Cab to Buckingham Palace		£0.60
			Bribe to sentry		£10.00
			TOTALS:	£18.75	£17.25
11/10	$96	£64	Remaining Cash £128		

HOW TO ESCAPE AND SURVIVE INDEBTEDNESS

We live in an era of profligate waste, which consumers are finally beginning to do something about. If, like me, you have been married to a self-made millionaire, people tend to think that you have lots of money and are used to it. But how do they think millionaires acquire their millions in the first place? By living on a permanent, lunatic, public-prosperity/private poverty breadline, in order that every available penny can be used for the Big Scheme, that *really* teaches you to make each one dollar do the work of five. I've also learned a lot about economy while living in our farmhouse in France. All the rich farmers never throw a thing away, not a bottle, not even a jam jar, and they even hoard bits of string. (I turned up my nose at this parsimony until I needed bottles for my elderberry wine, jars for my jam, and seemed to be in permanent need of string.) *No matter how tight your budget there is room for economy.*

If You're in Debt

Eliminating small things won't make much of a difference. Don't cut a tree here, a tree there; chop down a bit of the forest. In other words, *cut down on the big things.* Don't economize only on things that will hardly save more than a few cents, for instance, buying medium instead of large eggs. If life looks all black, never cut down on the little things that make life worth living: If your one joy is playing golf, don't sell your clubs. (However, if you belong to a country club, you should probably resign and play on the municipal links instead.) Tiny economies won't add up to much and will cause everyone to feel poor and depressed. The trick is to economize in as big a way as you can on something boring, getting the cooperation of the whole family while doing it.

Short of tearing paper napkins in half and rationing toilet paper, there are sensible economies that should arouse the enthusiasm of any right-minded family. Everyone can help to *cut down the bills of the rapacious utility and telephone companies.* Any step you can take to reduce energy consumption besides saving you money is almost a patriotic duty, and may be your ticket to survival some day.

You might consider reviving that ancient form of transport, your feet. If you really want to see someone face to face, and he/she lives not too far away, *walk or bicycle* over. If your job or commuter station is less than 30 blocks away, bike to it. Forming *car pools* can also save money and energy. However, whether it's a matter of getting bodies to and from work or visiting the supermarket or hauling kids to the lake or the movies, it will take some organization and patience.

IN THE CASE OF TEMPORARY FINANCIAL TROUBLES: You can attack this problem by examining your budget. Remember all those figures you were keeping in your housekeeping budget? (see p. 236) Now's the time to take a fresh look at them. The American family making about $20,000 per year (before taxes) spends nearly 25 percent of its after-tax income for food. Almost another 25 percent goes for housing, 15 percent for transportation, and the other 35 percent goes for everything else—clothes, medical care, grooming, recreation, and education (not including college), insurance, gifts, and contributions. How do you compare?

Check your Essentials/Necessities/Luxuries groupings (see p. 237). Put the fixed expenses to one side. You cannot easily make cuts on these—rent or mortgage, car payments, installment payments, insurance. But the flexible expenses could be subject to reduction. Will your financial strain be relieved if you cut 10 percent from your food costs? Or 10 percent out of clothes and upkeep? (Discount stores can help here.) If so, this is where you should start economizing.

IF YOUR PLIGHT IS MORE SERIOUS: In this case your fixed expenses must be tackled. Is a move to a smaller home feasible? Can you rent out a room to bring in some more money? Can you trade in your car for a model that is more economical to run and insure?

If you decide that you must move, do your research carefully. Be practical. Moving to the country may save money in some ways, but the dearth of big supermarkets and the consequent increase in traveling costs may offset the savings. Check out all financial aspects of a neighborhood (commuting costs, local taxes, schools, proximity to the supermarket so you won't need a car, resale possibilities if you are trading your mortgage in for a smaller one) so that one move will do the trick. Remember, moving is itself a large and costly decision.

Don't be sentimental or afraid of what the neighbors will think if you have to move for money reasons. You won't be around to hear them. It isn't easy. When Doomsday hit me I moved 5 times in 18 months. Oddly enough I was cheered by my lawyer's telling me how difficult *everybody* always finds it, not just me. "One of the most difficult things you can do," he said, "is to cut your budget drastically, because nobody ever thinks he is personally 'being extravagant' or he wouldn't live that way."

I was also cheered and urged on by another man who said, "Come on, Shirley, see it as a challenge. I mean you could have the most marvelous converted garage in town if only you put your mind to it." From then on I upset my mother dreadfully by drawing garage plans on the backs of envelopes and working out how 3 of us could live in an area 12 by 14 ft. But the point had been hammered home. Everything is easier once you face it and galvanize into action rather than being appalled and paralyzed by it.

What to Do on Doomsday

Doomsday happens in every family sometime—when Father's job is eliminated, Mother's secret extravagances come home to roost, you're hit with devastating medical expenses, the accountant turns out to have been a crook, you lost your case with the IRS, or whatever. The essential feature of the situation is that the money just won't go around, there are too many bills and not enough money to pay them.

When doomsday comes to your family you *can* cope with it, if you remember 2 basic facts. First, all the people you owe money to are chiefly interested in getting their money, not in suing you, which will only cost them more money. Second, as these disasters happen to everyone it's nothing to be ashamed of, but something to be calmly explained to your creditors as soon as possible.

MAKE A LIST OF ALL YOUR MAJOR CREDITORS: This would probably include installment debts, charge accounts, the mortgage, and such services as the telephone and the gas and electric utilities if you've let them run up. Also note how much you owe each of them. Then, make a careful analysis of your income, or your income plus savings if you have to, work out how much you can afford to pay each of them on an installment basis. This is called "keeping your credit good," and it could help to keep you off the dreaded credit blacklist or from going into bankruptcy that can make it tough as hell to get loans, credit cards, and mortgages for the rest of your life.

Write each creditor a letter. Direct your letter to the attention of the credit office. Explain that your family is in a financial crisis (no need to go into elaborate details), and ask whether they would accept payment in installments— quote the sum you have decided you can afford. Most reasonable concerns will accept this offer. Then it's simply a question of cutting down expenses until all your debts are paid. Two things to remember:

- Be sure to send your letter *before* the creditors start demanding money.
- Don't overestimate your income or underestimate the cost of living when working out what you can afford to pay off. Offer less rather than more, so as not to risk defaulting on your promise, in which case you might risk maximum wrath and penalties.

A GUIDE TO CREDIT AND BANKING

OUR SIGNATURE SOCIETY

Because paying in cash these days is somewhat suspect, carrying cash has become almost passé. In the smarter shops the salespeople turn their noses up at the sight of real dollars. We live in the "signature society" (we may soon see thumbprint credit cards). To be sure, there are special situations, such as gambling in Las Vegas or Monte Carlo or ordering a martini alone in a strange bar, where silver and the folding stuff are still held in high esteem. And, of course, you need the minted moolah for tips, taxis, exact change on buses, and the odd roll of Tums. Otherwise, the world economy, and our vital part of it, runs on *paper* (checks) and *plastic* (credit cards).

This is rather amazing when you consider that a decade or so ago only people like the Queen of England or a Mafia godfather dared venture forth without a penny in their pockets. But, BEWARE, that meal or that mink may seem like a Christmas gift when all you have to do is sign a tab or a check for it. Yes, Virginia, there is a day of reckoning, and that day cometh every single month.

IF YOU CHARGE IT: Doomsday doesn't fool around if you haven't paid your charge accounts by the date due; the computers are already preparing your next bill, and penalties lurk! They can run something like 18 percent interest on your unpaid balance, loaded on to the original charge. As weeks or months go by, this can mount up—you may easily have to pay interest on the interest. *Above all other short-term obligations, along with utility bills (your power and telephone can get cut off), pay your credit card bills first.*

IF YOU WRITE CHECKS: You will obviously need to cash enough for whatever ready money you need. Otherwise, you will have deposited your income or housekeeping money or IBM dividend check in the bank, which is where they all belong. As long as your checks never exceed your deposits, your relations with your bank will be serene, smooth, and anonymous (it sounds so easy). Unless you need to borrow large sums to expand your business or to buy a house, you may never meet your friendly banker face to face.

HOW TO CHOOSE A BANK

More and more, thanks to competition for our money, banks are dropping those nasty little charges—10 cents a check, or penalties if a minimum deposit (something like $500) falls below the specified sum for free checking. The pressure on banks to lend money has brought them back into the position of begging for funds. After all, *our* deposits constitute a massive lending pool for banks. Put succinctly, it's *our* money, loaned out to others, that brings them the interest that becomes their profits. Remember this when asking a banker to lend you back what is, in effect, your own money plus interest. Banks are only hiring out money like Avis rents cars. *Don't grovel.*

SAVINGS BANKS: In some states they are now allowed to act like commercial banks and handle regular checking accounts. Savings banks often permit free checking and no minimum balance if you have a savings account with them. The savings may have to meet certain standards— $400 minimum balance, or some such—but you want to maintain some savings base anyway and this is a good way to keep it sacred. This account, of course, pays you interest, so you gain twice: The checks and checking service are free, and the bank pays you up to 5.5 percent on your savings. So I like it.

BANK STATEMENTS: When you receive these monthly notices enumerating deposits and withdrawals, immediately check your bank's arithmetic. They're not very good at it and their computers can be even worse. During a 2-year period one of my banks paid $1,800 and $3,000 into someone else's account. (Never the reverse, I noticed.) I have framed their letter of apology, which hangs over my bill hook. Always check ALL your bank statements as carefully as you check your bills. (I *collect* computer errors. Last year I "saved" $9,000 by checking every single bill.)

CREDIT LINE: Of course, where you decide to stow your money will also be a matter of what banks with what services are available where you are. Once you have picked your bank, settled on the design and color of your checks, and received a checkbook, you are ready for your debut into the signature society. It is, shall we say, generally advisable to write checks for no more than the amount of your bank balance. However, if you want to be "toujours gai, wot the 'ell, Archie," and live dangerously and can manage it without headaches, ulcers, lower back pain, or awful quarrels with your spouse, banks will certainly be happy to assist you. For a fee—a steep one, 12 percent to 18 percent—banks will extend you a line of credit, also known as an overdraft, beyond the amount in your regular checking account. The fee is charged only when you draw on that credit.

CREDIT CARDS—PLASTIC MONEY

BANK CREDIT CARDS: You can, as explained above, work out an overdraft arrangement with a special line of credit approved by your banker. Or you can do it on one of the bank credit cards that you can apply for, Visa and Mastercharge, to mention 2 popular ones. These plastic cards are free until used, then you have to pay interest if the bill is not paid in full by the due date. However, there is an increasing tendency among banks to start charging for these cards if the holder doesn't use them.

When you get your card, there will be a specified line of credit you are permitted to draw on. Depending on the bank's interpretation of your prospective solvency and your character, you will get a credit line ranging from about $500 to $1,500 or $2,000.

Be wary of interest rates. The bank's very willingness to aid and abet you in getting credit should be a warning. The whole thing, if you use it, will cost you money and lead you into temptation, which is what you ask The Lord to lead you out of. If you accept that fact (but remember that interest on loans and installment accounts is deductible from your income tax), the cheapest way to use the card is to borrow money on it, as opposed to charging purchases in a store, because the interest on the monetary debt is less than the interest on purchases. In New York, for example, the banks charge 12 percent on money they lend you, but on charged store purchases, the interest can be all of 18 percent. (And you thought 12 percent was high!) Generally speaking, it's cheapest to borrow the necessary money from a bank.

This difference in interest rates is pointed up in the following example: You have decided on the spur to take a weekend jaunt to Sea Island or Bermuda. You dropped into the airline office and charged your $400 round-trip ticket on Mastercharge. You then went around the corner to the bank and charged $200 in cash on the same card. When the statement arrives, it lists the charges at 2 interest rates—the airline ticket at 18 percent, the money at 12 percent. (The related information in the following paragraph is worth reading. It may save you a lot of money.)

You decide to pay back the indebtedness a little faster than the recommended rate (the minimum payments are calculated on an annual basis), and you think you'd prefer to pay back the more expensive charges first. Forget it. For paying-off purposes, your 2 payments are lumped together in one sum, and the interest on that sum is calculated in proportion to each of the 2 charges, which would be an overall 16 percent in the example I've given here.

The moral is, write a check for the fare or else use the credit card to get cash at the cheaper interest rate, with which to pay for the ticket.

The only way to avoid paying the 18 percent charge is to pay the whole thing back at once, but even then by that time you've had a month's charge and you're somewhere into the second month.

The interest on these accounts is like a taxi meter—it never stops running. After you write your check settling the whole caboodle, you'll get another bill for something like $1.50—interest that accumulated while you were writing your check to pay off the borrowed amount.

OTHER POPULAR CARDS: But the bank cards are only one small segment of our plastic card world. There are other big names—American Express, Diners Club, Carte Blanche—dear to the hearts of the expense account crowd and jet setters. These require an annual fee, presently $20, which is paid by the cardholder in advance. These companies have also discovered the device of charging interest on unpaid balances—that 18 percent again. There is, however, at the time of this writing, no interest charged on American Express card accounts, which must be paid in full on receipt of your monthly bill. This is the one I have. (Although American Express has made embarrassing mistakes about it. I now carry their letters of apology when I travel abroad.) I only use it for travel.

Credit cards are certainly very helpful in business entertaining: By simply saving your receipts you have a record for your expense account, or for the tax man (if you are claiming unreimbursed entertainment deductions necessary for your business). They are also useful in traveling since you can charge meals and lodgings on the ubiquitous plastic and don't have to carry large sums of cash, or plan to take more than you reckon you need, in case of an emergency. (There never *is* an emergency and you always spend the emergency money.)

Then there are *gasoline credit cards.* Nearly all the major oil companies have their own credit card system, and these are invaluable. You can fill 'er up, buy tires, have your car serviced, and have limited repairs done on the road, without a cent ever changing hands. In the gasoline line, you should have all the cards you can garner if you plan to drive across the United States since many of the oil companies are regional. You will drive across many an invisible line where one company's stations end and another's begin.

Unless you have become a deadbeat in the midst of all this temptation to spend, these cards are childishly easy to collect. It's almost as though the credit cards reproduce themselves. The initial credit investigation for American Express is more probing than others, which may account for the fact that around the world it's the most universally recognized (this is important), accepted, and respected card. However, the most prestigious card of all is the International Air Travel Card, for which your company has to put a bond and to which you can charge just about anything.

Another part of the plastic world is represented by *department store charge account cards.* These are issued in different colors and with variations on the standard rectangle to demonstrate their exclusivity. They too have the 18 percent interest "penalty" for laggards, stiff enough to stimulate prompt payment. But there is no initial charge for these cards, nor is there an annual fee. You are billed only if you use it. And it can be a valuable credit reference. In Chicago, a Marshall Field card carries almost as much power as a reference from the President.

THE PERILS OF THE PLASTIC WORLD: You must exercise a certain amount of self-control. Don't use the cards just because they're there. They presuppose fiscal maturity. If you haven't got it, face it, and don't let one of those seductive shapes into your purse. *A cardaholic is a cashaholic on a time fuse.*

There is another peril. Your credit cards could be stolen. There are hairy tales of credit sprees taken by exuberant card-thieves who joyride to Nice and Hong Kong, throw parties at posh restaurants and hotels, and charge all manner of broads, baubles, and booze before the real world catches up. If your credit cards should be snatched NOTIFY THE ISSUING COMPANY, PRONTO. You will probably be liable only for the first $50 charged on each stolen card, and perhaps not even for that. But get them canceled immediately on discovery of the theft, and keep proof of your cancellation. (Naturally, you have all your credit card numbers listed at home in your organization file. Remember to note the telephone numbers and addresses of the issuing companies.) The fewer cards you have, the fewer you have to chase and replace if they are lost or stolen.

BORROWING MONEY

NEVER, NEVER borrow money from loan agencies to pay off your debts. Borrow from your bank, which can be a tidy way to consolidate your debts into one lump sum, enabling you to clear the debts and repay the bank on the installment basis. You may at least want to consolidate charge account debts (which carry heavy interest) into a single bank loan and a single interest payment. If you can handle the crisis yourself, you can spare yourself heavy interest payments, especially to those *usurious loan agencies*. Next time you watch one of those easy and persuasive gentlemen on television suggesting that you "just pick up the phone for immediate relief," remember that he is offering you long-term misery.

Although financial matters can never be straightforward, it's smart to have a simple guide for money matters. Besides such admirable and weighty books as Sylvia Porter's *Money Book* (Doubleday) and the *Book of Family Finance* (Time-Life), there are useful government pamphlets such as the U.S. Department of Agriculture, Division of Home Economics' *Managing Your Money*, available from the U.S. Government Printing Office, Superintendent of Documents, Washington, D.C. 20402, for the modest outlay of 25 cents prepaid, which is one way of getting some of that tax money back.

EMERGENCY PLANNING

A major theme of this book is that, as far as possible and reasonable, you should strive for independence. You should be able to take care of your home, performing certain easy-to-manage repairs without calling for help from expensive or unavailable experts.

In emergencies such as hurricanes, blizzards, floods, and earthquakes, the skills of self-sufficiency are more than desirable: They may be essential to you and your family's survival. Before, or until, a disaster actually strikes, people tend to be amazingly optimistic that it can't happen to them. Because people are unprepared, climatic disasters cause many hundreds of unnecessary casualties each year. You should draw up a basic survival strategy now.

A CHECKLIST FOR SURVIVAL

- You should always have ample reserves of food and drinking water on hand. You can't count on a freezer in case of prolonged power breakdown, so make sure you have sufficient supplies of dry and canned goods stored and in good condition.
- Keep a spare transistor radio, especially if you're in the country, with fresh batteries in some accessible hiding place. It might be a vital link to the rest of the world.
- The moment you hear of an approaching hurricane or blizzard, or feel quake tremors, sterilize all your bathtubs and sinks by washing them out with water plus 2 cups of chlorine bleach for the bath and 1 cup for the sink. Fill with water. Also fill sterilized plastic garbage cans with water. In case you need to purify water, keep some halazone tablets (available from drugstores) on hand in the medicine chest.
- Have alternate sources of heat and light: gas and electricity and firewood and a butane or solid fuel stove; and butane or kerosene lamps, candles, and a flashlight.
- Check your fire extinguishers to see that they are fully loaded and in good condition.
- Make sure your family knows exactly what to do in case of fire. Hold a fire drill at least every 6 months.
- If you have an all-mechanized kitchen, check that you have some old-fashioned, nonelectric tools such as an eggbeater, a bottle opener, and a can opener.
- Get a first-aid kit and manual. In addition to the standard first-aid items, consider stocking aspirin, Rhulicream (for poison ivy), rubbing alcohol, and an antidiarrhoea preparation.
- When severe storm warnings are broadcast, batten down or bring inside everything that might blow away, such as patio furniture, storm shutters, garden tools, awnings, garbage pails, and window screens. Put your car in the garage; flying objects, such as side-view mirrors, can be lethal.
- Keep a supply of books and, for small children, crayons, paper, and games (the kids may even forget all about TV).

To SURVIVE A FLOOD: If you are warned of a possible flood in time, and decide that you must evacuate your house, turn off the main electrical switch to your house. Tape plastic wrap around electrical outlets. If possible, move appliances, mattresses, and valuables to the top floor. Then evacuate.

To SURVIVE A HURRICANE: If ordered to evacuate, turn off all gas and electric appliances, and leave at once. Otherwise, stay indoors and keep a door open on the *leeward* side of the house, the side opposite the direction the wind is coming from. Batten down or remove all possible flying objects.

To SURVIVE AN EARTHQUAKE: Put all fires out (such as stove and fireplace), turn off the gas supply and do not light matches. Explosions from ruptured gas mains are a major threat. Crawl under a table, preferably in an inner room, to avoid falling debris. If electrical wiring is shorting out, turn off the power at the meter box. If you should be caught in a car, stop immediately and *stay inside*; if a power line falls on the car, wait for help.

DURING AND AFTER A DISASTER, YOU WILL NEED HELP: Listen carefully to your radio; if you have to evacuate, broadcasts will tell you where to go. If the telephone lines are not down, call the local or state civil defense agency or the Red Cross for details of available aid, such as shelter, medical care, food. Needless to say, keep cool and cooperate with the authorities to help those worse off than yourself.

After the disaster, as soon as possible notify your insurance agent of any damage. Your policy may cover such postcrisis costs as staying in a motel until you can move back into your house. Keep an exact record of your losses, for the insurance company and for your income tax returns, on which you may enter losses over $100 due to acts of nature, as deductible items. If your locality has been declared a disaster area, you may be eligible for low-interest government loans to help you repair your home or business property. The Department of Housing and Urban Development may provide up to $5,000 for family or individual relief, which does not have to be repaid. Check your local government to find what relief is available and how to apply for it.

To SURVIVE A POWER FAILURE:The great blackout of 1965 which supposedly caused the Great Birthrate Leap in 1966 and left thousands of households in the northeastern U.S. without electricity for many hours, could happen again anytime. Shorter blackouts occur all the time, all over Canada. Against this kind of emergency, and others, such as hurricanes and floods, that can knock out your power supply (see "Crisis" chapter), you should have a variety of strategies. Make sure you have alternative methods of lighting, heating and cooking. (Apart from its other merits, one reason I prefer a gas range is that it doesn't fold up in a blackout.)

Lighting: Be sure to have plenty of candles on hand. Instead of throwing them out, you might just as well save the ends of dinner-party candles in a paper bag for emergencies.

Keep a propane camping lantern around. Hide a box of matches, a flashlight, spare battery and candles some place where the menfolk can't find them. Keep two flashlights for the entrance hall.

Hide away a cheap-o transistor radio and separate batteries; as the only means of knowing what on earth is going on in a blacked-out world, a radio can be a sanity-saver. Don't forget to check the batteries occasionally.

Heating: Various "space heaters" that use wood, coal, gas or oil are available. Any portable space heater must be used with caution as it uses up the oxygen in a room and gives off combustion gases which can be suffocating. If you use an unvented (not connected to a chimney or other outlet) space heater, make sure that the room is well ventilated.

An old, dependable heat source that has come back into importance as fuel costs have mounted is the wood burning stove. These are readily available (through large mail-order stores, for example) and serve the dual purpose of providing heat during a power failure and of supplementing the central heating during exceptionally cold weather. You can get various modifications of the charming old Franklin stove (which you can also cook on, by the way). If you have fireplaces, always keep a handy pile of dry logs and kindling, in case the furnace goes on the fritz. The reason that the nineteenth century made such a fuss about dust is because there was such a lot of it, due to wood and coal burning fires.

Cooking: Apart from making tea and coffee and heating his shaving water, you should have no real need to cook food—only heat it——during a blackout—provided you have ample supplies stored for just such emergencies (see "Food" chapter). However, if you want to live it up with hot meals as usual, you can always tuck a billy can into the fireplace and put saucepans on top of a Franklin stove or potbelly stove. I have a small camping gas burner, with cylinders of gas.

WARNING! Make sure that ALL appliances are unplugged during a blackout. They can be damaged, or even catch fire, when the power surges back. (What to do with your freezer during a power failure is discussed in "Crisis" chapter.)

THE MOST DANGEROUS GAME (HOME HAZARDS)

Do you tempt fate? Why should the gods be specially kind to you and protect Grandma from breaking her neck on your loose stair carpet or keep your 2-year-old's nightgown from catching fire? (Fifteen seconds is all it takes for a child to burn to death.)

Here is a checklist of causes of the most frequent home accidents. Give yourself one mark for each of the hazards that apply to your home. If you score more than 10, you may be living in a deathtrap and should do something about it.

Making your home less dangerous than a freeway on a foggy holiday isn't difficult, it merely involves correcting the hazards listed below, most of which can be checked out any rainy weekend and dealt with on subsequent ones. Others involve personal habits that you can change immediately.

HAZARDS THAT CAUSE FALLS

- Loose stair carpet.
- Frayed or worn patch of carpet.
- Missing floor tile or loose brick on front steps.

- Faulty stepladder.
- Using swivel chairs or stools instead of a properly balanced stepladder.
- Slippery floor, especially if you have scatter rugs.
- Spills that aren't wiped up immediately.
- Cleaning equipment left in unexpected places, such as a broom or bucket at the bend of a stairwell.
- Trailing electric extension cords.
- Poor lighting in hallways and on stairs, especially if you have a lurking cat.
- A step in an unexpected place that the family knows well, but has therefore forgotten to warn a visitor about.
- No grab bars on bath or shower wall, particularly for the very young, the very old, and the very pregnant, or those who are apt to feel dizzy after a too-hot bath or from getting up suddenly. People of all ages and conditions slip in the shower or tub—it's one of the commonest causes of accidents in the United States— so put in solidly mounted grips or grab rails (*not* towel rails). Use nonslip, rubber suction-cup mats in tub or shower. Better yet, put in permanent, nonslip strips or decals.

HAZARDS THAT CAUSE CUTS

- Razor blades left lying around.
- Broken glass left unswept.
- Sharp knives left in a kitchen sink full of murky water.
- Sharp cooking knives left in a kitchen drawer. Keep them in a jar, blades down, or buy a knife-holder for countertop or wall.
- Walking barefoot or kneeling without a mat when cleaning.

HAZARDS THAT CAUSE FIRES, BURNS, SCALDING

- Unscreened fires of all types.
- Cigarette butts that aren't properly snuffed out, particularly in bedrooms.
- Clothes left to dry in front of an open wood fire or electric heater.
- Newspapers or books left in front of an open fire.
- Furniture left too close to a fire.

- Careless use of an electric iron, such as leaving it on a working surface or table without switching it off; accidentally standing a switched-on iron on top of its cord.
- Faulty electrical equipment, particularly frayed extension cords and make-do plugs and sockets.
- Jugs, bowls, and pans containing scalding fluids left any place where small children can reach up and pull them over onto themselves.
- Saucepan handles sticking out from the stove.
- Grease-filled frying pans left unattended over a gas burner.

CHILD HAZARDS

- Children need protecting from their own passion for picking up, sticking fingers into, disassembling, or eating anything within reach of their tiny tentacled hands. All *electric outlets* should, ideally, be above adult waist height and preferably of the shuttered type that children can't poke with their fingers.
- All *breakables* and *medicines* should be kept out of children's reach. Pills should always be bought in containers with kiddie-proof tops.
- Don't leave *plastic bags* within reach of children. If a child puts one over his head, he may suffocate.
- A baby should not be given a *pillow* until after his first birthday, as he might easily roll over and smother himself (besides, it's healthier for babies to sleep flat).
- Don't give a baby any *lumpy food* until he's old enough to chew. Never leave a young child alone while he's eating.
- Don't leave a child alone in the *bath*—let the phone or doorbell go on ringing.
- Never leave *sharp objects* where children can reach them. That includes knives, pins, needles, safety pins, nails, saws, scissors, axes, and meat-grinder blades.

SENIOR CITIZEN HAZARDS

- Older people are in constant danger of falling and breaking their brittle bones, especially if they stubbornly refuse to face the fact that they aren't as •rightly as they used to be. *Nonslip bath mats* are essential. In addition to these and bathtub *grab bars*, a handgrip mounted next to the toilet bowl can be a great help to the elderly.

- Use a *nonslip polish* on your floors. Make sure scatter rugs are firmly anchored with nonskid rubber backings. Make sure banisters are solid.
- Don't leave toys, shopping baskets, or other *obstructions* in hallways or on staircases (which should be well lit). Plug a night light into a bathroom socket.

KITCHEN HAZARDS

- Most common *household cleansers are poisonous* and must be kept out of the reach of young children. It may seem a ludicrous idea—you may sniff and call me the Mary Poppins of the Cleaning Closet—but speaking as one who has been poisoned, I urge you to have a lock on your cleaning storage cabinet. If possible do not keep cleaning materials in a dark clutter under the sink, but on a pull-out shelf, where they can be properly organized and picked out. If (as is highly likely) you haven't got a high pull-out shelf, use a big cheap supermarket tray or cat-litter tray and stand your cleansers in that, or use a couple of square pails.
- As previously noted, don't let *saucepan handles* project over the edge of the stove to be bumped into: The hot contents of the pan could spill over you or your child.

ELECTRICAL HAZARDS

- *Always* switch everything off before investigating any electrical trouble. Check for loose connections, frayed wires or extension cords, and possible electrical overloads. (Like you, there's only so much a circuit can bear.) Never put electrical appliances into water.
- *Don't* lace your rooms with intricate snaking writhes of extension cords, which you can easily trip over. In the case of semipermanent installments like lamps, radios, and TV sets, get the wires off the floors by stapling or taping them to a molding. Even when you temporarily plug in a stereo or movie projector, wind the excess cord around a cheap plastic spool.
- If a plug feels warm, if an appliance fizzles or crackles, TURN IT OFF. Have the appliance, as well as loose sockets or cracked plugs, adjusted immediately.

- *Don't* clean an electric stove until you have disconnected it, or you'll risk an electric shock.
- *Don't* fill an electric kettle when it's plugged in.
- *Never* use a portable electric appliance near a water source without extra caution. This particularly applies to plug-in heaters or radios in the bathroom.
- *Never* touch a switch with a wet hand or damp cloth. Never leave an electrical lead plugged in, and switch on with the other end of the lead exposed.

GAS HAZARDS

- Never look for a *gas leak* with a naked flame or Pffffttt!!! Use a flashlight.
- Always light the oven as soon as the gas is turned on. Never leave *gas burners* on when you have finished cooking—they can dangerously deplete the oxygen in a room.
- If a *gas jet* isn't working efficiently, get it fixed. Your appliance dealer or utility company service representatives will usually be available to check appliances.
- *If you smell gas,* open all windows and doors, turn off the main switch, and phone the utility company for emergency service. In most cases the company will send a radio-connected team faster than you can say HELP. If gas runs out for any reason, make sure to check that all outlets are turned off. When the gas comes on, **remember to rekindle the pilot lights.**
- If you want to *locate a leak* rub a piece of wet soap or dishwashing liquid along a suspected gas pipe leak; bubbles should form at the leak! If it is a small leak it can be *very temporarily* sealed with chewing gum or a Band-Aid until the service people arrive.

FIRE PREVENTION AND PROTECTION

Nearly 7,000 people lose their lives in home fires each year in the United States. Most of them are the very young or the very old. Most of those lives could have been saved. For you, fire prevention and protection is not a matter of statistics but of elementary precautionary planning that can and should keep superwoman and family out of the obit columns.

Obviously, you're not going to drop this book the moment you finish this chapter and rush around your house making like a junior fire marshal. But you should start thinking about fire—the sooner the better. It would take you all of 10 minutes to check obvious fire violations.

FIRE HAZARDS

- Don't overload any domestic appliance: If your washing machine or clothes dryer is designated to cope with 10 lb. of laundry, find out how much this is translated into towels and shirts, and never feed it more. Otherwise the motor could burn out and start a fire.
- Empty the lint trap of the clothes dryer or the engine can overheat.
- Don't hesitate to repair any electrical equipment that shows scorch marks or emits a burning smell. Something is wrong somewhere, and if it is scorching now, it might burst into flames next time.
- Don't allow the extension cord from an electric kettle or frying pan to drag across the stove.
- If an extension cord or cable is not long enough, get a new one, rather than joining 2 short ones together.
- If you *must* use multiple socket attachments, remember that a lot of appliances wired to one outlet can overload the circuit and blow a fuse, or overheat and start a fire. The safest method is one appliance, one socket.
- Never leave candles burning unattended.
- Keep matches and lighters out of the reach of children.
- If you have to run an extension cord under a carpet check the state of the cord at least 4 times a year.
- Don't deliberately dim a table lamp by covering it: Buy a lower wattage bulb.
- Gas and air form an explosive mixture. If you have a gas furnace, water heater, or stove, make sure you are ready to light it BEFORE you turn on the gas. If the pilot light does not ignite the burners at once, turn

it off and see whether the pilot is properly lighted.
- Don't dry clothes over a stove.
- If you have to leave a frying pan filled with hot fat unattended, turn off the heat and move the pan away.
- If you have an open fire, your chimney should be cleaned once a year. Keep the hearth and surrounding area clean and empty.
- Don't hang a mirror over the fireplace—it invites people to get too close and risk getting burned.
- Don't put anything on a mantelpiece that a child might try to reach up and grab.
- Never put furniture or clothing close to a lighted fire.
- Never leave a room without putting a screen in front of an open fire. Don't build the fire up too high—the chimney might catch fire, or burning logs or coal fall out. Don't use gasoline or kerosene to light the fire— you might set fire to the room.
- Never leave a lighted cigarette on an ashtray where it can fall off. *Never empty ashtrays or throw matches into a wastepaper basket or a plastic garbage can.*
- Don't smoke in bed—it causes thousands of fires a year, many with fatal results.
- Don't leave cleaning or lighter fluid lying around. Lock it up.
- Keep aerosol-type pressure containers away from heat. *Never* burn or puncture them.

How to Handle a Fire

QUICK ACTION IS ESSENTIAL WHEN SOMETHING CATCHES FIRE: YOUR REACTION SHOULD BE AUTOMATIC, SO CAREFULLY READ THE NEXT SHORT SECTION.

The main thing to remember is to check your fire escape method and fire extinguishers. Make sure (1) that means of escape from second- or third-story rooms have been provided (one of those folding ladders or even a knotted rope); (2) that fire extinguishers are checked about every 3 months and refilled, if necessary, according to the manufacturer's instructions. Every household should have at least 2 fire extinguishers, and everyone in the house should know where they are kept and how to work them; (3) that each family member knows what to do in case of fire. My father used to enjoy drilling his 6 children: We all had fun throwing dirt from the plant pots on the carpet, aiming a soda syphon at the armchair, and being awarded chocolate cookies for the fastest times with the extinguisher. (Mother didn't enjoy the fire drills so much.)

IF A PERSON CATCHES FIRE: Stop the victim from running, which only fans the flames. Don't try to strip his clothes off. Never throw water at him as the extra shock can be more dangerous than the flames, and even fatal. Smother the flames by rolling the victim on the floor in a coat, rug, blanket, curtain, pillow, or anything similar that is at hand. When the flames are out, make sure that no part of the clothing is still smoldering. Call for an ambulance.

When buying children's clothing, check the label to make sure the garment is "flameproof." (Keep in mind that "Tris," a flame-resistant treatment, has been banned by the federal government as a suspected carcinogen.)

SMALL FIRES: A cup of water, some baking soda, salt, sand, or even earth thrown from a plant pot may be enough to stop a small fire. Or you may be able to suffocate it with a cloth, rug, curtain, or coat. Shut doors and windows to prevent it from blazing again.

To extinguish a fire in a wastepaper basket, cover it with a tin tray, a drawer, a telephone directory, or another wastepaper basket.

If a frying pan catches fire, turn off the heat, douse the fire with salt or smother the flames with a doormat or rug. When fighting any small oil, paint, gasoline, or grease fire, never use water, or the liquid will probably splash and the fire will spread. Use an extinguisher.

If the fat in a frying pan overheats, turn off the heat, but DO NOT MOVE the pan because movement of air against overheated oil can cause it to burst into flames.

If your barbecue catches fire, it can be put out with water or sand. Be especially cautious in dry weather.

If an electric appliance catches fire, DON'T POUR WATER ON IT. Use a fire extinguisher. Unplug the appliance or turn off the main switch.

If a chimney catches fire, close all windows and doors. If possible (and it probably won't be), close the top of the chimney with bricks or wet sacks; wet sacking or rags pushed into the chimney will help to slow down the fire. Close the damper to shut off air, if possible.

Lots of salt and sand will extinguish a fire in the grate. After the fire is out make sure no woodwork in or around the chimney is smoldering.

If *curtains catch fire*, pull them down before attempting to quench the flames.

If *a television catches fire*, throw a blanket, rug, or thick coat over it, and unplug the set.

BIG FIRES: If you can't *immediately* extinguish a fire, get everybody out of the building in whatever they're wearing, no matter how little. Never stop to dress or rescue valuables. Call the fire department at once from the nearest outside telephone. Don't assume someone else has already done so; 2 calls are better than none. NEVER GO BACK INTO THE BUILDING, not for the family jewels, documents, or pets.

When an alert is sounded, never leave a buiding via an elevator. The power might fail, the elevator might stop between floors, and you'd be trapped; *use the stairs or fire escape.*

If cut off by fire, close the door of the room and any other opening and *block up any cracks* with bedding, towels, rugs, clothes.

If you're trapped in a building, try to attract attention from the windows. If the room fills with smoke, *lean out the window.* If you cannot do this, *lie close to the floor,* where the air is cleaner, and *take short breaths* until you hear the fire engines.

If you have to escape before help arrives, *make a rope* by knotting together sheets or similar material and tie it to a bed or other heavy piece of furniture. If you cannot make a rope and the situation becomes intolerable, drop cushions or bedding from the window to break your fall. But don't try jumping from any height above the second floor unless firefighters are there to catch you.

If you do have to jump, wait until the very last moment, and then lower yourself out, feet first. Hang by your arms from the windowsill, then try and go limp as you fall.

WHICH FIRE EXTINGUISHER TO CHOOSE: Water and sand are the oldest, simplest fire-fighting tools, especially when in a pail. But you'll also need a more modern alternative, and there is a bewildering array from which to choose.

There are *3 basic types of fire* in the home: *Type A* consists of fires involving combustible solids, such as woods, textiles, paper, and garbage; *Type B* involves inflammable liquids, such as paint, grease, oil, gasoline; *Type C* includes electrical wiring or appliances

There are 5 *different types of fire extinguishers:* ranging from the old-fashioned water type, which can be used only to fight Type A fires, to the foam variety, which is effective against Types A and B but can cause electrical shock if used against Type C.

So, instead of getting 5 different types of extinguishers, *get one multipurpose type.* This should be labeled ABC. It should bear the stamp of the Underwriters Laboratory UL or Factory Mutual FM. It should come with precise directions, not only for use but also for refilling when necessary. With a single multipurpose unit one farmer friend has several times saved his whole house from going up.

CAUTION: The National Fire Protection Association warns against those small extinguishers in aerosol cans, which are inadequate and unreliable.

Recommended. A dry chemical 5 lb. all-purpose rechargeable unit. Cost (with mounting bracket): about $22. You should have one in the kitchen and at least one upstairs, *conveniently placed for use but also strategically located so that you can use it on the way to an escape route.*

Remember. Everyone in the house should know what to do in case of fire. Your family should have fire drills at least twice a year, so that everyone understands clearly how and where to get out, with both primary escape exits and alternatives in case, say, the stairs are burning or the fire is on the roof. You should also tape fire exit instructions in your guest room, as they do in hotels.

Fire Detection

A vast and costly complex called the Early Warning System is supposed to protect us from a Russian invasion. A small and inexpensive EWS should, right now, exist in your home, to warn you of fire in time to put it out or escape.

Smoke and heat detectors have been hailed by fire prevention experts, police, insurance analysts, and consumer groups as one of the greatest fire-fighting weapons since water (which, as we know, is not always very effective in fighting fire).

These clever gadgets *do not prevent fires or put them out;* rather, they are *fire protection* devices. They are attached to the ceiling, and on detecting smoke, sound a piercing alarm. Since 1973, California has made smoke alarm devices mandatory in all new houses and mobile homes. The National Fire Protection Association estimates that wide public use of smoke detectors could reduce fire-caused fatalities by 50 percent to 60 percent a year.

Fire marshals and other safety experts all recommend battery-powered units, preferably those that show a light or chirp at you when the battery runs down. To be sure you have to replace the batteries about once a year (put it on your New Year check list) but on the other hand, the alarms will work if the power is cut off.

A happy footnote to this gloomy subject is that 6 out of 10 top casualty insurance companies will give you a 2 percent rebate on your home policy if you have installed fire detectors. At about $30 each, smoke detectors can actually save money as well as lives.

SHORT, SHORT FIRST AID

In an Emergency

Keep calm. Control yourself. Call a doctor or ambulance as soon as possible. Your main job is to soothe and reassure. If you can't keep calm (and it's not easy when you see your child's face covered with blood), you won't think sensibly. SO DON'T YOU MOVE. FORCE YOURSELF TO THINK FIRST. Don't move the victim—he might already be injured, and further movement might rupture his spleen or something. (Watch injured ice hockey players. They're never moved until the doctor comes.)

Most people die in accidents during the first 7 minutes, so you must move fast. Because you probably won't be able to recall complex instructions in a crisis, here is encapsulated, emergency first aid:

- Avoid further injury. Turn off power if the victim is suffering from electric shock. (Don't touch him with your bare hands before doing this or you may be electrocuted.)
- If the victim is unconscious, prevent his tongue from blocking airways by tilting his head backward. If no breathing is apparent, apply the kiss of life (see below).
- Control bleeding by pressing hard around the wound. Apply bandage firmly and raise the bleeding limb.
- Turn an unconscious victim into the "coma position." Stomach to the ground, with one knee bent and drawn up to waist level. Turn his head sideways so the victim doesn't choke on his own vomit. Pull elbows away from the body.
- Immediately send for help.
- Keep back crowds, if necessary.

COMA POSITION

The Kiss of Life

If you think the victim may have stopped breathing, apply the kiss of life as follows:

Lay the victim on his back, open his mouth, and press down his tongue to check that nothing is blocking the air passage; tilt his head backward with your hand under his neck. Kneel or lie down by his side. Expand his chest by slowly blowing hard into his mouth (about 10 times a minute for an adult) while you *pinch his nostrils shut so that the air goes into his lungs,* not out his nose. Keep it up until a doctor arrives. First aid is to be given while awaiting medical help, *not instead of it.*

Shock

Every injury or accident brings with it a certain degree of shock (sometimes even to onlookers who are otherwise unharmed), which leaves the victim shaken, giddy, very pale, with blurred vision, shallow breathing, and sometimes loss of consciousness. Reassure the victim. Lay him flat on his stomach, loosen constricting clothing, cover him. Turn his head sideways so that if there is any vomiting it won't choke and suffocate him.

Give nothing by mouth, *particularly not any alcoholic beverages*. Don't apply hot water bottles to the victim's body. Remember that shivering is nature's way of keeping the metabolism going. If the injury is severe, don't let him drink anything as he may require a general anesthetic later, and this must be given on an empty stomach. Severe injuries, which may be internal and not immediately obvious, induce a more severe form of shock in which the casualty collapses and becomes deathly pale, a very serious condition. Make certain that professional help is summoned.

HOW TO DELIVER A BABY

(Even if you're not a cop or a cab driver it's something you might want to know.)

- Get the mother to lie down on her back (preferably on a bed) with her knees bent back to her chest. Reassure and soothe her; sound firm, calm, and optimistic; encourage and praise her.
- DO NOT TRY TO PULL THE BABY OUT.
- As the baby starts to appear, support it with your cupped hands and then forearms so that it doesn't flop around or fall into the blood or other waste material coming from the mother.
- DO NOT PULL OR CUT THE UMBILICAL CORD.
- If the baby appears with the *water bag or membrane* over its head or face, take hold of the sac between your fingers and tear it (it's easy), so that the water can run out and the baby will be able to breathe.
- Immediately the baby is free from the mother, make sure it's breathing. Drain off any fluid in the baby's throat or nose by wrapping a towel around its feet and hold the baby by the ankles, upside down. DO

NOT PULL ON THE CORD. The baby should start crying and breathing as the fluid runs out—but you may find you need to stroke its throat up toward the mouth to clear the fluid.

- Give mouth-to-mouth resuscitation if the baby doesn't breathe or cry quickly. Lie the baby flat on its back and cover nose and mouth with your mouth and gently breathe short puffs into his mouth—about every five seconds. Stop as soon as the baby starts to breathe.
- Wrap the baby in a towel, blanket or newspaper, then give it to its mother, gently laying him on his side across the mother's stomach with its head lowered and facing away from the mother's face.
- The placenta (afterbirth) will be pancake sized and is expelled from the mother's womb about twenty to thirty minutes after the birth, and will still be attached to the baby by the cord. DON'T CUT THE CORD. Wrap afterbirth separately in a bit of cloth or plastic bag, but leave the cord to hang slackly from the baby. Put the wrapped afterbirth next to the baby and then wrap them together securely in a towel or blanket: This will stop the placenta from falling and pulling on the cord.
- If no help arrives after a couple of hours, cut the cord by tying a piece of string or clean strip of cloth about 4 in. (10 cm) from the baby's navel. Cut on the side of the placenta, using a knife or pair of scissors which you have sterilized by holding in a flame or boiling in water.

And I hope they ask you to be godmother . . .

EQUIPPING A FIRST-AID KIT

Waterproof adhesive bandages, such as Band-Aids

Waterproof adhesive tape

Absorbent cotton

Sterile gauze

Scissors

Thermometer

Antiseptic cream, such as Bacitracin

Painkiller, such as aspirin

Milk of magnesia (anticonstipation)

Kaopectate (antidiarrhea)

Disinfectant, such as hydrogen peroxide (for

Tweezers (for bee stings, thorns, splinters)	cuts and scrapes)
Fine needles	Bicarbonate of soda
Eyewash and cup	Ointment, such as
Pen light	Rhulicream (for insect
Medicine glass	bites, poison ivy and
Safety pins	oak, sunburn)
Rubbing alcohol	Smelling salts
Cough medicine	Petroleum jelly
	Tourniquet

Keep out of reach of children, but *not* in a locked cupboard and not in the bathroom where a child might get to it and gorge on aspirin.

First-Aid Measures for Specific Injuries

ANIMAL BITES: Wash the wound with clear cold water, being careful not to disturb any blood clots. Pat dry and cover with a bandage. Go to a doctor or nearest hospital. Tetanus or antirabies injections may be necessary. If possible, catch the animal and have a veterinarian test for rabies.

BURNS: The cause is either dry heat or hot fat or oil. A burn or scald is automatically a sterile area, which is a great help in healing the wound.

A *scald* is caused by moist heat, as from a kettle. Hold such burns under cold running water, then apply antiseptic cream, such as Bacitracin. In the case of a *burn*, wash your hands, bathe the burned area with cold water, then cover with dry sterile gauze or a piece of freshly laundered linen. DO NOT APPLY ANY LOTION OR OINTMENT TO A MAJOR BURN. Bandage lightly if the skin is blistering, firmly if no blisters are present. Treat the patient for shock.

If a person is badly burned, either call an ambulance or wrap him in a sheet and rush to the hospital.

CHOKING: In polite Emily Post society, if you choked at the table you could turn the color of a turkey and be speechless, yet the people on either side of you would consider it polite to ignore you. *Any choking can be fatal and should be dealt with immediately.* You can die in 4 minutes.

Try to remove the obstruction. The newest treatment, known as the *Heimlich Maneuver,* is very effective. Stand behind the victim; grip him around the waist, below the rib cage; form a fist with one hand; cover your fist with the other hand; push suddenly and firmly INWARD AND UPWARD. When the choking has subsided, give the person a glass of water. If the victim has turned blue, rush him to the hospital.

CONCUSSION: A blow to the head can result in loss of consciousness. Place the patient in the coma position and keep him warm. Watch to see that breathing continues. If it doesn't, apply the kiss of life.

CUTS: Clean the wound with warm water and soap and cover with sterile gauze. Press edges of the wound together and apply pressure on a wound that won't stop bleeding (first make sure there is no foreign body in it, such as a glass splinter). For the really ghastly cut/hole, make a king-size wedge of some absorbent material (e.g., gauze, clean towel, or handkerchiefs), and hold or bandage over the hole with firm pressure. Don't waste time trying to clean the wound: The body is built to cope with quite a lot of dirt. Just concentrate on covering up the wound so that no more dirt gets in or blood gets out. The emergency-room doctor at the hospital can clean it when he stitches the wound and gives an antitetanus shot.

DIABETIC COMA: Give the patient a couple of lumps of sugar or a piece of chocolate. Call a doctor.

DROWNING: If the victim is breathing, place him on his stomach with his head turned to one side—water from his lungs will be expelled spontaneously. If the patient is not breathing, place him on his back and give the kiss of life. Call for an ambulance.

ELECTRIC SHOCK: Don't touch the victim before switching off the electric current or pulling out the plug, unless you wear rubber gloves, or *you* risk getting a shock. Pull the patient away. Apply artificial respiration (kiss of life procedure). Treat the patient for burns, if necessary, then for shock. Call for an ambulance.

FAINTING: Loosen any neckwear, and put the patient's head between his knees. If a HEART ATTACK is suspected, prop the patient up and on no account move him until an ambulance arrives.

FRACTURES AND SPRAINS: These are generally caused by a fall. Symptoms of a *fracture* are pain, tenderness, swelling, deformity of the limb, loss of movement and function of the limb, and ghastly bone-on-bone sounds. DO NOT MOVE THE CASUALTY OR ATTEMPT TO SET THE BONE STRAIGHT. Be very gentle and do not bandage the suspected fracture. Stop any bleeding and treat for shock. Call for an ambulance.

Firmly bandage a *sprain* and, if possible, immerse in cold water. Treat the patient for shock.

HYSTERIA: If a person becomes hysterical it is usually because he is making a bid for attention. Give it to him. Soothe him, but don't catch his hysteria (it's very contagious), and he will calm down and not cause other people to panic. Get the hysterical person away from any crowds to a quiet place as quickly as possible. Sit him down, give him a hot (nonalcoholic) drink, and keep soothing him.

NOSEBLEED: Don't hold the head back—the blood will be swallowed. Sit the patient down and calm him. Don't let him blow his nose. Pack the bleeding nostril with absorbent cotton and exert pressure against it for a few minutes.

POISONING: Call a doctor immediately, telling him, if you know, what poison the victim has taken. For instructions and antidotes for specific poisons you can also contact your local Poison Control Center (listed in the phone book). It would be a good idea to include this phone number in your household files (see p. 16).

If the person is found with an empty bottle of pills, call an ambulance (not a doctor) and save the bottle to give to the attendants. Make every attempt to keep the patient awake, such as making him stand up. If he's asleep, do your best to wake him.

Noncorrosive poisons. These include tranquilizers, sleeping pills, even aspirin, lead-based paint, and poisonous plants. They should be vomited up. Start by sticking 2 fingers down the patient's throat. If possible make him *repeatedly* swallow glasses of warm water with 2 heaping tbsp. of salt, and *repeatedly* vomit. If the casualty is unconscious, place him facedown with his head turned to one side in the coma position so he can breathe easily. If his breathing becomes very slow and feeble, apply kiss of life.

Corrosive poisons. If corrosive poisons—disinfectants, cleaning fluid, gasoline—have been taken, the lips and mouth may be burned. If the patient has taken one of these or has burned lips, do not make him vomit. Make him drink lots of water in order to dilute the poison. If unconscious, place him in the coma position. If his breathing stops, give the kiss of life.

GAS AND EXHAUST FUME POISONING: Get patient to fresh air and give kiss of life.

SOMETHING IN THE EYE: Don't rub the eye. Bathe it with an eyewash, preferably with a weak solution of salt water. Look under the eyelid if necessary. If the object can be seen (hair or grit), try to remove it with a *soft* material, such as a tissue or the corner of a clean handkerchief. Never use a hard implement for removing an object from the eye. If you can't see anything in the eye, get the patient to the emergency room of a hospital.

For eye ache or temporary blindness from too much chlorine in a swimming pool, get basin of clear (non-chlorine-treated) water, immerse face in it and open eyes.

STINGS:

Bee. The bee leaves the actual sting behind in the flesh, so extract this first with clean tweezers. Apply ammonia solution, bicarbonate of soda, or Rhulicream. Contact a doctor if you suspect an allergic reaction.

Wasp. Apply vinegar or lemon juice.

Jellyfish. The acid left on the skin should be removed with oil as soon as possible.

Mosquito. Apply ammonia solution, bicarbonate of soda, or Rhulicream.

SUFFOCATION: Remove obstruction such as plastic bag or cord. Apply the kiss of life immediately. Call for an ambulance, if necessary.

If in doubt about any first-aid treatment, telephone a doctor or the emergency room of your local hospital, which is on call 24 hours a day.

The Red Cross and other institutions offer courses that teach basic and advanced first aid, which you might want to investigate. The life you save may be your own.

THE MARAUDERS (Burglars)

The best way to foil burglars is not to have any valuables —or so says my neighbor the judge. But my girl friend

Jenny, whose San Francisco garden apartment gets burglarized every few months, says she never thought she *owned* anything valuable until she had to replace it all. You need only to be burglarized once to know that it is upsetting not just because your possessions are missing but because an aggressor has been in your home. It has the feeling of a rape, and the trauma can upset you for a long time afterward. Consider yourself lucky if your home isn't ransacked and vandalized in addition to being burglarized. My place was stripped clean in 20 minutes one Christmas Day; the only thing they left in my jewelry box was the plug to the plastic wading pool. (But oh, what fun I had with the insurance money.)

What It's Like to Be Burglarized

Probable scenario for a devastating burglary: It most likely takes place between 2 and 6 P.M. A burglar rings the doorbell; if there's no answer, he opens the door with a strip of plastic. He enters and heads straight to the back door (if there is one) or to a window that leads to a fire escape, which he opens as an escape route. He proceeds to the main bedroom, spreads out a sheet, empties the drawers on the floor, picking out jewelry and other valuables. He removes the cashbox from the wardrobe (or checks under the bed or mattress for it). Any valuable furs or clothes are stuffed into one of your suitcases. He checks the living room, attacks the desk (more drawers upturned), and picks out the goodies (he also checks for secret drawers—he knows about them.) He then leaves, taking everything of value you own along with him. This whole scene is usually played out in less than 2 minutes.

To Discourage Burglars

Most thieves are scared and in a hurry. Often, if it takes too much time to gain admittance, a smart break-in man will give up and pass on to the next front door. A burglar alarm is no guarantee against burglary, it may at best deter an amateur. A simple latch lock is no deterrent either; nor are most window locks of any use—a burglar can get through a 9 in. square window opening.

There's only one way you can definitely protect yourself, and all for as little as $100. What you need, provided that your door is thick enough, is an *automatic deadlock*. With this type of lock part of the latch remains rigid if a piece of plastic is pushed through. And there's a second, mortise lock with a hardened steel insert. You're supposed to have the lock fitted at knee level, so that the burglar can't put his full weight behind his knee and heave the door open. The disadvantage of this lock is that you risk slipping a disk or dropping your shopping bag every time you bend to unlock the door.

Internal *handles* should be out of reach of a wrench lowered through the letter slot from the outside.

Lock *inside doors*. Although the intruder can break them, it makes the job more difficult for him.

Violence attracts violence. Unless you're Kojak tough, never try to grapple with a burglar. He's probably more frightened than you are and will do almost anything to get away—and a frightened man hits harder. Let him escape, but try to remember enough of his looks in order to give the police a good description.

According to the police, nearly half of all burglaries could be prevented if people didn't make it easy for the criminal.

DOS AND DON'TS OF THEFT PREVENTION

- *Don't* advertise your absence.
- *Don't* leave bait such as a hi-fi, TV set, or typewriter sitting in full view of a window. If you go away, hide these valuables.
- *Do* fit a magnifying peephole and safety chain to the front door (and back door if necessary), and use them, however silly you feel.
- *Don't* open the front door to anyone if you are alone, unless it's on a chain.
- *Don't* let strangers into your house, however plausible their stories may seem, without checking their credentials. Any genuine charity fund solicitor, social worker, or meter reader should automatically show identification.

If you live alone, you could get a good siren burglar alarm that will wake you and half the neighborhood.

- *Don't* run out for 5 minutes shutting the front door but leaving the back door and windows open.
- *Don't* leave doors unlocked while taking the kids to school, running to the corner grocer or newsstand, or anywhere else.
- *Don't* sit in the backyard or on an upstairs terrace without locking the front door and windows.
- *Don't* leave the garage or toolshed open. It offers burglars a beautiful choice of break-in tools—especially the ladder, ax, screwdriver, or even the garden spade, with its great strength and leverage.
- *Do* turn on a light upstairs when you are out at night; draw the bedroom curtains, but not too closely. If you're going to be away for several nights, you can attach a time switch to a lamp that will turn it on every evening and off again every morning at 2 A.M.
- *Don't* leave a light on in the hall only. Burglars aren't idiots. They're fast, sharp, crafty, nasty, and clever, just like the villains on the tube.
- *Don't* keep the TV turned up loud downstairs at night when the upstairs windows are open.
- *Don't* keep cash in the house. Don't think you can fool a burglar by taping a bundle of green stuff under the wardrobe or bed. When you're burglarized, anything locked is smashed, including interior doors, wardrobes, jewelry boxes, and strong boxes.
- *Do* take snapshots of any irreplaceable valuables. Make a list of your paintings, objets d'art, silver, jewelry, cameras, TVs, radio. The police suggest you make a note of the numbers of all your machines. You can have your name and social security number stenciled on valuable machines, which makes them harder for a thief to get rid of.
- *Do* check whether any appliance you have rented or borrowed is covered under your insurance. It's your responsibility, not that of the owner.
- *Don't* take so many burglary precautions that you make your life a misery. Besides being a potential burglary victim, you're prey for those who sell costly burglar preventers. (I spent a great deal of money having special locks put on each window and internal door, and installing diamond-shape grilles like those they put on ghetto stores at night. All that happened was that we quickly lost the keys to the locks, and

for 2 years we never went into the garden and hardly
opened a window because it was too much trouble.
Then we all locked ourselves out one night and my
12-year-old son shinnied up a drainpipe, broke a
panel of glass, and was inside in 3 minutes. So we
just said to hell with it.)

Before going away for a weekend or vacation:

- *Do* stop newspapers and any other telltale regular
  deliveries, such as milk.
- *Do* take any valuables to the bank, if they aren't
  already there.
- *Do* lock all doors and windows. Leave a key with a
  neighbor, and ask her to hop in every few days to
  check that all is well.
- *Do* turn off the water and drain the pipes if you're
  going away in winter. Burst pipes can be an expensive proposition as well as reassuring an intruder that
  you haven't just stepped around the corner.
- *Do* tell the police you're going away, but only if you
  live in a small town or suburb where the police (1)
  can be trusted, (2) know you, and (3) regularly patrol
  your neighborhood. Don't tell the police about your
  impending vacation if you live in a big city; it'll do no
  good, and besides, even police officers talk.

Aftermath of a Burglary

Almost as bad as a visit from a burglar can be the subsequent visits from the police (a messy business, fingerprint-
ing, and you're not supposed to clean up until the cops
have left).

The visit from the insurance company team might be
even more upsetting. (It's wise to overinsure rather than
underinsure.) If the appraisers glance around your pad
and decide from its general appearance that the stolen
goods must have been worth less than the amount for
which you were insured, they simply halve your claim
even before they start hacking here and there for depre-
ciation. (The portable TV might be 5 years old, but by the
time they've agreed to pay you 1/10 of its original cost—
forget it! If you argue, they tend to make you feel that
you are the criminal.) They finally beat you down until

you may find that all your accumulated and vanished valuables were worth maybe, according to their arithmetic, 10 bucks.

On top of this, they always ask you for receipts, as if you were a company filing system. So, if you insure, try to keep a box somewhere for shoving receipts into in any old order. It's easy once you've pasted a label marked "receipts" on an empty coffee can. (See also household filing system, p. 16.)

COMPLAINING

If you are not satisfied with the job a professional has done, or if you feel that a firm has not lived up to the terms of the warranty of an appliance, do not hesitate to make a fuss. However, you should do this in a calm and systematic way, as lashing out in anger will probably get you nowhere.

Just about every profession or trade has an association to which reputable members belong; you should complain to the appropriate association. But the professions gang together. You're in for a tough time if you want to complain about a doctor and it's very, very, very, very difficult to get anywhere when complaining about a lawyer.

If your complaint concerns a piece of malfunctioning equipment that either has never worked properly or that you cannot seem to get serviced satisfactorily, write to the manufacturer's local representative. If that gets you nowhere, write to the service manager at the manufacturer's headquarters. When complaining to a large company I find that it's best *not* to go straight to the man at the top. Try the head of the department, then proceed not to the president but to the president's secretary. The secretary's job is to prevent trouble from landing on the boss's desk, in addition to putting the fear of the Almighty into anyone else in the firm by mentioning this possibility. If all of this doesn't do it, try writing directly to the president of the company. (Look up the name in the annual report of the company or in a business directory at the public library.) In all cases, send copies of estimates, bills, and previous correspondence.

Three appliance manufacturers have around-the-clock toll-free "hot lines" for complaints: Westinghouse (800) 245–0600, Whirlpool (800) 253–1301, Admiral (800) 477–1305. The appliance industry also supports an association known as the Major Appliance Consumer Action Panel (MACAP) to which you can call in complaints.

Many newspapers and television and radio stations now have hot-line departments to which an aggrieved consumer can complain—often with striking results, because of the damaging publicity to the guilty retailer or company. Consumer protection programs often use volunteer staffs, so, if you want to help your neighbor or yourself, check what programs are available in your area.

If you still haven't made any headway, try contacting a local consumer group (your local newspaper can probably supply you with names).

Use the people whose job it is to protect you. Almost every community has a Better Business Bureau, a Consumer Agency, a State Attorney General, and, of course, a District Attorney. If you have had serious trouble with a local firm, call the Better Business Bureau so that they can warn potential customers to steer clear of the offending outfit.

If all else fails, you can always sue in a small claims court without having to hire a lawyer. However, never resort to the law unless you are prepared to lose at least $150, 3 working days, and your battle on top of it. I use this measure as a personal restraint.

If properly handled, the *unspoken* threat of going to the law is just as effective, but the threat of it usually gets the other side's back up, so avoid mentioning it.

The one thing YOU must do is COMPLAIN. If you don't assert your rights, then no one is going to help you. Don't waste time threatening an inefficient, or possibly unscrupulous, firm; threats will get you nowhere—ACT!

How to Complain—and Win

A travel agent once told me that the secret of successful complaining is having a reasonable complaint, being brief and persistent, knowing your own nuisance value, and knowing what you want. Don't complain without knowing what you want to get as a result of your complaint—an apology, a replacement, or financial compensation. Ask for it outright.

The first battle is lost by the one who loses her temper; once this happens you are vulnerable. The second battle is lost by the one who loses her nerve, so *don't be intimidated*. Don't be frightened by teachers, presidents, or other petty deities.

BE PREPARED: When complaining you should state your situation to the correct person—that is, someone who can do something about it.

State your *complaint*.

State your *witnesses*.

State your *requirements*.

Don't state anything else.

For example, say that the stereo doesn't work; don't tell the whole story: "I had my husband's family to dinner on Thursday and a friend from San Francisco, he's staying for 3 weeks, said after the evening meal, 'Shall we play a record . . .?' " Having marshaled your facts check that they are accurate and that you have dated everything, and identified everyone, including your witnesses.

BE PATIENT: As I write, it has taken British Airways 10 weeks to answer a letter about my luggage that they had mislaid. The correspondence will continue.

TELEPHONE TECHNIQUES: If complaining by telephone, make sure you identify the recipient of your complaint. This can be difficult, so ruthlessly pursue his identity. If the anonymous whine on the other end asks, after a long pause, "Why do you want to know my name, I'm only on the staff?" you reply smoothly, "I like to know who I'm speaking to. Have you any reason for not giving me your name?" If you don't get a name, hang up, telephone again (immediately), and ask for the head of the department (anonymous whine is obviously going to do nothing about your grievance or else is planning to quietly leave at the end of the week).

To complain by telephone, call as early in the day as possible, when they're all opening their mail and organizing themselves, and before they've started to deal with the day's frustrations. Never complain after 3 P.M., when everyone, including yourself, is likely to have used up all his reserve of patience.

Don't sound as if you are whining, but as if you are inquiring. You are seeking the truth.

Try not to put the other person in the wrong because they will only become more defensive. When you reach crunch point, *immediately* give the other side some letout. "I know you must be understaffed" or "Of course we must allow for human error." (Note that plural.) Never admit anything, ever, in a case which is likely to involve an insurance claim (especially not in an auto accident).

As with rape, so with complaining: the better part of valor is to avoid trouble in the first place. Do this by always getting written estimates from workmen in advance of letting them undertake a job, and by dealing only with reputable firms that will stand behind the products and services they sell.

For more detailed guidance, a definitive book on this subject is *The Consumer's Guide to Fighting Back* by Morris J. Bloomstein (Dodd, Mead).

WHERE TO GET FREE ADVICE AND HELP

You can get a lot of information from those little booklets and pamphlets that manufacturers print up to be handed out in hardware stores ("How to Wallpaper" or "Weatherstripping Tips"). And some of the big chain discount hardware/building supply stores have their own *do-it-yourself pamphlets* on plumbing, electrical repairs, carpentry, insulation, roofing, and just about every other field you can imagine.

The public libraries are well stocked with *how-to books* on all subjects, and it is a good idea to spend some time reading up on a subject before you tackle a specific project. You will probably find that some of the books are so useful to you that you'll add them to your personal bookshelf, right alongside the cooking and gardening books.

The government publishes an absolutely overwhelming amount of material, and you can buy some very helpful booklets from them for very little money. They have information on just about any subject and your public library should have a catalog of U.S. Government Printing Office publications. A catalog called *Consumer Interest*, listing more than 200 low-cost booklets, is available free from the General Services Administration, Washington, D.C.

THE HUSTLE JUNGLE SURVIVAL KIT

We live in a jungle of hustlers. Every time we buy anything we are wide open to deception, manipulation, intimidation, trickery, fakery, fraud and outright swindle. The best businessman is still the honest one. But the opportunities to bamboozle are so fat and so safe—and the victims so many and so unsuspecting (such as yourself)—that the marginal and crooked operator will, like the Great White Shark, always be with us.

Remember that the predator feeds on the Three I's: the Innocent, the Ignorant and the Impatient. And, alas, the Three I's include graduates and Ph.D.s. The kind of people who are apt to be too busy with the Big Overall Picture to wear snakeproof boots in the jungle. You, as a consumer, owe it as a duty to yourself not to be fleeced. So, in all you buy and consume, be governed by these 7 survival points:

- 1. *Decide precisely what things you really need.* Make priorities. (A new TV would be nice but the roof leaks.)
- 2. *Never buy a major item in a hurry.* Take time to explore the relative merits of competitive products. Price may not be the determining factor; the manufacturer or retailer may be just as important.
- 3. *Determine how much of a product you need.* Don't buy an 18 cu. ft (0.5 cu. m) freezer if a 6 cu. ft (0.2 cu. m) size will do. Remember the running costs and energy consumed.
- 4. *Shop around for the best price.* A friend of mine, shopping for a new Renault stationwagon found a $300 differential between the prices asked by two equally reputable dealers within ten miles of each other.

- 5. *Always read the contract and/or warranty that accompanies a purchase.* The time to read the boring fine gray print is BEFORE you buy—not when something goes wrong. Remember that there is no such thing as an "unconditional guarantee." The important point is to find out what is *not* covered by a warranty or contract. Ask the seller if you have doubts. Ask him for it in writing. Is the entire product covered, or only parts? Who pays for the labor costs during the warranty or contract period? Is there an authorized service representative nearby?

- 6. *Never buy anything ever from a stranger who appears unsolicited at your door.* Above all, never give that glib salesman a deposit, except perhaps the verbal equivalent of a well-placed boot. This may seem simplistic, but it is very important advice, and I urge all starry-eyed consumers, such as myself, not to ignore it.

- 7. *Old Mother Conran's Condensed Self-help guide to dealing with hustlers.* Don't be hurried. Don't be embarrassed. Don't be frightened of his disapproval. Don't be ashamed. Read the fine print. Be on your guard. Say you'll think about it.

The commonest form of hustling—with infinite variations—is as old as time. It is called bait-and-switch. An ad for a swimming pool may offer the lowest-priced full-sized model in the world at $549 (REDUCED FROM $1,900) for $10 down and $1 a week. *Deep down in your intelligence, you know this is ludicrous.* And yet . . . you call the company, which duly sends around a salesman, who—if you insist on that all-time $549 miracle bargain—will explain that the firm is fresh out of that particular model, BUT—he does have an infinitely superior bargain at $7,345. Two fast-talking hours later, *you* swallowed the bait: *he* switched.

A more seductive method of bait-and-switch is employed by the salesman who offers to charge you *less* than the "regular" price for a specific product or service. He may persuade you that you need new siding on your house and explain that he can drastically cut the price because he can use your refurbished mansion to demonstrate the value of new siding to neighbors (who will, of course, pay the full price, making you a conspirator), or else as "a model to be used in advertising."

If you succumb to such tactics, you have totally ignored the six-point guide and are a sucker besides. *Why* should this stranger give *you* this amazing offer, instead of one of his friends or deserving relations? After asking yourself this question hustle to the telephone and call your local consumer affairs office—Bait-and-switch sales are illegal.

Hustle-jungle tactics work, because they play subtly on your pride, shame or simple stupidity. Why, Ms. Goodbody, with your standing in the community, you wouldn't want to drive a junky car, or have the cheaper grade of carpeting, or pass over a truly fine buy at a price you must promise never to mention?

The slickest sales pitch of all may never be delivered in person: it may arrive in the mail. Though any sales offer through the postal service that is blatantly fraudulent is illegal and may be prosecuted under the criminal code, an enormous amount of marginal, misleading and hoked-up advertising gets to you via junk mail.

This is because every time you sign your name to practically anything, from a wedding licence or a birth certificate to a magazine subscription or an automobile registration, your name, address and vital statistics—even in some cases your income—are peddled to one or several compilers of mailing lists. There are thousands of mailing lists in the U.S. and they are valuable commodities.

If you do not relish the idea of your private statistics being peddled by companies and government agencies that have no business doing so, or if you also loathe junk mail, you can turn off the torrent quite simply. Write to the Direct/Mail Marketing Association, 6 E. 43 St., N.Y.C., N.Y. 10017, asking for a Name-Removal Form and fill it in.

As I have repeatedly said in this book, industry and government at every level have become markedly more responsive to consumer complaints in recent years. Between ombudsmen, hot-lines and media consumer advisers (see p. 290), not to mention the traditional Better Business Bureau and Chamber of Commerce, no legitimate, properly detailed gripe should go unanswered. But unfortunately, such agencies receive hundreds of letters whose writers do not make clear *what* they are complaining about, and *why*, and *against whom*.

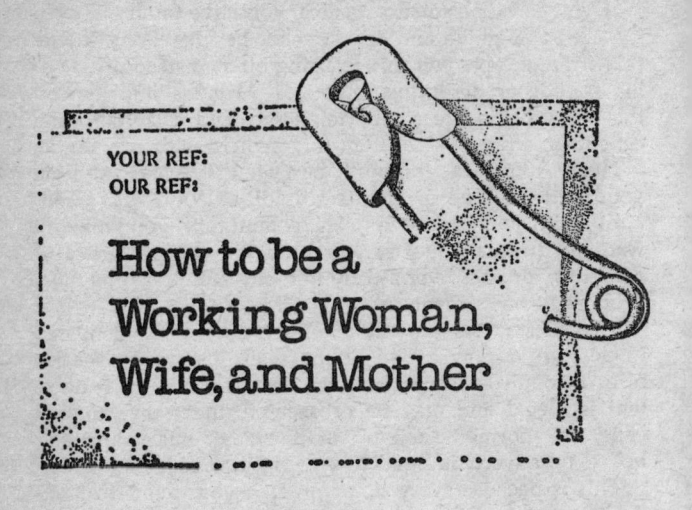

YOUR REF:
OUR REF:

How to be a Working Woman, Wife, and Mother

ADVANTAGES OF A WORKING MOTHER

HAVING ONE: There are some obvious disadvantages to a child in having a mother who works outside the home, but there are less obvious advantages. Children with working mothers don't suffer from smother-love, or overfussing. They learn to be realistic, independent, responsible, and sometimes stoical, no mean preparation for the possible toughness of life.

My children have flourished under this system of self-reliance: They use their initiative, are responsible for their words and deeds, accountable for their money, and supportive of the family. They have also been taught that they owe me nothing and no one owes them anything. I focused on what I considered the essentials (aim low and you're more likely to succeed), and just hoped for the best with everything else.

BEING ONE: Children of working mothers don't have a permanent in-house punching bag, but they do have a mother who is likely to have a younger outlook, and who is more likely to be open to new ideas. She may seem freer, happier (nagging is often a symptom of frustration) and have more things to talk about.

A working mother may turn out to be a more respected and valuable adviser in later life; you have to rely on reason, not authority, if you hold down an outside job.

Working at a job also demands that a person develop self-control and discipline, qualities which should be as useful and important to a woman—especially a mother—as they are to a man.

The woman with training is equipped to lead a full, useful, self-sufficient life. It should be reassuring for a man to know that his wife could support herself and the children, and even him, should disaster strike.

Men in our society have always tended to die earlier than women. For the future welfare of a family, job-training and/or continuing education for the woman can be better insurance than insurance itself if a man dies, is disabled, divorces, or simply disappears. And it means the woman won't feel useless and unwanted when her children grow up and leave home. A working woman is not as likely to cling to her children when it's their turn to leave the nest; she has her own interests.

The average female lifespan is now 76 years. Your child-care years could be over at 36. What is Ms. Average going to do for the next 40 years?

Seventy percent of women analyzed in a *Family Circle* survey found that when they had jobs they were happier and more interesting, and their children were more self-reliant. This is not really surprising, considering that, generally speaking, household management is vastly under-rated. Amazingly, the U.S. Labor Department rates house-work at the bottom of its scale of complexity for 22,000 different occupations, along with poultry-offal shovelers and rest-room attendants.

A growing number of women who feel they're taken for granted, unappreciated, or neglected in the home, are starting to find that be it ever so hectic, there is no place like *work*. Work is where you're needed. Work is where you're welcomed. Work can heal wounds; it can soothe, it can be a means of forgetting your troubles, your despair, your loneliness. It can be a comfort, a strength, the basis of self-esteem and fulfillment, and certainly work can provide rewards. What makes a job worthwhile is the enthusiasm it generates, the job satisfaction, the sense of achievement and the MONEY.

EVERYBODY'S ATTITUDE

I've read a lot about women who serenely cope with the three roles of full-time working woman, wife and mother. However, I've never actually met one. All the ones that I know feel inadequate.

Going back to work after having children is a practical and emotional problem and both its aspects are interrelated. You risk worrying about the children when you're at work and about work when you're at home, and end up being happy in neither situation.

Two requisites for a working mother are stamina and an understanding family. Sympathetic they may be until it comes to your interests versus theirs, but they still want their evening meal on time and they don't want to hear about the traffic jam that made you late. (A husband who cooks and doesn't mind the occasional snack meal in a crisis is worth his weight in caviar.)

What a working mother risks if she goes out to work and doesn't look after herself is her health. She needs to be an efficient and well-organized person to survive and even if she manages the mechanics she will probably have emotional problems. Her biggest, probably unrecognized problem may be to get a certain amount of private time to herself every day, which is essential.

Apart from that, what a working mother needs is the tangible support of a family that shares out the household tasks and takes as much pride in your achievements, as you do in theirs.

YOUR ATTITUDE

In a perfect world I wouldn't have to write this but in all matters, especially domestic, I like to deal with fact as well as theory. Today everybody knows that a woman's place is not necessarily in the home. Sometimes, home is where the harpy is, and sometimes she has good cause to be bitchy. However, it's no use pretending that our world is set up to welcome, accept and help the working mother, and, while pressing for fair play, I think it's easier to live in the world as it is and not as I'd like it to be.

Even if household tasks are shared and the screwdrivers are marked His and Hers, it is generally the woman partner who bears the responsibility for organizing the domestic three-ring circus and this is the exhausting part.

It seems to me that the homes of non-working mothers are seldom any more neat or clean than those of working mothers: in fact, it is possible for non-working housewives to be just as lazy housekeepers as those working, and some of them are not around the home that much more. They may be out socializing, earnestly playing tennis, earnestly seeing their psychiatrist, home fantasizing (matching the candleholders to the drapes, combing the town for the right-sized pine cones for the open fireplaces, etc.) or drinking.

Agreed, working mothers often feel inadequate and exhausted but I have noticed that many non-job mothers constantly convey a different sense of inadequacy and exhaustion. Instead of the working mother's anxiety as to whether she can juggle the whole lot simultaneously, it's a restless feeling that she should want to do more, but that she has no idea how to get started.

Working mothers may have a more valid reason for fatigue but this is physical, and therefore remedied by a long night's sleep or a day spent alone and doing nothing or with friends.

If a job gets to feel too much for you, you had better consider getting another job, one which is perhaps less demanding and emotionally exhausting (see also "What to do if you can't cope," p. 324).

I know this sounds glib in days of unemployment and

inflation, I know that this isn't the attitude of the Woman's Movement, and were it a perfect world I wouldn't suggest it but the fact is that I don't believe women have (or should have) the job-pride which men have and can more easily shift "downwards" in employment, especially if it's going to improve the quality of home life for their children. When I felt that my children needed me more, and I needed a less demanding job, I moved to a job that paid 30 percent of my previous salary. I hated it and they hated it, "You're always hanging around us . . . ," "Why don't you go back to nerve-racking newspapers, we're happiest when you're happy . . ." but I have never regretted that when I thought it was necessary I did in fact try it.

Anyway, if a job gets too oppressive to the point of not coping I would quit and try to get temporary work close to home under less pressure. This comes under the heading of "simplifying your job" and it should always be considered as a worthwhile alternative.

If you know that you would consider this, you are less likely to be anxious and it is less likely to happen.

It is important that you shouldn't feel guilty about working—and this may be impossible. You have been conditioned to feel guilty. Don't fight it, you can either go into psychotherapy or simply accept it. The generation that *won't* feel guilty is, we hope, the one that we're bringing up right now.

Children instinctively know that your guilt about your work is your Achilles heel and will use it, when they are bored, or cross, to have a crack at you. "Why don't you ever bake *cakes* like *other* mothers?" once nagged my son, who hates cakes. A doctor once told me to do as much as you can for your children but never make gargantuan sacrifices because they will resent it. Women who martyr themselves harm not only themselves but possibly their families as well, if the children are left with the uneasy feeling that mother has sacrificed herself for them, which may be 95 percent untrue. Mother has probably done exactly what she wanted to, no matter what she says.

The sort of woman who *really* has to make sacrifices for her children and is *really* prepared to do that makes sure that her children never know. He also told me that children have a very good basic set of priorities. They don't care about mess or dust as long as they feel loved and if they are secure in this then it doesn't matter much what else you do, because that's the only thing that really matters. This seems so obvious that one is left wondering what you've been so worried about all the time. However, it's a good thing to remind your eldest when, raising an eyebrow, he runs his forefinger along a window ledge like a situation-comedy mother-in-law.

YOUR CHILDREN'S ATTITUDE

There is the distinct possibility that your family may never regard your work as anything but tiresome. There are certain occasions when you would, of course, never think twice about asking for time off work: for anything special which involves your husband's work, any special occasion involving your children at school, or when a child is ill. Before you start a job you may have to sort out that odd days such as these come out of your holiday time. Incidentally, I found that as my children grew into teenagers, they needed *more* of my time and undivided attention. Their needs were more complicated, and obviously at this stage they needed *me*, not just my services. You can't tidy a child into a drawer when it suits you, so never be surprised or exasperated when a child needs more of your time than you can afford.

Except for emergencies *and recognized, prearranged tasks*, I have found it easier not to expect any household help from my children and then I neither irritate them nor rely on them. I find that it is difficult to slow down to a small child's pace. Very small children are *no use* in an efficient domestic routine. They are slow and messy and they break things. What children over seven *can* be expected to do is to provide a certain amount of self-help. They can make their own beds and tidy their rooms, and Heaven help them if they don't leave the kitchen tidy. Over ten they can wash up, but if younger, I find it's not worth the effort to get them to do it, and then have to check it, and then redo it. Teenagers can be careless and reluctant, if not downright resentful of a succession of time-consuming little chores and with good reason if they have a full quota of school work (as they should).

If you've had a hard time getting back to work and staying there, make sure that your daughters get a thorough education before leaping into bridal white: a good early grounding can make all the difference to the sort of job which she can aim at twenty years later. If she has a thorough professional training then later on when she goes back to full-time work after child-rearing, she can afford labor-savers (including human ones) that make it possible and enjoyable.

Your children's teacher is tremendously important to you because (one hopes) he or she has a balanced, objective view of your offspring and their problems. Ask his or her advice if your children develop any antisocial habit, such as bullying, or if they seem to be doing badly at school, or if you have any misfortune, such as divorce, that will affect the children.

YOUR MAN'S ATTITUDE

There's no more worthy and enjoyable job than making a happy home. If you don't want to work outside it, that's fine by me. I stopped full-time work just as soon as I could afford to do so, when my eldest son was fourteen.

But if you *are* working outside your home, then you may, without realizing it, have problems with your man. Generally speaking, the husband of today's working woman genuinely likes the idea of a self-reliant wife (and a self-reliant mother) who can command a second income (not least as an insurance policy in case of illness or death), and whose interests and skills range beyond the kitchen, and who can understand the burden of responsibility at business and help to lighten it at home.

The Reluctant Husband

But many men subconsciously resent giving up any of their traditional rights in order to allow their mate a separate identity. They want to have their cake and eat it (just like women). Most hubands, *even* if they say that their wife has a right to work, *even* if they enjoy a two-paycheck life-style, *even* if they're proud of her, would prefer that she didn't work. A husband likes to come first. (*Anyone likes* to come first.)

We all know what an enlightened man's attitude *ought* to be, but that isn't going to help you if his attitude is different. There are three types of husbands: Type (1), liberated; Type (2), unliberated; Type (3) (Reluctant Husband), the man who thinks he's liberated but is unconsciously resentful of any of his mate's interests if they interfere with his life as he would ideally like it led. If your mate is a Type (3) Man then you might have a serious emotional conflict because your man will probably deny it, if challenged about his attitude; so it will be very difficult to discuss.

This problem can be difficult to resolve because if you continue to work he's going to continue to unwittingly resent it and if you stop work there's a good chance that *you* will unconsciously resent it.

A partner with whom you live, as opposed to a spouse, is far less likely to have a Reluctant Husband's attitude because it seems only to accompany that age-old institution, marriage. There seems to be less mutual accountability in a live-with situation. If a woman is living with a man, and she has her own job and income, then the man knows (because this is recognized among men) that he has to be more courteous, careful and respectful, in all the proper senses of these words, because if he isn't, she can pack her bags and go off any time, because she's free to do so. So the freely consented to, live-with situation, is a continued relationship on both sides, which is clearly understood.

Reluctant Husbands usually keep their ambivalent feelings secret except when with other men. They certainly never voice them to their unknowing wife. They say what they know they *should* say, what is socially acceptable. So if your husband starts acting in a bewildering, contradictory manner after you've had a salary rise or some public praise, DON'T LISTEN TO WHAT HE SAYS, WATCH WHAT HE DOES.

The Reluctant Husband can be expected to demonstrate that intellectual agreement of equality is not emotional acceptance of it by carefully sabotaging his share of the household chores. Although he is an intelligent man and not clumsy in other areas he will demonstrate this by burning meals, breaking dishes, dropping loaded trays or doing sloppy, inefficient cleaning. (Scientists can be particularly ham-fisted. There they are, mixing a milligram of this with a microgram of that in a delicate little test tube all morning, splitting the atom all afternoon, then having these incapable hands in the evening; they don't even match, you see.) Expect such a man to justify his resentment with pseudo logic, and keep alert for well-worn phrases such as "sheer selfishness," "lack of responsibility," "not identifying as a mate," "duty as a mother," and the trump card "I don't like to see the children suffer."

What these men don't like about their wives working boils down to three main threats: (1) the threat to male authority as the one-and-only King of the Castle, Benevolent Provider and Resident Tarzan; (2) the threat to their spending power (there may be two incomes but she's going to want to decide jointly what they're spent on); (3) the threat to their sex life (statistically, when a woman works outside the home she is twice as likely to have an affair than the stay-at-home wife) and any man who works in an office, or travels, knows this without statistics.

Some men certainly feel ambivalent about sharing family power. (Remember, "Remember your father's always right dear?") There are, thank Heaven, few family dictators today but, by some strange accident of genetic memory, some men look back longingly to when they were looked up to by a wife who was culturally indoctrinated to be dependent. Perhaps this is because some husbands tend to confuse independence with power and muddle assertion with aggression.

One of the secret male fears is *supposed* to be that one day she will no longer need him. This theory, that a woman only needs a man as a crutch, is just as weak an argument against women's independence as the old-fashioned woman's reasoning "If I'm weak and dependent then he will be strong and I can depend on him." As an attitude this is one hell of an illogical gamble which, of course, can leave her helpless and stranded if it doesn't come off, and he goes off.

Some men don't like their wife shouldering part of the family money-making responsibility. In theory they eagerly agree that she has a right to spending decisions: in fact, a husband can resent it bitterly (whether or not he tells her, whether or not he realizes it) if his wife wants to buy something or invest her money in something that he doesn't want.

Many men consider that being a successful provider is proof of virility (culture indoctrination also accounts for this) and secretly resent it if the wife works because they *both* agree that they need the extra money or because it provides luxury extras. In the latter case, a husband, while enjoying the higher standards of life that his wife's salary makes possible, might also feel alarm and anxiety at the idea of getting used to living beyond *his* income. This is comprehensible, although not logical.

The most illogical of male anxiety areas is when a man objects to his wife earning *more* than he does. Logically, he should be delighted, but, to him, it means that she therefore has more power than he does (money power, leading to other powers). As he sees it this means an actual reversal of the traditional cultural role of male dominance. (Women don't usually see such a situation in this way.)

A man does not want a mate who is a threat, in terms of the outside masculine world. Most men are fiercely competitive and they don't want to sleep (on a long-term basis) with someone who's got a better job, a better salary and more success, recognition and responsibility than they have.

If a man, however covertly, doesn't want his woman to be successful at her job, or if he seeks her dependency upon him, this is diagnostic of his own, almost certainly unadmitted, lack of self-confidence. This can be associated with a fear of domination. Culturally, he's expected to be dominant, he may have been conditioned by a dominant mother—using blackmail dominance ("How *could* you hurt your own mother, like that?" "How can you *think* of doing that when you know it will hurt me?") and he then finds that his wife is becoming threateningly powerful (as he intuits it—not as he *sees* it, because he doesn't see it, he imagines it). She is being increasingly powerful simply because she is escaping from the cultural situation on which his cultural dominance is dependent. In other words, she's escaping from her domestic overlord.

The boy who is (as I've suggested above) submitted to domination by his mother is in a culture which still expects a male to be dominant, not dominated, so that his experience and his expectations of himself in regard to women are confusing and contradictory: hence his lack of confidence, and possible bewilderment.

His wife may unwittingly manifest her increasing freedom and escape from her cultural role limitations by remarks, apparently innocent enough in themselves, but which sting him and alarm him. These could be as trivial as not answering simply "yes" or "of course" to his suggestion, BUT

> "I agree" (indicating that she has an equal right to do so)
> *or* "No, I don't think so . . ."
> *or* "No, I'm not going to do that because I've arranged to do something else . . ."

A very unhealthy situation. Beware of causing it in your own sons by desisting from dominating for your own convenience and according them respect but not adulation.

If your man feels jealous and resentful but he doesn't feel that he should say so, then you certainly have a problem. The problem is that you probably can't tackle it logically—because it isn't a logical problem, it's an emotional problem.

And men don't want a tired, preoccupied mate: understandably, what they would really like is the laughing, carefree and passionate girl they married. Ho Hum. Most of all a man can resent your being tired. This is another reason why it is vital to share the housework. Then you aren't tired: of course *he* may be. It makes an interesting change.

Men can take out their resentment in their sex life (absence of), which is, of course, attributed to the new, non-effacing independent wife. I asked three psychiatrists about this and they all confirmed that they had yet to hear of a genuine case of impotence that stemmed from a wife's working and certainly not from her independence. It may be the new, fashionable male excuse but it isn't much help to know this if you are stuck with the consequences.

There may be other reasons for resentment. A husband may resent a wife travelling on business, he may resent working hours that don't coincide with his. An insecure husband in a low-earning job may feel that it is humiliating to his God-given status as Head of the Family to be seen doing household chores or going shopping.

Openly or otherwise, men often resent "menial" household chores on principle (except that they're not menial when wives do them, then they are tangible proof of love, unmentioned though it may be). Some men regard domestic jobs as time-wasting when *they* do it, and resent it accordingly. And although not all men resent looking after their own children they may well be amazed by the time, energy and patience that they find it requires.

In any of these situations a man who lacks self-confidence may easily become jealous, resentful, self-pitying and avenging. That's what you've got to watch out for, ladies.

But your husband may not admit to this—especially not to himself. After all, he's not supposed to be emotional, is he? Tarzans don't get upset: he's supposed to be the logical, stainless-steel brain of the household, isn't he?

If that's your problem, it may take a little time to sort out, but it's an understandable problem—and a solvable one.

However tolerant and understanding a husband is about his wife's job, there's almost bound to be *some* area of resentment as a result of early indoctrination for men born before 1955 (which means that they were over thirteen in 1968 when the Woman's Movement got under way).

If this is your case, it's important that you shouldn't get resentful or indignant. What you must realize is that he is being *unconsciously* selfish, emotional and unreasonable. It is unreasonable to expect an unreasonable man to be reasonable. Don't try to deal with the situation logically: you have to deal with the situation as it stands and you are unlikely to resolve it by yourself because *you* are the person he secretly resents.

If a man wants you to quit your job (or you think he does) because it "isn't working out," try following Elinor

Guggenheimer's advice (see p. 70). If that doesn't work, head straight for professional counsel, starting with your local doctor or Family Service Association who will indicate whether something more, such as psychotherapy is required.

YOUR STAND-IN

The lack of enough affordable day nurseries and day schools and child-care arrangements is what prevents most mothers who would like to do so from returning to work.

Looking after a family and taking care of children is obviously the most important job in the world. Unfortunately, society only pays lip service to this. It doesn't pay us for doing it and it is not particularly interested in seeing that it gets done: otherwise day-care centers would be every city's priority. Many mothers have no choice as to whether or not to work. But, whatever City Hall says, City Hall's motto seems to be "Women and children last."

Anthropologist Margaret Mead goes so far as to say that lack of day care is "a new and subtle form of anti-feminism in which men—under the guise of exalting the importance of maternity—are tying women more tightly to their children than has been thought necessary . . ."

The second great drawback to full-time work for mothers is what to do with the vacation periods. (For the woman who works in a school or college, the vacations are no problem, which can be the major advantage to this sort of job.) Again, this situation could be resolved by government action and local centers.

Camp can account for some of the time and children generally love camp, but it's not a cheap solution and it doesn't solve all the vacation problems.

These two main problems for the working mother could both be resolved by official action, that won't happen unless the voice of the community calls for it. Any woman who has any time for any voluntary work should consider giving priority to getting more adequate, cheap local day-care nurseries under way. (We really owe it to our daughters—the future mothers of America.) Once set up they could probably all be run by working mothers.

Employers should also be firmly encouraged to provide day nurseries—they are actually obliged to do so by law in Italy and Turkey if they employ more than a specific number of married women. (Alternatively, the manufacturer has to pay a levy toward the cost of a state day nursery.) Often, several firms join forces to start one nursery available to all their female employees. Over 40 percent of French firms that employ over 500 people provide child care.

Apart from the needs of a young child, a mother probably prefers to be with her baby until it is 3 years old, or she probably wouldn't have had it to begin with.

However, some mothers have no choice. They are obliged to go out to work, often because they are the breadwinners. In the United States, 7.2 million families are now dependent on the earnings of a woman.

And if a new mother has the choice but finds that the bliss of looking after a baby twenty-fours hours a day isn't so fulfilling as she had expected, if it becomes clinically depressing,* it would be wonderful to know that the end can be nigh in only 3 years: she could draw up a 1095 day check-off calendar immediately.

Some states now have laws that pertain to the working mother. If you are employed in a full-time position, you can collect part of your salary (about half) for a period of 4 weeks before and 4 weeks after delivery of your child. Your employer must grant you a leave of absence for a reasonable amount of time (approximately 3 months) if you request it—yes, your job will be waiting for you.

Womankind *has* taken some giant steps: In addition to pregnancy-related "disability" pay, some of the cost of child care is tax deductible. If you spend money for baby-sitters, nursery school, day-care centers, or summer camp so you can work full or part time or go to school, don't overlook the child-care credit when filing your tax return.

Now, what can you do regarding your daily domestic situation? If you can afford it, I think the best home help is a *daily housekeeper*, rather than a nurse or nanny, because children, no matter how young, shouldn't get used

---

* Easy to sniff at and impossible to ignore if you've never experienced it.

to a lot of attention. But the housekeeper should understand that the children come before the home. She should speak good English (or your children may grow up talking pidgin English), know exactly what to do in an emergency (have a few trial runs), and, if necessary, be able to drive in order to take your turn in the car pool.

If you pay more than the going rate you will not be popular with your neighboring working mothers, but, on the other hand, you will generally find someone who is somewhat more responsible. I always award a money present at Easter (not Christmas or summer vacation, when extra-to-the-contract money can be almost regarded as a right, or when, after pocketing the money and visiting their folks, they find the temptation to stay with them or continue lounging at the seashore often too great). Pick your own bonus system; relate it to achievement. Never deduct money from the salary, even if it's deserved, even if it's been prearranged; it simply isn't worth the hassle and the resentment.

Professor Virginia Tiger, married to sociologist Lionel, employs her baby-sitter on a yearly basis, with an end-of-year bonus. She gets reliability and her children get the same person. A good idea.

If you want to employ a *foreign housekeeper*, make sure she is certified as an alien and has a permanent resident's visa. *Ask to see this.* If you want to import a foreign helper, go to a reliable employment agency and be prepared for a lot of paperwork, a big bill (about $300 plus air fare, at the time of writing), and to pay a minimum salary of about $120 for a 5-day week. She can legally walk out the month after her arrival—many do—and you will have paid all that advance money for nothing. I wouldn't do it. Whoever you hire, ask for at least 2 references and check them carefully.

As to *evening baby-sitters*, either you can afford them and can get them or you can't. And that's the cost of having children. Raising a child in modern times can be more expensive than running a Lincoln Continental, especially after 6 P.M.

If you employ home help make sure that your stand-in likes and is liked by the children, whether or not she is particularly efficient with the housework. Don't be jealous of your children's affection for their minder—you want them to feel affectionate toward lots of people.

Check on your surrogate: There is no reason to trust her until she is proven trustworthy. If you can't hop home unexpectedly yourself, get someone else to do so. This sounds nasty, but they're **your** children and you have a duty to them and you can't take risks. Also check carefully with other parents about your child-minder, play group, day-care center, or nursery school. *Never stop checking.*

CHILD-CARE ORGANIZATIONS

- *A preschool playgroup.* A center organized by parents in premises that have been approved by the local authorities. It takes children from 3 to 5 years old for about 3 hours in either morning or afternoon, so it's suitable only for mothers who do part-time work. Nominal fees pay for light, heat, toys, modeling clay, paints, books, and other equipment. The children are taught no formal subjects, but they learn to relate to one another, to accept authority, and to be imaginative and unselfish. If there isn't one locally, how about starting one, either on a cooperative basis with other mothers or as a business venture?
- *City day care.* Noneducational in the same way as play-groups. These are for priority cases—for children whose mothers must work or are ill. They take children from 3 months old for up to 8 hours a day. Get further information from your local health department or newspaper offices.
- *City nursery schools.* For 3- to 5-year-olds, normal school hours, but there is a great shortage.

If you don't have a local day-care center or nursery school, start campaigning for one.

- *Private local nursery schools.* You can get details of these from the local newspaper or health department.
- *A registered child-minder.* Can look after your children for up to 8 hours daily in her home. Costs can be from $90 per child per week, including food. There are bad child-minders and there are good ones.
- *A nonworking neighborhood mother.* Mothers who have no home help might pay one of these woman to cope with their children as well as her own. There's sometimes still a grandmother or aunt to look after the children, but nowadays there's a good chance that

grannie is busy running her own boutique and auntie is a trainee computer programmer.

SOURCES OF INFORMATION ON DAY CARE

- *Day-Care Services.* U.S. Department of Health, Education and Welfare, Office of Child Development, P.O. Box 1182, Washington, D.C. 20013. Free.
- *Federal Interagency Day-Care Requirements.* Same as above. Free.
- *What Is Good Day Care?* Same as above. Free.
- *Standards for Day-Care Service.* Child Welfare League of America, 67 Irving Place, New York, N.Y. 10003. $2.50.
- *Guide for Establishing and Operating Day-Care Centers for Young Children* by Dorothy Beers Boguslawski. (How to set up a center, decide on its design, staff it, and plan for daily activities.) Same as above. $2.50.
- *A Catalog of Selected Day-Care and Child-Development Publications.* Day-Care and Child-Development Council of America, 1426 H Street N.W., Washington, D.C. 20005. Free.

HOW TO RUN A HOME AND A JOB

Funnily enough, money is no panacea (although people who haven't got any never believe this). You just have to organize the help as well as the children, and if you're not careful, you have *their* psychological dramas dumped in your lap just as soon as you get back from the office. If you have living-in older help they often get jealous of you, your job, and your sex life and security and start sniping at you; if the help is younger—such as a student au pair— she often isn't sufficiently experienced, interested or responsible (and neither were you at seventeen) and you'll spend half your time worrying about her sex life or maybe turning up the television full blast so that you can't hear it.

Women hate being efficient in the home and they tend to feel uneasy if they hear the word "organization." Lists and routines simply do not fit into the pink-checkgingham-and-lace mental picture of the soap opera mother, which so many of us were brought up to be.

When you become a working mother you will with any luck get twice as much out of life, but you can't run your house as if you weren't working. A working mother has to work faster and more efficiently in the home and she has to be *twice* as reliable outside it, because people expect her not to be.

I have evolved my own set of guideline rules for housework, which I slowly slip away from, but it pulls me back to reality at regular intervals, and Heaven knows what I would be like without it. Here it is.

CONSERVE YOUR ENERGY: Realize that you can't do everything, like those ladies in the glossy magazines seem to. A-day-in-the-life-of always seems to start with Her, at dawn, in immaculate leotard: she bakes a cake, takes the kids to school, does a little light voluntary work and has a face-pack before catching the 8 o'clock train to her office (meditating or studying during the journey) where she goes through a similarly impossible day before, serene and relaxed, swooping back (TM on the train) to give a dinner party in the evening (which she sometimes prepares before breakfast when she isn't being photographed). Don't you believe a word of it. They're either outright liars or ruthlessly selfish and I've noticed (because I've covered dozens of newspaper stories on them) that their families seem a bit frightened of them.

KNOW YOUR LIMITATIONS: I have low blood pressure and I can't do a lot of work at a stretch. I get a lot done in the time available to me but I have to keep resting in between and this is much more difficult than it sounds, particularly if I'm on tour or attending official luncheons. It was easier to deal with once I faced up to it, rather than try to will myself out of it or pretend it wasn't necessary.

Try to evolve your own basic lifestyle which allows for the fact that you can't get a quart out of a pint jar, and plan around your *own* capacity, and weaknesses, not someone else's set of oughts and shoulds.

The secret of getting things done is to *know what to leave undone*, and the secret of that is learning to sort out your priorities fast. Decide your basic priorities. I decided that my children came first, and apart from that, nothing came before my job, which was a reasonably responsible one, working to national newspaper deadlines.

- *Disregard what you're SUPPOSED to do.*
- *Consider what you can't avoid doing.*
- *Consider what you CAN avoid doing,* e.g. daily cleaning, drying up, most of the ironing, and producing *two* hot meals a day. Remember, however, that evening candlelight or soft lamplight may be kind to your face and your standards of housework, but it can't disguise canned spaghetti *ad nauseam.*
- *Eliminate THINGS as well as tasks:* The less you have the less you have to take care of.
- *Everything you dread doing you must do STRAIGHT-AWAY,* then things seem immediately much better.
- *Never leave anything until the last minute.* It is a straight gamble with fate and time and the dice are NEVER weighted in your favor.
- *Encourage self-discipline:* It's simply that nothing else works . . . And as war leader Winston Churchill said in his speech to his old school "Never give up—Never. Never. Never. Never. Never." That's all he said, but it is enough to live by.
- *We are all too often too tired, but try never to let the phrase cross your lips:* Try going to bed really early once a week immediately after work. It's amazing what a treat it feels.
- *Never rely on your memory.* Nobody has one good enough to retain all the tedious clutter that your work involves. Keep a notebook in your purse and don't let anyone else get at it.
- Keep a notebook and ballpoint pen (pencils break) *attached* to the telephone. Train the family to write in it. Everything they want you to know or do! Look at it as soon as you get in. Train them to do the same.
- *Your lunch hour is for lunch and relaxation:* Try to keep shopping out of it.
- *Making more time:* The choice is to get up early or go to bed late. You are either a lark or an owl.

Voices of Experience

Larks can't keep their eyes open in the evening, but they cheerfully perform amazing feats such as laying breakfast at dawn. If you are not a lark you might have to invest money in getting up: try a costly telephone alarm call or one of those radio-alarm clocks that keep coming on again, however many times you shut them up.

I know a poet housewife who works from 5 A.M. to 7 A.M. Perhaps only someone with the soul of a poet can do that, but if you can't summon up enough energy to get up early then you can go to bed later, a regular 2 A.M. owl. If you do neither, then you don't really want to be a poet or study Mandarin or whatever. *The Times* columnist Bernard Levin told me this and I was furious with him for months because he was right.

Conran's Law of Housework is that it expands to fill the time available plus half an hour: so it is obviously never finished. The important thing is not to do the housework but to decide how much *time* you are going to allow for your housework (See "The reason why," p. 5). What doesn't get done in that time is left undone (perhaps for next time, perhaps not). Keep housework in its place, which you will remember is underfoot, and regard it not as a reflection on your worth but as the minimum essential support-work to keep the place functioning as a background to living.

Penelope Perrick, who wrote *The Working Wives' Cookbook*, told me: "For me, the clue to being successfully organized lay in realizing that my work must be my hobby." She believes in a once-a-week preparation time for food and realizes that the best day to do the bulk of the shopping and a good bit of housework is Saturday. (The only day? For most people, yes.) "Any meals that have to be prepared on Saturday must be fitted in between painting the ceiling and washing the dog. I reserve Sunday morning for fixing casseroles and baking pies and all the other things that result in stacks of dirty dishes. Then I tackle this chore in one fell swoop."

A fellow writer once told me that her organizational secret was never to take her coat off until she had laid the table and the evening meal was well under way. Otherwise she would have flopped into an armchair with a drink and the meal would have been extremely late, if indeed, it appeared at all. A famous architect, Lady Casson, told me that she never entertains; never, ever. She sends flowers, notes and gifts to her hostesses, but she never asks them home, and eventually this has been accepted by all the friends she has left

Try to avoid always cooking a hot evening meal.

On Monday serve a casserole you prepared with the weekend cooking.

One evening serve carry-out food.

One evening leave it to your man—enthusiastically eat whatever turns up.

One evening serve cold food.

One evening go out (if you can afford to).

Use as many semi-prepared foods as possible.

Buy the classic Peg Bracken's *I Hate to Cookbook* (published by Fawcett Crest, $1.25).

Consider cutting out anything that makes work (polishing silver; open fires). Use the maximum labor-savers but the minimum number of machines (there will then be fewer to break down).

Make use of available services, such as the window-washer or carpet-cleaning firm.

Every member of the family must help with the housework.

Share the work: calculate the time these jobs take you and apportion jobs according to hours. Most husbands say they are willing to share the chores and actually do so, although they don't assume equal hourage: the best you can hope for at the moment is one husband hour to two or five and a half wife hours at housework. (And I have the statistics to prove it.)

When proportioning equal shares of housework relate it to hours not to tasks. You can't really work out any other way (except with money via paying someone else to do it) whether mending the vacuum cleaner is equivalent to getting breakfast.

The question of whether or however the husband should help around the house can be solved by jointly paying someone else to do it: I don't know about your principles, but so long as people want cleaning work I don't see why there shouldn't be cleaners (personally, I prefer to hire male cleaners because they are stronger than me.)

JOB	HOURS A WEEK
Shopping	....
Meals	....
preparation	....
cooking	....
clearing up	....

Clearing up kitchen ....
Clothes ....
   cleaning ....
   mending ....
Floor care ....
Furniture care ....
Cleaning bathrooms ....
Making beds ....
General tidying ....
Auto care ....
Domestic maintenance, furnace
   and machinery care ....

In *my* wardrobe I keep an emergency clean set of clothes for each child, even if it is only cotton underwear, jeans and a T-shirt. Also a spare shirt, set of underwear and cuff links for my husband.

Never return to an unmade bed, it's so disheartening. Make them fast rather than not at all. (Get continental quilts.)

A FEW FAMILY MOTTOES:

- Don't put it down, put it away
- If you leave things on the floor they get trodden on by clumsy grown-ups
- First thing first, second things never

Yes, here's another of those sermons about using business methods and writing notes in order to run a house better. Only those articles are generally written by a business consultant who doesn't do much housework, or he would realize that what can disorganize the Chase Manhattan Bank in a year is *nothing* to what can disorganize your organization (through no fault of your own) over a family weekend, every weekend.

SITUATION

- In the limited time available you have an unlimited number of things to do and every day they become more.
- Nothing you're doing can sensibly be labeled productive, non-productive or counter-productive, hence those days when you seem to have worked your

whatsit off but at the end of it can't quite see what's been achieved.

- The secret of finding the bluebird of home happiness is to:

    Set your priorities
    Ruthlessly simplify
    Allocate your time specifically
    Delegate

- The secret of mother power is to:

    Rethink your priorities and cut out what you don't *have* to do
    Decide what you *do* want to do
    Don't bother too much about the rest

- Buy a big purse (or smart tote bag) and use it as your organization center. Carry that notebook in your purse. Make lists in it.

Don't forget Conran's Second Law of Housekeeping, that *possible* Daily Output is always halved by Unforeseen Interruptions. (Although halving the things on your list doesn't seem to deal with that problem.) Conran's Third Law: However much you halve your list you will *still* only get half of it done.

Keep your lists and at the end of the week see what got crossed off and what didn't and ask yourself—why? Check *all* your lists quietly at the end of the week, over a drink. Check why certain things didn't get done. Were you not tough enough with yourself? Too easy on other people? Check that you're not striving for perfection. (That way madness lies.)

Ask yourself whether you are deleting and delegating enough of your housework. Think of a mother not as the family servant, but as the family housekeeper. Traditionally, a housekeeper's job is to organize, delegate and supervise. Of course, getting a child to do some simple chores frequently (see p. 299) takes three times as long as doing it yourself (to begin with, anyway), but anyone takes longer to do anything the first time around (consider your first use of any new appliance), and anyway you should be bringing up the kids to do things for themselves, which leads to self-reliance. It is NOT quicker to do it yourself. It's quicker not to do it. Accept the fact that your helpers may not do things as well as you. Simply remember (1) that you are not doing them; (2) to handsomely praise effort (which is what you wish people would do for you).

Try different work systems until you find one that suits you. I do a great deal of work and a great deal of entertaining and get help from whoever is in the house on Saturday morning (which is when as much of the housework gets done as is going to get done). I have trained my children to shop and cook for themselves and for me: they have done so since they were twelve. It is good for all of us, especially me, and they like the system because they learn to cook, they get to eat what they want and they get paid for their work. Accept the fact that, like the Sunday newspapers, you are not indispensable. Then you will feel less guilt about your shrinking lists. It's more fun having spare time than wearing an invisible martyr's crown.

Another way of lessening your work is to learn to say NO, and to keep saying it, cheerfully, but firmly, whenever *anyone* asks you to do *anything* that isn't on your lists. The trick here is to say "NO" as the first word, followed, perhaps, by an explanation, although no explanation is necessary, just a repetition of your first monosyllabic message, or perhaps "I'm afraid not" or "I'm sorry I can't." Say this charmingly and firmly, then *stop*. (That's the second trick.) Then let the other person speak. If you are immediately asked again, immediately repeat the routine.

Don't Alter It the Second Time

No matter how worthy other people's problems are, their A, B, C and D lists are not your concern. Don't let other people delegate to you.

Learn to protect your time, because your time is what you need first of all, in order to achieve *anything* . . . Today's time, that is. The way to stop wishing you'd done more in the past, or thinking in terms of vague daydreams for the future, it is to stop and start those lists TODAY. You have nothing to lose, except your life.

Cautionary tale: When I stopped full-time work and

started working from home, by writing this book, I made one big, basic mistake. I realized that I would have to be my own secretary and maid, so I used to play that role in the morning and leave the afternoon free for my work, which brought in the money. The drawback was that I never finished the morning's work until 6 o'clock. What I had to learn was to reverse the procedure and do my productive work in the morning and the system support-work afterwards.

CHOOSING THE BEST WORK PATTERN

Should you work part time or full time? It depends on your needs. When I had my first baby, I did part-time design work at home. Then I worked full time in an office with resident home help. Then I worked full time at home with no home help. Now I work at home full time when my youngest son is at school and theoretically not at all when he is home on vacation (hohum). I have found it easiest (but not always possible) to go out to work full time and pay for adequate home help. For me working part time seemed to involve twice the work for half the money, with none of the office perks and protections.

I am not the only woman to have found that part-time work at home is 10 times more difficult than it sounds. It's because you are trying to do at least 2 jobs at once. Of course the children interrupt you and so does the phone, whether you're trying to start a business or write a short story in your kitchen. Of course you answer the phone, the door, take in your neighbor's laundry, and stave off various door-to-door salespeople. It certainly seems easier to work part time if you leave home to do it.

I know one author of detective stories who leaves her home every morning at 11, catches a bus to a room she rents, and works until 2 P.M., when she returns home. If renting a room is a prohibitive expense, try swapping homes with a friend who also wants to work (you'll have less difficulty dealing with her domestic responsibilities and interruptions).

Working at Home

After my home business got groggily on its feet, I found I could afford a secretary, who now comes in one day a week. I feel I'm not struggling along entirely on my own, and knowing that I'm going to have Nicola's help on Mondays acts as a good discipline for me to get all my office work ready in time for that day—no matter how early I have to get up—when it gets polished off in one swoop.

Apart from the problem of interruptions, there's nothing basically difficult about working from your home—almost all businesses were run from home cottages until 1840 and the advent of the Industrial Revolution. There are many businesses that could be run from home today provided local zoning laws allow for it, for instance, a travel agency, public relations firm, real estate agency, and any kind of design work, fashion or otherwise.

One of my neighbors got tired of producing make-believe costumes for the local kids (fairy, witch, knight, wizard, Superman, spaceman), so she had cards printed, took sample kits to local shops, and now works almost all year round running DRESSING UP, INC., from her rumpus room.

There are many other part-time jobs or services that can be managed from home, but beware of the following pitfalls:

- Any grand title (such as Market Research Agent) in an advertisement. They're usually disguising door-to-door or telephone selling on commission.
- Any advertisement involving a registration fee for being put on their list. Any request for money.
- Advertisements that promise amazing results. You are unlikely to make "hundreds of dollars" in your spare time. (Check the *Hustle Jungle Survival Kit*.)
- Being led by advertisements into purchasing expensive equipment to make items, such as knitwear or toys.
- Unlicensed employment agencies.
- Correspondence courses that offer to turn you into a Top Model or Harold Robbins within months. A lot of women try to get back into the job market via a vocational school. If so, make sure you speak to some-

one well established in the particular industry you're aiming at or to the commercial establishments for which you wish to work as a result of the training, and find out if any of them are hiring people who are graduates of that school. Speak to other people who have gone to the school and find out if they got their jobs as a result. There have, for instance, been occurrences of training on computers that were so obsolete that the whole course was useless. Be very careful of training at vocational schools. Get advice on contracts, make sure you don't sign anything too easily (beware of the salesman's smooth pitch).

Only a working mother understands the weight of anxieties such as how-can-I-get-time-off-to-take-him-to-the-dentist. *You* could be the neighborhood home sitter: For instance, women who are at work can't be at home to receive deliveries, get meters read, or accommodate the repairman.

Then, too, evening door-to-door salesmen are very successful, and many companies are aware of the vital fact that the housewife with the fattest wallet is most likely to be at home in the evening. So why not try some job that services the working woman after 6 P.M.?

Anyway, remember that somebody, somewhere, needs you, and there are plenty of ways of meeting up with that person apart from agencies, advertising in local newspapers, leaving your brand-new calling cards all over town, and telephoning everyone you know in the neighborhood to tell them (briefly) of your plans.

IF YOU PROVIDE A SERVICE:

- Have a telephone answering machine or service; one no-answer is enough to put off a would-be client forever.
- Organize an office area in your home, even if it's only a drawer.
- Be reliable. Don't have an amateur, pin-money attitude about your job. People are going to expect you to be unreliable (and in my experience, I'm sorry to have to admit, part-time women workers are, more often than not), which is all the more reason why you shouldn't be. Remember NO EXCUSES ARE EXCUSES.

ADVICE FROM THE TOP

Where home and job juggling is concerned I think you can serenely keep 2 balls in the air simultaneously (job and children, job and mate, children and mate), but 3 is very difficult.

It seems to me that there might be 2 main reasons for this: (1) There are not enough day-care-center facilities provided for working mothers (nursery schools, preschool playgroups, regular vacation playgroups) and (2) Where a mate is involved, there is still some predetermined code of gracious living to live up to and a whole lot of guilt if you don't. It can be much easier to run a place in a relaxed and logical fashion if there isn't a man around.

There's Nothing Like Learning from a Good Example

If your man is enlightened, if he salutes all the shoulds and oughts, well, that's wonderful. But what can you do if he doesn't? I asked Elinor Guggenheimer, former New York City Commissioner for Consumer Affairs, a mother and grandmother who has been champion of the day-care-center movement since the late 1940s and has a demanding weekly TV and radio schedule, as well as being a member of nearly 24 organizations.

I learned long ago that you can't juggle a husband. You have to lay down the ground rules at some point and come to an understanding. My husband used to get very, very angry if I got home after he did, so eventually I sat down and I said to him, "O.K., my marriage means a great deal to me. Do you want me to give up my career? If so, I'll do it. I'm not going to be so happy, because I need to be busy, but I will not have a career and a feeling of guilt tied up together because it's not worth living that way.

"Guilt is the most devastating thing to live with and one should never have to do it. You've got to accept that there are times when I'm going to be coming in late because I can't compromise with my job."

She advises women who can't get or afford day care to form their own small group, which is what her daughter-in-law did.

There were 8 mothers and 2 of the mothers would be on duty for one week a month, so that the other 6 mothers had 3 weeks off. And those 2 mothers planned a whole set of activities, working in pairs. They sent for books and learned how to do crafts and about nursery school programming. They managed it by working in pairs of friends, and they only did a morning-only program; they didn't attempt it for a whole day. What you have to watch for, in *any* sort of voluntary work, is not to take on too much of it to begin with and to understand the responsibility. You must pledge yourself to take it seriously and be totally dependable. You can't have someone producing even a *good* reason for not doing it. You have to be as dependable as if *you* depended on your work.

You must sort out your priorities. Nobody gets *everything* they want; you must decide what you want *most*. I have cut out a lot of our social life. Also, I say beforehand to friends, "I'm sorry, I know you think that your party won't be a success unless we stay until midnight, but we are going to leave at 10:30 because I need 8 hours' sleep a night, and if that upsets you, then you musn't ask us again." I wish I could cut down my sleep but I can't, and you have to admit that you're not Napoleon and it's important to recognize how much sleep you need: If I have less than my needs I feel tired the next day, which sort of wrecks that day.

I have long learned to condense the early mornings; I can now get dressed, have breakfast, and be out the front door half an hour after waking up. I don't do exercises and I always bathe at night.

You need some time of the day exclusively to yourself: You really need it. It's more difficult to get if you have small children, but then it's more necessary that you get it. For me, when I come home tired, 20 minutes is spent in the bathtub—I pour everything in it—it smells of flowers, it's colored, it bubbles! It's the one piece of cosmetic nonsense I go in for, and every woman needs a bit of frivolity, as well as time to herself.

And we don't go in for Gracious Living, but we always have a Gracious Cocktail Time. It might be wine, it might be tomato juice or martini or scotch, depending on our mood, but it's the time that we sit down and do *nothing*. This also is essential, just sitting down and relaxing and chatting together; even if we're going out, we always do it for 10 or 15 minutes.

If you want to enjoy a busy life you have to become fast and efficient and discipline yourself to getting the good things as well as avoiding the bad.

I have learned that there is no *one* right way of doing things. Everything depends on who you are and the way you want to live. Nobody can tell you totally how to organize yourself because it depends on what you like doing and why and what you want and what you don't. You have to find out what *your* needs are and then you formulate your own private rules.

At home I don't do anything I hate. I've always loathed making beds so we never sat down and talked about it, but my husband makes the beds. He hates washing dishes, so I do it. Everybody has to work out his own values and compromises.

If you have to continue housekeeping with a job, you become fast and efficient because you can't manage otherwise. You learn 2 things which give you a huge advantage over the wife who has no outside job; you learn how to make decisions quickly and you learn not to waste time. I have a friend who doesn't do anything and who can spend her entire day doing it. Most working women can do the same amount of work that a nonworking woman can do in half the time.

On the other hand, you pay for this time-saving, because you spend a bit more in some ways, although less in others. I spend more money than I need to because I lack the time to do what I advise every consumer to do—comparison shop.

I use a mail order all the time, because it's so easy, from buying panty hose onwards. I also buy over the telephone a great deal. I have a contact in the dress store I deal with regularly who I'll call up and say

"Have you anything for a gala opening or a farm in the Midwest in July?" and she'll say "NO," so I say "Well, could you please find me something," and she will. That way I save time but I may spend a few dollars more. On the other hand you save money, because you're not in the stores being tempted to buy, so I think things balance out.

I don't spend much on food and we eat simply—dishes that can be put together quickly. When we're alone together we eat in the kitchen from plastic plates. I must admit that I have moved very far away from elegant living. I love looking at those home magazines with candles and everything matching, but when we're home alone it's the last thing we bother about. Because for me, Gracious Living has nothing to do with whether you eat from a plastic container. It has to do with the feeling of fulfillment, of time for yourself, work for yourself, leisure for yourself.

WHAT TO DO IF YOU CAN'T COPE
(Including How to Avoid a Small Nervous Breakdown)

Unless you live in a convent in the country you will need, in these depressingly stressful times, to make a conscious effort to relax, to unwind, to combat tension and frustration. So what can you do when you're exhausted and shortly have to scintillate again?

2-MINUTE FRESHENER: If you're tired at any time—even if it's when you wake up—dash to the nearest source of fresh air and take half a dozen deep breaths. Breathe in as slowly as possible, hold the breath for 10 seconds, then breathe in yet more, and hold it. Then expel all your breath as slowly as possible. When you think all the air has left your lungs, try to squeeze still more out.

15-MINUTE FRESHENER: Take your shoes off and loosen your clothes, especially around your waist.

As you won't have time to reapply makeup, dampen your face with a sponge or cloth wrung out in cold water, a premoistened towelette, or a splash of eau de cologne. *Allow 2 minutes.*

Draw the drapes, lie on the floor, put a blanket over yourself—relax in the dark and think of black velvet. *Allow 5 minutes.* (Use a kitchen timer so that you won't be anxious about overdoing it, which will keep you from relaxing properly.) Then, still on the floor, s-t-r-e-t-c-h like a cat, several times. Stand up with legs apart, hold arms over head, and stretch again. *Allow 2 minutes.*

Tuck a towel around your shoulders, lean over a basin, and with cold water lavishly sponge the back of your neck and wrists. If possible, sponge your ankles, it's not as inconvenient as it sounds. *Allow 2 minutes.*

Adjust your clothes, check your makeup. *Allow 4 minutes.* If you have time, walk slowly around the block, breathing slowly.

30-MINUTE FRESHENER: Warm a room and pull the shades or drapes. Take off your shoes, loosen or take off your clothes, and put on something loose, light, and comfortable, such as a dressing gown. Lie on the floor (on a rug if there's no carpet) with no pillows and no sound, not even radio music. Try to make your mind utterly blank—concentrate on thinking of gray fog, black velvet, or soft white light.

Try to relax your body bit by bit, letting each part go completely limp in turn from your toes up. Concentrate firmly on *relaxing* each bit of your anatomy in turn, especially your neck. It sometimes helps to tighten each muscle, then relax it. *Allow 10 minutes.*

Stand up and stretch slowly with your eyes shut; then work through the following simple yoga exercises very slowly, stretching as much as possible.

- *Relaxer 1.* Sit up straight. Keep shoulders straight. Slowly roll your head in a circle, 6 times clockwise, then 6 times counterclockwise. Try and stretch your neck as far forward, sideways, and backward as it can go. *Repeat twice.*
- *Relaxer 2.* Sit up straight. Hunch both shoulders forward and then slowly rotate them at the same time. Do it 6 times, then hold your shoulders as far back as they will go, and rotate them backwards 6 times. *Repeat twice.*
- *Relaxer 3.* Stand up without shoes. Flop downward from your waist, arms down—don't try to reach the

floor, just let your weight sag toward the floor. Stay there for 1 minute, then *very slowly* pull yourself straight again, take a deep breath, and stretch your hands to the ceiling. Try to touch it, stiffen kneecaps and bottom. Higher . . . now higher. (Don't stand on tiptoe.) *Repeat twice.*

* *Relaxer 4.* Stand with legs slightly apart. Clasp your hands behind your back (palms facing floor), and slowly lift them backwards and upward as high as you can (keep elbows straight). Lean forward from the waist, raise your clasped hands as far as possible. You should feel the weight of your hands pulling your arms over your head toward the floor. Count to 30 slowly. Slowly straighten up. *Allow 10 minutes.*

* *Relaxer 5.* Lie on your back, hands at your sides, and *slowly* suck in your stomach for a count of 10, breathing in. Slowly breathe out. Don't be afraid to push your stomach out as far as it will go. *Do this exercise for 1 minute.*

* Lastly, lie flat on your back and think of nothing for an additional *5 minutes.* You should then rise a new woman. Allow *5 minutes* to dress again.

OTHER TENSION RELIEVERS: These include soothing, slow, repetitive work with end results, such as *knitting, tapestry work,* and *embroidery*—sewing, painting, and writing aren't mindless enough. Some people find gardening is good therapy, as well as a way of getting exercise in the sun and fresh air.

Novelist Mary Stewart has the most immaculate garden possible, because whenever she gets stuck on a story she goes out and fiercely weeds.

Before she was married, Tish Baldridge (who was Jacqueline Kennedy's social secretary at the White House) used to invite herself to different friends' houses to do their gardening. She would mow and rake, weed and prune, until she was exhausted and could sleep like a log.

You might also try to escape the insatiable demands of civilization for a few days. Here's how to:

* *Ignore the telephone.* Take it off the hook.
* *Ignore the mail.* Put it, unopened, in a basket and deal with it all next Monday morning.
* *Ignore the television.* Unplug it.

- *Ignore the newspapers.* Put them in the basket until next Monday morning. Then throw them away.

If you are really near screaming point, the best tension reliever is to *remove yourself from the action.* Go anywhere—but go. This isn't easy if you're surrounded by yowling toddlers, but if this isn't the case, you ought to be able to quietly excuse yourself, or loudly storm out, or rush away to cry in private. But *go.* It may be for a calming walk around the block, an hour's trip on the river, a bus ride, a weekend in the country, or Back To Mother, but take however long you feel you need. It's only common sense to remove yourself from what's driving you out of your skull because of pressures, indignation, noise, or exhaustion. Whatever you do, don't jump into the car and externalize your feelings on the accelerator.

Pressures and tensions are not confined to women with jobs or women with young children. Historical biographer Elizabeth Longford had 8 children. They are all dispersed now, and the weekday turmoil of her early writing days has quietened, but there is still such a lot to be done on weekends when grandchildren arrive. She says,

Sometimes I wake up early with "morning panic." I survey what's got to be done in the rest of the week and I (madly) go on to the rest of the month and finally I am in a state of absolute panic and see that I can't possibly get it done at all. But as the day proceeds I will slowly stabilize it and realize that things perhaps can be done. I make an "effort of concentration"; it used to be against the children, but now that they are gone it's an effort of concentration against just—all the things that keep coming up.

But what when an effort of concentration no longer helps? What should you do if you can't manage a husband, children, and a full-time job? Signs of overwork are nervous tension, irritability, exhaustion, indigestion, severe headaches, insomnia. If you reach this point, not only will you be suffering, but your family will be, too.

Try to simplify your home life. Try to simplify your job, or take a part-time job near your home. (This is especially easy if you have secretarial qualifications.) As I keep saying, what a working woman needs is a fast and unerring sense of priority. Often a woman feels that she can't cope because she's expected to cope with too much. Often, the person who expects her to do it is the woman herself. In which case try the Conran Power of Negative Thinking (do less and achieve more), and go back and reread the introduction to this book. Remember that a superwoman is someone who knows her own limitations and has the strength of character to stay within them.

If you ever feel you have too much to do, if you can't get to sleep, or if you keep waking up at night wondering how you're going to cope, why then stop coping. Stop doing all of it. Get off the frenetic treadmill.

If stress is a problem, try TM classes—you can learn to meditate and relax in six easy lessons. Look up the center nearest you in the phone book under Transcendental Meditation or Maharishi International College (MIC).

HOW TO HAVE A SMALL NERVOUS BREAKDOWN

The following method can't help you avoid a Grade A clinical nervous collapse, but, through self-analysis and a medically approved treatment, it really *can* help you avoid a breakdown caused by too much day-to-day stress. It is extreme advice for an extreme condition and 3 days would be the minimum time for the treatment at home. (If your condition is even worse, you probably need at least 7 days at a clinic, rest home, health farm, or hospital.)

- *First day.* Give yourself half an hour to cancel everything you've arranged for the next 3 days. If you have children, dump them, delegate them, or hire someone else to look after them. You can't afford not to if you're really at the breaking point.

  Draw the shades or drapes; take the phone off the hook; warm the room if necessary. Take a warm bath (not hot). Climb into a clean nightgown and go to bed.

  Lie in bed all day. Keep the room dark. Don't read, write, or listen to music or the radio, and try not to think. Don't plan revenge, accusations, vacations, how to get him back, or your way out of this mess. DO NOTHING. Don't take pills. Don't drink alcohol. Drink orange juice, weak tea, or hot milk with a little honey.

- *Second day.* Write down the main things that are worrying you. Try to reduce them to 3 sentences with no subclauses.

  Check out guilt. Remember that Woman Is Imperfect. Remember that you've done an awful lot of "wrong" things in your life and (like most of us) you're probably going to do a lot more. We all make mistakes, all the time, and always will. Remember that it is pointless to blame yourself for anything that has happened and is past.

  Check out self-pity. Remember that it is dangerous, self-indulgent, and renders you unable to assess a situation correctly. This form of ego massage does you no good and *can* do you a great deal of harm.

  If someone's treating you badly through ignorance, envy, fear, or sheer basic nastiness, they've got the real problem, not you. Don't give them the satisfaction of letting yourself get upset because of their bad treatment. Get indignant, stick pins into a wax doll, pummel the pillows, but try not to let this sort of unfair unpleasantness get to you, upset you, because it's pointless.

  Remember that the President is elected to look after the rest of the world, not you. Mind your own business. Other people's problems are not your affair at the moment.

  Lie in bed all day. Keep the room dark in the afternoon. Don't read. Don't talk. DO NOTHING.

- *Third day.* Have another look at those 3 sentences you wrote yesterday summing up what's wrong with your situation.

Talk to your nearest and dearest about them. If your dearest isn't near enough, or you haven't got one, call your doctor and ask his advice.

Then make a few lists. Write down all the things you want to do, all the things you enjoy doing, all the things you don't much like, and all the things you hate. Concentrate ruthlessly on eliminating the things you hate. Then figure out how you can get other people to do the things you hate but can't eliminate, and work out how much it would cost you in terms of money and spirit. Develop the fine art of farming things out.

If you feel you can do it without bursting into tears, sit upright in bed, propped up by the pillows, and ask yourself:

Who am I?
What am I doing?
Where am I going?

Or maybe leave that till next month. Today, remember that from now on your motto should be: ONE THING AT A TIME AND THAT WELL DONE.

There are two sorts of crisis; there is the personal one, such as the loss of a job or of a loved one by death or divorce, or the communal one, such as an expressway that rips through your suburb, or a flood, or a war. But there always seems to be some sort of crisis.

There's nothing like being personally machine-gunned on your way home from school (as I was during the Second World War) to make you realize that someone is actually—amazingly—unreasonably out to get you, and that you had better do something about it fast. But it's much harder to be wiped out (emotionally, physically or financially) than you ever suspected.

Obviously what you gain from a crisis is self-knowledge and greater independence and self-confidence, since your own resourcefulness has now been tested. You also gain the knowledge that when the time comes to face all the dreaded nightmares, they're not nearly as bad as you've imagined.

Once out the other side of the tunnel, a sort of survivor syndrome sets in. You have come through.

CRISIS AVERSION

You can sometimes prepare for material mishaps, or prudently ward them off or deal with them in practical ways. As far as material mishaps are concerned, I go into procedures and preparations to safeguard yourself in almost every chapter of this book. You can, of course, be *over*-prepared; you can have an atomic fall-out shelter in your garden and buy two of everything in case one breaks, in which case you'll have half as much money and twice as many things to look after, worry about and insure, but for disasters that affect your ego and your emotions, you can only prepare a broad psychological strategy. The first thing to realize is that only YOU can mentally prepare yourself for great personal wounds and losses, and you'd also better face up to the fact that in life they are bound to happen.

When personal disaster strikes, you probably need sympathy and practical help; but there is a distinct possibility (especially if everyone else is also swimming for the life-boats) that the only person who is always interested in you, and able to provide you with sustained help is . . . YOURSELF.

Don't think "somebody ought to do something about it" or "the government should see to it." Start thinking in terms of self-reliance. What *you* can do and what *you* can't do—that may be all you can count on. Whatever your crisis, force yourself to look cheerful. Shakespeare said: "There is nothing either good or bad, but thinking makes it so," and Napoleon added that "the moral is to material as three to one." I would also say that the quickest facelift is a smile. Go on—try it, just for today SMILE and try to find something good instead of something bad in every new situation.

I'm not suggesting that when disaster strikes you can Pollyanna your way through; in fact, it may be a great mistake to think that you can instantly surmount your troubles. As the distinguished psychoanalyst Karen Horney wrote in *Self Analysis*, "The blitzkrieg approach to problem solving is never a good method . . . The person who is overconfident believes that he can eradicate his problem by direct action as simply as he switches off an electric light To some extent this expectation is based on wishful thinking; he would like to remove quickly the disability that disturbs him; and he likes to think that apart from this outstanding disturbance everything is all right. He does not like to face the fact that an overt difficulty may be merely an indication that something is basically wrong with his relationship to himself and others."

Again, I'm not suggesting that you should rush off to a shrink, but *do*:

LOOK ON THE BRIGHT SIDE. I firmly believe in the silver lining of adversity, because there always *is* a bright side, however minor. If your husband disappears, at least you won't ever again have to watch football all Sunday.

FACE YOUR CRISIS and don't hide your head in the sand, ostrich-like. Don't cross your fingers and hope for the best. Face what is here and prepare for what might be coming.

And troubles have a habit of multiplying faster than fieldmice. When you think things simply can't get any worse—*that's* when the roof falls in. And then it starts snowing.

BE CONSTRUCTIVELY SELFISH: Think of yourself first. If you're not healthy and functioning efficiently, you can't look after your family or do your job. Ignore accusations of selfishness, egotism or ruthlessness from those who resent that you won't do what they (selfishly) want you to do. The need for self-preservation forces everyone to be selfish.

DON'T HOPE TO CHANGE ANYONE OR THEIR ATTITUDES: It will probably be an exhausting waste of time.

DON'T HATE ANYONE: It's a destructive waste of energy. Try to ignore that person and try to make sure that you are no longer vulnerable to him or her.

RECOGNIZE YOUR PRACTICAL AND EMOTIONAL LIMITATIONS: If you can't control your temper, look for ways to avoid losing it. Don't allow yourself to be tempted or bullied into any emotionally upsetting situations which you can avoid.

DON'T HOPE. Hope is dangerous if it is over-optimistic, and can stop you viewing your situation realistically.

TRY NOT TO WORRY. It can't do any good and it's often only a habit. ("Your mother's a worrier.")

DON'T TALK ON AND ON ABOUT IT. People may get bored or embarrassed. So keep it to yourself. Especially divorce.

DON'T BE SELF-PITYING. You don't need pity; you need clear thought and action.

"Thought must be the harder; the heart the keener.
Courage must be greater as our strength grows less."

A fighting Anglo-Saxon chieftain said that; whoever he
was, he sounds like a survivor.

MAKE ALLOWANCES FOR YOUR WEAKNESSES: It's unrealistic to
give up smoking to save money now, if that's the only
thing that takes your mind off your problem. Just make
sure you don't start smoking more.

COUNT YOUR FRIENDS: Whatever your crisis, it is important
to realize that it has happened before. Trust your true
friends to understand and sympathize, although it may
not be within their power to help in practical matters.
Don't mind asking for simple practical help when it is
needed. At the worst, they can only say no. Some people
in this world *are* selfish, but it *helps* most people to give
help when it's in their power. Those who have been
through hard times are glad to pay back the help they've
had from others. This is the way the help chain works.

DON'T ASK TOO MUCH OF YOUR RIGHTS: The less you rely
upon them the less you risk disappointment—when a few
dollars takes months to come through or someone else's
inefficiency negates your claim.

COUNT YOUR RESOURCES: Your money, time, talent, possessions and family help. Write them down in a list. Mine
started with "mother" and ended with "electric blanket."
I looked at this long list (there were other things in between) and thought, "How dare you feel sorry for yourself?"

GET EXPERT ADVICE: A survivor must be practical. Assess
your immediate problems, write them down and seek objective advice to clarify your situation. No one can think
clearly when disaster strikes. You might need to visit a
specialist, solicitor or accountant.

Be careful of those old Dutch Uncles. It may be better
to *hire* one, with professional experience in the area you
need: He might be a family counsellor; he might be a psychiatrist (you might ask him about group encounter
therapy which many people find more stimulating and rewarding than conventional therapy, as well as being possibly quicker and definitely cheaper). Your Dutch Uncle
might even be a career consultant: there's nothing like a
new job to reinflate your ego.

You must also realize that you might be in a state of shock, which is a physical illness. Don't hesitate to go to a doctor if you have any unusual symptoms and be sure to tell him the whole problem, not just the physical symptoms. Again, don't be proud or ashamed, or feel that you are wasting his time. He's heard it all a million times before and your problems will obviously be treated as confidential. To pride yourself on *not* going to the doctor or to think you are making a fuss, might harm you and might impair your efficiency for dealing with your crisis.

MAKE YOUR OWN DECISIONS: Although specialists may be useful to analyse a situation and suggest solutions, they cannot run your life for you. Once your choices are clarified, use your common sense to make your own decisions. Then force yourself to be pessimistic, *to look for the snags* in the arrangements and face them. Don't opt out because you don't understand your position: Make your adviser explain it all again until you *do* understand it, and so can be responsible for deciding which path you want to take. Be prepared to be responsible for your own decisions. Life is a risk. Nothing is certain in this world, and there is no guaranteed security, financial, intellectual or emotional. Security lies in your own self-reliance to deal with the problems of life. You will make some right decisions and some wrong ones. Pay the penalty for the wrong ones, cut your losses and start again.

Never make a major decision under pressure or if you are upset. Wait at least twenty-four hours until you can think more clearly. Also wait twenty-four hours before sending an emotional letter. Then tear it up.

THE ADVANTAGES OF A CRISIS

A crisis can be a blessing in disguise if it makes you stop and take a long look at your life, and then cut out the clutter.

CUT OUT WASTE: Don't waste money, resources, time or friendship. You can now stop feeling obliged to do things just because others expect them from you. There are now plenty of reasons and excuses.

There are a lot of things in life that you needn't do. You don't have to cook a hot lunch on Sunday or return the Jones's invitation, or attend parties if they make you nervous, or functions that bore you.

DON'T WASTE TIME: And if you've suddenly got more of it than ever before, try to look upon it as a life-enriching bonus. If you've wished for more time in the past—now's your time to use it.

Use that time for more creative leisure, active sports and hobbies, doing things *with* your children instead of *for* them, or taking an inexpensive, stimulating course. Think of something rewarding to do and start DOING IT NOW.

STOP WANTING THINGS: Are you wasting time, effort and money doing things and buying luxuries that you don't really need? After all, your grandparents got along without a freezer or air-conditioning; try switching off the sound on the TV commercials for a start and then start trying to tell the differences between a wish and a want. A wish is not a true need, but can be an artificially stimulated status symbol. In other words, unnecessary.

WHEN RECOVERING FROM A CRISIS, you should be somewhat like Hercule Poirot solving a murder. In trying to figure out What Went Wrong, you can sort out, analyse and examine all the clues (i.e. has anything like this ever happened to you before?) and separate the outside causes of calamity from those which may have come from within yourself. (If in doubt, charge them up to yourself.)

If your disaster involves guilt and self-hatred, however far-fetched and pointless ("But I thought he knew how to swim"), then you should see your family doctor.

If your disaster involves your pride (loss of job or lover), accept the fact that your ego may have taken a terrible blow, that it's just had major surgery and needs time to recover from the wound.

A main problem may be to restore your eroded self-esteem. Just how do you get the gilt back on the gingerbread? Family, friends and lovers can help but it's sometimes easier to seek objective, professional advice (and I don't mean an astrologer) as well as love and sympathy. Without being self-pitiful or making excuses for yourself, perhaps it's simply time to be nicer to yourself? Perhaps no one else has been for some time?

If so, prepare a few little treats for yourself. Buy a stack of paperbacks, buy yourself some flowers, go on a boat trip, *get outside the front door*.

It's tremendously good therapy to get involved with something outside yourself. Try working for the community chest or the local cancer drive or your church and you'll not only be helping people, but also you'll maybe see how minor your troubles are, compared with those of others! And you'll also find out that casting a little bread upon the waters *often* brings back caviar on toast, just so long as you never count on it.

IN A COMMUNITY CRISIS

SHARE YOUR TROUBLES AND SHARE THE SOLUTIONS TO THEM, whether it's grouping together to buy groceries in bulk or passing on a good recipe. All over the country people may be having similar problems. Pool your resources. Start lending things, the way people did in wartime.

Share clothes; advertise in your local paper right now for a swap baby-sitter; baby-sitter-swapping is *far* more liberating than wife-swapping. If one person answers the ad you can take turns to sit for each other. If two or three people answer it you might as well be a bulk baby-sitter if you're stuck doing it anyway. You could each of you look after three babies a morning, or afternoon or day and have the rest of the week free. Wouldn't that be nice for a bit? If more than one person answers the advertisement, start a pool. Don't wait for someone else—*you* do it. Nothing gets started unless somebody starts it, and if nobody else seems to have thought of it, why shouldn't that someone be you?

Today we are threatened on all sides by pollution, inflation, economic uncertainties and political malaise. However, you aren't the head of General Motors or the Prime Minister. Let those people continue to shoulder all *their* responsibilities. What *you* can do is mind your own business, check the kitchen cabinets and the electric blanket (crises are always cold) and start digging a vegetable garden. Voltaire said: "*Il faut cultiver notre jardin*," and I'm sure that if that sensible man were alive today he'd tell us to turn it over to vegetables.

THE SIMPLE LIFE

and do you want it?

This book is about eliminating unnecessary worry, upkeep, and maintenance time. However, it's when the monthly bills pour in that you often think of dropping out, selling out, and heading out—maybe for a commune in California.

It is probably unnecessary to tell you that unless you are very young, adaptable, and accustomed to an austere rustic life, a utopian commune in which you own nothing and have no rights to anything (not even to your own child), you, like thousands of others who have tried the collective life, may be bitterly disappointed.

I used to worry about the bomb. Not if it *got* me, of course, but if I survived and had to lead the simple life. My problem would then be how would I get to the mountains in order to start procreating with the other few survivors? So I went out and bought myself a pair of stout walking shoes for women at an explorers' shop (these are every bit as flattering to the ankle as they sound). I real-

ized that I would have to take them off fast if I was ever
to get anyone to procreate with me. It's a bit of a strain
to lift either foot when I'm wearing them, but they stopped
me from worrying about the bomb, just like that.

I also bought a book on self-sufficiency, which, with
my shoes, makes up the complete survival kit. This book
tells a sheltered female like me, brought up on meatballs
and television, just the sort of thing I might find expected
of me when I eventually arrive in the mountains, late as
usual. Undoubtedly everyone else would already have
gotten there first and collared the best jobs, like editing
the *Survivor's Daily* or being Chief Wife. But, survival
book in hand, I would know how to slit the throat of an
ox, I would be able to gaff salmon, and know what to do
if a cow gets diarrhea (and to think that once I couldn't
even *spell* it).

Wise words would drip from my lips ("When you have
got the cow there is no more care about manure."—Wil-
liam Corbett), and I would cultivate popularity, when not
slitting throats, by making delicious butter, cream, cheese,
bread, beer, and wine, and growing parsnip, elderberry,
and potent rhubarb, all according to the instructions (with
none of your spoonfuls of this and that. Now I would be
into the 60-gallon-vat league.

I would also produce pickled herring and smoked
salmon. If the children were good, I might let them tend
my underwater fish farm. I would start an orchard and
keep the bees humming in their hives underneath the fruit
trees. I would gather the peaches, walnuts, and water-
melons, and feast on asparagus tips (my own), and maybe
trap pheasants when I got bored. Frankly, what with feed-
ing the pigs, hoeing the garden, patching clothes, and running the still, I don't see when I would find the time to
procreate.

But fantasy aside, you must face the realities if you're
pining to get rid of your troubles and go back to the land.
It's not as easy as it sounds. There will be a whole lot of
new troubles waiting for you. You must realize how *complicated* the simple life is, you must make sure that you've
been adequately trained to cope with it, and you must give
it a trial run first, because for most of us that isn't the
simple life at all. The simple life is far more likely to be
found in your own home because, paradoxically, our com-

plicated civilization is the only life that we have been trained to lead, and which, for us, is as simple as we care to make it. Better the complexity you know than the so-called simplicity you don't.

Obviously, your present worries may be either emotional or material. First, check the emotional area because you won't shed those problems by leaving, you will carry them with you. On the other hand, problems may be an accumulation of material and financial woes, obligations, and chores. If so, consider this checklist for ways to drastically simplify and uncomplicate your life-style. It should be a life (yours) and style (yours), not some souped-up form of living beyond your means that may be dictated to you by other people. You may be unnecessarily overspending in terms of emotions, energy (mental and physical), as well as time and money.

THE SIMPLIFY-LIFE CHECKLIST

Do you want it? Do you need it? Can you live without it? Will discarding it save you money? Time? Worry? Upkeep? Insurance? In the list below I've starred my own crossed-off items, just to give you something to argue about.

- ★ Jewelry
- ★ Big parties (going or giving)
- ★ Theater
- ★ Movies
- ★ Concerts
- ★ Excess furniture
- ★ Excess rooms
- Personal Transportation
- ★ Inessential home equipment (Conran's last Law says there's always one machine not working and in need of attention)
- ★ Houseplants (very, very reluctantly)
- ★ Pets
- ★ Snacks
- 3 meals a day
- Excess clothing
- ★ Lower temperature central heating
- A second house
- A second anything (or anyone)

However, the things that weigh you down so heavily that you don't have enough free time may not be the case of material possessions but excessive demands on your emotional strength. Perhaps you happily submit to these demands? If so, learn to say NO (with no qualifications) and then learn not to feel guilty about it. Guilt is a point-less waste of time.

THINK METRIC—A Guide to the Metric System

After interminable delays, Congress is expected in the next year or so to approve legislation that would lead to ultimate adoption in the United States of a decimal-based system known as S. I. (from the French name, Système International d'Unités), a modernized version of the metric system that is now used by *all* advanced industrial nations *except* the United States; (Canada is in the process of converting to it). Amazingly enough, the British found the switch almost painless.

In fact, Americans are well on their way to metricization. Speedometers on many new cars use "dual graphics" to record kilometers as well as miles per hour (in contrasting colors). More than half of all canned goods are now labeled in both metric and conventional units. The space program uses metric measurement. And there have always been 100 cents in a dollar.

The reason, of course, is that the crazy-quilt ancient British system is just too awkward and time-consuming.

The great point about the metric system is that it is logical and not based on the length of the big toe, pole, or perch of somebody's Saxon ancestor. The French worked it all out according to reason, just after their Revolution in 1791.

Basic Metric Vocabulary

LENGTH: How long or far is it? Measured in *meters*.
AREA: How much surface does it occupy? Measured in *square centimeters, square meters,* and *hectares*.
VOLUME: How much space does it occupy? Liquid volume is measured in *liters*.
WEIGHT: How heavy is it? Measured in *grams*.
TEMPERATURE: How hot or cold is it? Measured in *degrees*.

All decimal calculations are made in units of 10 and each unit of calculation is interrelated.

The Rock Bottom Basic Metric Measurements

(The only ones you need to remember)

Metric units are in 10s.
1000 millimeters = 100 centimeters = 1 meter
1000 meters = 1 kilometer
1 meter = 1.1 yards (approx.)
1 liter = 1.75 pints (approx.)
1 kilogram = 2.2 pounds (approx.)

Metric System Abbreviations

LENGTH		AREA	
mm	millimeter	mm²	square millimeter
cm	centimeter	cm²	square centimeter
dm	decimeter	dm²	square decimeter
m	meter	m²	square meter
dkm	dekameter	dkm²	square dekameter
hm	hectometer	hm²	square hectometer
km	kilometer	ha	hectare
		km²	square kilometer

VOLUME		WEIGHT	
ml	milliliter	mg	milligram
cl	centiliter	cg	centigram
d	deciliter	dg	decigram
l	liter	g	gram
dkl	dekaliter	dkg	dekagram
hl	hectoliter	hg	hectogram
kl	kiloliter	kg	kilogram

Precise Measurements in Metric System

A little memory aid to help you remember the metric order: *"Kitty, How Does My Dog Catch Mice?"*

The capital letters are those of the metric system in descending order: kilometer, hectameter, dekameter, meter, decimeter, centimeter, millimeter.

The italicized measurements are current usage.

LENGTH

10 millimeters	=	1 centimeter
10 centimeters	=	1 decimeter
10 decimeters	=	1 *meter*
10 meters	=	1 dekameter
10 dekameters	=	1 hectometer
10 hectometers	=	1 *kilometer*

AREA

100 square centimeters	=	1 *square meter*
10,000 square meters	=	1 *hectare*
10 hectares	=	1 square kilometer

VOLUME (Liquid Measure)

1 milliliter	=	1 centiliter
10 centiliters	=	1 *deciliter*
10 deciliters	=	1 *liter*
10 liters	=	1 dekaliter
10 dekaliters	=	1 hectoliter
10 hectoliters	=	1 kiloliter

WEIGHT (Dry Measure)

10 milligrams	=	1 centigram
10 centigrams	=	1 decigram
10 decigrams	=	1 *gram*
10 grams	=	1 *hectogram*
10 hectograms	=	1 *kilogram*

TEMPERATURE
(Celsius is the same as centigrade)

Some Useful Temperatures

C stands for Celsius, F for Fahrenheit.
  0°C (32° F) is the freezing point of water.
  10°C (50°F) is the temperature of a warm winter day.
  20°C (68°F) is the temperature of a mild spring day and
      the new recommended central heating living room
      temperature (cooler than we've been used to).
  30°C (86°F) is the temperature of a hot summer's day.
  37°C (98.4°F) is normal body temperature.
  40°C (104°F) is heat-wave hot.

43°C (110°F) is hot bath temperature.
49°C (119°F) is hand-hot water temperature.
100°C (212°F) is the boiling point of water.

Aids in Converting to Metric Measurements

A brilliant little wallet-sized *quick guide* to the metric system is obtainable from the Superintendent of Documents, U.S. Printing Office, Washington, D.C. 20402. Enclose a self-addressed stamped envelope and 25 cents.

COMPARE METRIC AND CUSTOMARY UNITS

	Length	Volume	Weight	Metric Units are in 10's
				1000 millimeters = 100
				centimeters = 1 meter
Metric	*Meter*	*Liter*	*Kilogram*	1000 meters = 1 kilometer
Customary	Inch	Teaspoon	Grain	1 meter ≅ 1.1 yards
	Foot	Tablespoon	Ounce	1 liter ≅ 1.1 quarts
	Yard	Cup	*Pound*	1 kilogram ≅ 2.2 pounds
	Rod	Pint	Ton	(≅ approximate)
	Mile	*Quart*		
		Gallon		

You can also get a slim pocket 6″ *converting ruler* (see a bit of it below) for metric measurements from the National Bureau of Standards, Washington, D.C. 20234. Send 25 cents and a self-addressed stamped envelope.

Useful Equivalents—Metric to Imperial System

In changing from our current system of measurement (the Imperial System) to the Metric System, it is not enough to know the arithmetic but to have a little picture in your head of what a liter of milk looks like (a bit more than a pint), how far a kilometer is to walk (a long half mile), and what size bra you will need if your bust now measures 90 cm (36″): Standard beauty queen measurements will now be 91-66-91, and we'll be hearing that joke a lot.

LENGTH

Centimeters	Inches
2.5 cm	1 in.
15 cm	6 in.
20 cm	8 in.
25 cm	10 in.
30 cm	12 in. (1 ft)
35 cm	14 in.
60 cm	24 in. (2 ft)
90 cm	36 in. (1 yd)
100 cm (1 m)	40 in.
1.2 m	4 ft.
1.5 m	5 ft.
1.8 m	6 ft.
2.0 m	7 ft.

TRAVELING LENGTHS

Kilometers	Miles
8	5
16	10
48	30
80	50
120	75
161	100

AREA

1 sq cm	=	0.15 sq in.
1 sq m	=	10.8 sq ft = 1.2 sq yd
4,000 sq m	=	approx. 1 acre
1 ha	=	1,000 sq m = 2.5 acres

VOLUME

1 ml	=	a few drops
5 ml	=	1 tsp (standard medicine measurement)
1 l	=	1.06 qt
4 l	=	1.06 gal (4 qt)

(So a 5-l can of paint holds 1.3 gal)

WEIGHT

25 g	=	just over 1 oz
100 g	=	3.6 oz
400 g	=	just under 1 lb
1,000 g	=	1 kg
1 kg	=	2.2 lb

(Relatively) Easy Calculator

It's *really worth* spending two minutes to try this out, using my ABC calculator. As one example, here's how to convert 16 inches, then 5 teaspoons.

(A) 16 in . . . multiplied by (B) 2.5 is (C) 40 cm

(A) 5 teaspoons . . . multiplied by (B) 5 is (C) 25 ml

THE INSTRUCTIONS

Shortened symbol	A Take the number of . . .	B Multiply by . . .	C To find the equivalent number	Shortened symbol

Length

in.	inches	2.5	centimeters	cm
ft	feet	30	centimeters	cm
yd	yards	0.9	meters	m
mi	miles	1.6	kilometers	km

Area

in.^{2}	square inches	6.5	square centimeters	cm^2
ft^2	square feet	0.09	square meters	m^2
yd^2	square yards	0.8	square meters	m^2
mi^2	square miles	2.6	square kilometers	km^2
m	acres	0.4	hectares	ha

Volume

tsp	teaspoons	5	milliliters	ml
Tbsp	tablespoons	15	milliliters	ml
fl oz	fluid ounces	30	milliliters	ml
c	cups	0.24	liters	l
pt	pints	0.56	liters	l
qt	quarts	1.1	liters	l
gal	gallons	4.5	liters	l
ft^3	cubic feet	0.03	cubic meters	m^3
yd^3	cubic yards	0.76	cubic meters	m^3

THE INSTRUCTIONS

A Take the number of . . .	B Multiply by . . .	C To find the equivalent number of	Shortened symbol

Weight

ounces	28	grams	g
pounds	0.45	kilograms	kgr
short tons (2000 lb)	0.9	tons	t

Temperature (exact)

Fahrenheit temperature	5/9 (after subtracting 32)	Celsius temperature	°C

It's also worth spending *another* two minutes, so that you can do it in reverse. Just follow the instructions, D E F. For example:

1) 25 mm . . . multiplied by . . . 0.4 in . . . is 1 in.
2) 140 g . . . multiplied by . . . 0.035 oz . . . is 4.9 oz.

D	E	F	
Take the number of . . .	Multiply by . . .	To find the equivalent number of	Shortened symbol

Length

millimeters	0.04	inches	in.
centimeters	0.4	inches	in.
meters	3.3	feet	ft
meters	1.1	yards	yd
kilometers	0.6	miles	mi

D	E	F	
Take the number of . . .	Multiply by . . .	To find the equivalent number of	Shortened symbol

Area

square centimeters	0.16	square inches	in.^{2}
square meters	1.2	square yards	yd^2
square kilometers	0.4	square miles	mi^2
hectares (10,000m^2)	2.5	acres	

Volume

milliliters	0.03	fluid ounces	fl oz
liters	1.75	pints	pt
liters	0.87	quarts	qt
liters	0.22	gallons	gal
cubic meters	35	cubic feet	ft^3
cubic meters	1.3	cubic yards	yd^3

Weight

grams	0.035	ounces	oz
kilograms	2.2	pounds	lb
tons (1000 kg)	1.1	short tons	

Temperature (exact)

Celsius temperature	9/5 (then add 32)	Fahrenheit temperature	°F

QUIETLY GOING METRIC IN THE KITCHEN

For converting your own recipes from conventional to metric quantities:

Recipe translators generally use 25 grams as a basic unit in place of 1 ounce (rather than the 28 grams which is the accurate equivalent), 575 milliliters in place of 1 pint, (rather than the more accurate 569 milliliters.) The 5-ml and the 15-ml spoons are used in place of the old variable teaspoons and tablespoons. (They will give slightly smaller quantities.)

However, if *you* are translating your recipes, all quantities should be rounded off, *either* upward *or* downward (but only one or the other), so that the *comparative* quantities will remain the same.

Cooking Conversions

Use the following rounded-off measurements.

5 milliliters	=	1 teaspoon
15 milliliters	=	1 tablespoon
50 milliliters	=	¼ cup (60 ml, to be exact)
100 milliliters	=	½ cup (120 ml, to be exact)
200 milliliters	=	¾ cup (180 ml, to be exact)
250 milliliters (approx. ¼ liter)	=	1 cup (240 ml, to be exact)
500 milliliters	=	1 pint (1.06 pt, to be exact)
1 liter	=	1 quart (1.06 qt, to be exact)
4 liters	=	1 gallon (1.06 gal, to be exact)

Recommended Metric Equivalents for
Dry and Liquid Ounces

Dry ounces/ Fluid ounces	Approximate g (dry) and ml (fluid) to nearest whole figure	Recommended conversion to nearest unit of 25 g or ml
1	28	25
2	57	50
3	85	75
4 (¼ pt)	113	100
5	142	150
6	170	175
7	198	200
8 (½ lb) (½ pt)	226	225
9	255	250
10	283	275
11	311	300
12 (¾ pt)	340	350
13	368	375
14	396	400
15	428	425
16 (1 lb) (1 pt)	456	450
17	484	475
18	512	500
19	541	550
20	569	575

When converting quantities over 20 oz, first add the appropriate figures in the center column, *then* adjust to the nearest unit of 25.

Where the proportion between liquids and solids is critical, particularly in baking recipes, an accurate conversion is necessary.

Dry Weight Equivalents—Pounds and Ounces to Grams

0 lb:

1 oz = 28.3 g
2 oz = 56.6 g
3 oz = 85.0 g
4 oz = 113.3 g
5 oz = 141.7 g
6 oz = 170.0 g
7 oz = 198.4 g
8 oz = 226.7 g
9 oz = 255.1 g
10 oz = 283.4 g
11 oz = 311.8 g
12 oz = 340.1 g
13 oz = 368.5 g
14 oz = 396.8 g
15 oz = 425.2 g

1 lb:

0 oz = 453.5 g
1 oz = 481.9 g
2 oz = 510.2 g
3 oz = 538.6 g
4 oz = 566.9 g
5 oz = 595.3 g
6 oz = 623.6 g
7 oz = 652.0 g
8 oz = 680.3 g
9 oz = 708.7 g
10 oz = 737.0 g
11 oz = 765.4 g
12 oz = 793.7 g
13 oz = 822.1 g
14 oz = 850.4 g
15 oz = 878.8 g

2 lb:

0 oz = 907.1 g
1 oz = 935.5 g
2 oz = 963.8 g
3 oz = 992.2 g
4 oz = 1020.5 g
5 oz = 1048.9 g
6 oz = 1077.2 g
7 oz = 1105.6 g
8 oz = 1133.9 g
9 oz = 1162.3 g
10 oz = 1190.6 g
11 oz = 1219.0 g
12 oz = 1247.3 g
13 oz = 1275.7 g
14 oz = 1304.0 g
15 oz = 1332.4 g

3 lb:

0 oz = 1360.7 g
1 oz = 1389.1 g
2 oz = 1417.5 g
3 oz = 1445.8 g
4 oz = 1474.1 g
5 oz = 1502.5 g
6 oz = 1530.8 g
7 oz = 1559.2 g
8 oz = 1587.5 g
9 oz = 1615.9 g
10 oz = 1644.2 g
11 oz = 1672.6 g
12 oz = 1700.9 g
13 oz = 1729.3 g
14 oz = 1757.6 g
15 oz = 1786.0 g

4 lb:

20 oz = 1814.3 g

Oven Temperatures—Converting from Fahrenheit to Centigrade

		To Cook
Very cool	240°F = 116°C	Stews, meringues
Cool	275°F = 135°C	Casseroles, milk and
	290°F = 144°C	egg dishes
Slow	325°F = 163°C	Lamb and slow beef roasts
Moderate	350°F = 177°C	Cookies, cakes, pies
	375°F = 190°C	Fruit cake
Moderately hot	400°F = 200°C	
Hot	425°F = 218°C	Soufflé, flan, short pastry, sponge cake
Very hot	450°F = 232°C	Fast roasts, bread, flaky pastry
	475°F = 246°C	

All ovens aren't the same: Some tend to be hotter than the temperature at which they have been set; allow for the idiosyncrasies of your oven in using the table above and follow manufacturer's instructions.

Meat Roasting

A meat thermometer takes the guesswork out of roasting, but if you don't have one, here's a timetable guide for traditional ovens. It allows for wrapping meats or poultry in foil and unfolding the foil during the last 20 minutes of cooking so that the meat will brown.

The following times are for average taste (if you like your meat rare, cross out the timetable and pencil in your own) and for roasts of average family size—3–5 lb.

	Quick Roast at High Temperature	*Slow Roast at Low Temperature (reduces shrinkage)*
	(425°F = 218°C)	(325°F = 163°C)
Beef and venison	15 min per lb + 15 min (rare) 20 min per lb + 20 min (well done)	25 min per lb + 25 min
Lamb	20 min per lb + 20 min	30 min per lb + 30 min
Veal	25 min per lb + 25 min	35 min per lb + 35 min
Pork	25 min per lb + 25 min	35 min per lb + 35 min (not for crackling)
Chicken and duck (including wild)	15 min per lb + 15 min	25 min per lb + 25 min
Turkey and goose	15 min per lb + 15 min	25 min per lb + 25 min (under 14 lb) 20 min per lb + 20 min (over 14 lb)

(Before cooking a fat goose, stab the bird with a fork all over so that fat oozes through and bastes itself.)

	(400°F = 200°C)
Game and quail	15 to 20 min
Pheasant	15 min per lb + 10 min

HOW TO GET HOLD OF THE VIP'S IN YOUR LIFE

(*You* fill in these telephone numbers)

Accountant ....

Air-conditioning repair ....

Airport(s) ....

Ambulance service ....

Appliance dealer ....

Attorney ....

Bank manager ....

Bus terminal ....

Butcher ....

Carpenter ....

Car rental ....

Clubs ....

....

....

....

Credit card companies...

....

....

Day-care center ....

Dentist ....

Doctors (all sorts) ....

....

....

....

Drugstore ....

Dry cleaner ....

Electric company ....

Electrician ....

Employment agency ....

Fire Department ....

Florist ....

Furnace repair ....

Garage ....

Gas company or bottle gas dealer..................................

Hairdresser ....

Hardware store ....

Heating oil supplier ....

Hospital ....

Housepainter ....

Insurance agents (life, property, house, car).....................

....

....

....

Laundry ....

Lawn care company ....

Library ....

Liquor store ....

Milkman ....

Minister or rabbi ....

Newspaper delivery ....

Plumber ....

Poison control center ....

Police station ....

Power company ....

Pump or well repair...

Railroad station ....

Rapid transit authority ....

Roofing contractor ....

Schools ....

Septic tank service ....

Special machinery repairs ....

Stockbroker ....

Swimming pool supplier ....

Taxi ....

Telephone company ....

Thrift shops ....

Town or city hall ....

TV repair ....

Veterinarian ....

Water softener dealer ....

Window cleaner ....

Fill in the following according to your needs, i.e., piano tuner, carpet cleaner, baby-sitter, flower nursery, local newspaper classified department:

....

....

....

....

....

VITAL FACTS ABOUT YOU

Important Numbers

Car or motorcycle number..

Car engine number ....

Car or motorcycle license plate number.........................

Automobile insurance firm and policy number.....................

Life insurance firm and policy number.............................

Health insurance firm and policy number..........................

Dental insurance firm and policy number.........................

Home insurance firm and policy number...........................

Social security number(s) ....

....

Passport number(s) ....

....

Savings account numbers ....

....

Savings bond numbers, issuing agency, date of issue..........

....

Checking account numbers ....

....

Store account numbers ....

....

Credit card numbers ....

....

Blood types of family ....

....

Renewal Dates

Car license ....

Dog license ....

Insurances (life/home/auto/etc.) ....

Other Numbers

....

....

....

If you own a lot of stocks, list them separately. Similarly, list securities and investments under columns headed:

    Number of stock
    Type
    Company
    Purchase price
    Purchase date
    Dividends

For the following lists, if you have additional entries, tape in extra pages.

Family Buy Now—Pay Later Schedule

This is for any installment purchase, such as property, car, stereo, refrigerator.

Item ....
Purchased by ....
Purchased from (name of firm and contact)..............................
Address and telephone number of firm and contact............

....
Date of first scheduled payment..
Amount of regular payment (i.e., $200 monthly)..................
Documents relating to purchase..
Documents held by (i.e., attorney or bank)..............................

Item ....
Purchased by ....
Purchased from (name of firm and contact)..............................
Address and telephone number of firm and contact............

....
Date of first scheduled payment..
Amount of regular payment (i.e., $200 monthly)..................
Documents relating to purchase..
Documents held by (i.e., attorney or bank)..............................

....

Family Insurance

Item insured ....

Agency or company ....

Amount of insurance ....

Policy number ....

Premium payment ....

Date on which policy expires..

Household Insurance

Item insured ....

Agency or company ....

Amount of insurance ....

Policy number ....

Premium payment ....

Date of expiration ....

If you have more items to be insured (car/house/health etc.) than there is room for on this page, then either tape in a separate page or start a file on insurance (see Organization, p 11).

Item insured ....

Agency or company ....

Amount of insurance ....

Policy number ....

Premium payment ....

Date of expiration ....

Don't leave insurance information hidden in the pages of your policies. Extract the information and clarify it for yourself by writing it above.

Personal Insurance Policies

Insured ....

Beneficiaries ....

Agent or company ....

Policy number ....

Policy is at...

Date on which premium started.....................................

Date on which premium expires ....

Amount of insurance ....

Premium payment ....

Other notes ....

In Event of Death

CONTACT THE FOLLOWING:

Name and telephone number

Nearest relative ....

Accountant ....

Attorney ....

Banks ....

....

Clergy ....

Doctors ....

....

Executors ....

....

Guardians ....

Insurance adviser ....

Stockbroker ....

Trustees ....

Other people to contact ....

Last will and testament is deposited at..................................

Safe deposit box site and number ....

Get key from ....

Safety deposit key number...

(You obviously won't want to fill in all of these or it won't be a very safe box, but you must ensure that someone at least knows of the existence of your safe deposit box.)

Insurance Policies Relevant to Death

Insured ....

Beneficiaries ....

Agent or company ....

Policy number ....

Policy is at...

Date on which premium started..

Date on which policy expires...

Amount of insurance ....

Premium payment ....

Other notes ....

If you have more insurance than I provided room for, tape in an extra page.

And So Farewell...

with the joke that never fails

As we prepared lunch for 20 teenagers, when only 7 had been expected, an old school friend of mine hissed that what she wanted to read in this book was a joke that she will continue to think funny every time the milk boils over. So here's my favorite cartoon:

An astonished husband has returned home from the office to an amazing scene in his kitchen. Two little children are murdering each other while another tot is garotting the cat.

There is a pile of last night's dirty dishes and a heap of dirty laundry. Pans are burning, clouds of smoke and steam are rising, the floor is covered with smashed crockery, and the dog has just upset the trash can.

In the middle of this chaos is his wife, sitting in an easy chair with her feet up on the table. She is reading a novel and dipping into a box of chocolates. She says, "I thought that the best way to let you see what on earth I do all day was not to do it."

THE END

INDEX

ABOUT THE AUTHOR

SHIRLEY CONRAN is the well-known British journalist and textile designer. She writes regularly for the *Observer*, was the first woman's editor of the *Observer Colour Magazine*, and woman's editor of the *Daily Mail*, where she launched the first weekly women's magazine. She lives in London with her two sons.

Hair-raising happenings
that guarantee nightmares!

You'll be fascinated by unearthly events, intrigued by stories of weird and bizarre occurrences, startled by terrifying tales that border fact and fiction, truth and fantasy. Look for these titles or use the handy coupon below. Go beyond time and space into the strange mysteries of all times!